SOCIAL SYSTEMS AND SCHIZOPHRENIA

SOCIAL SYSTEMS AND SCHIZOPHRENIA

Selected Papers

H. Warren Dunham

PRAEGER

PRAEGER SPECIAL STUDIES • PRAEGER SCIENTIFIC

Library of Congress Cataloging in Publication Data

Dunham, Henry Warren, 1906-
Social systems and schizophrenia.

Includes bibliographies and index.
1. Schizophrenia--Social aspects. 2. Social psychiatry. 3. Epidemiology. I. Title.
[DNLM: 1. Schizophrenia--Collected works.
2. Social conditions--Collected works. WM203
D917s]
RC514.D86 616.89'82 80-14193
ISBN 0-03-056134-5

Published in 1980 by Praeger Publishers
CBS Educational and Professional Publishing
A Division of CBS, Inc.
521 Fifth Avenue, New York, New York 10017 U.S.A.

0123456789 145 987654321

Printed in the United States of America

To the Memory
of
Jacques S. Gottlieb

ACKNOWLEDGMENTS

Of the 12 chapters in this volume, all except Chapters 1 and 8 have been published previously. Thus, I wish to express my gratitude to those journals for their permission to reprint the following: to the International Journal of Social Psychiatry for Chapter 2, "Methodology of the Sociological Investigation of Mental Disorder"; to the American Sociological Review for Chapter 3, "The Ecology of the Functional Psychoses in Chicago"; and for Chapter 7, "A Research Note on Diagnosed Mental Illness and Social Class"; to the Milbank Memorial Fund Quarterly for Chapter 9, "Social Structures and Mental Disorders: Competing Hypotheses of Explanation"; and to the Archives of General Psychiatry for Chapter 10, "The Epidemiology of Psychiatric Disorders as a Contribution to Medical Ecology"; and for Chapter 12, "Society, Culture, and Mental Disorder."

I wish also to express my thanks and appreciation to the following publishers for their permission to reprint several of my papers included in their books. Thus, I thank Holt, Rinehart and Winston, Inc. for Chapter 5, published in Changing Perspectives of Mental Illness, edited by Stanley C. Plog and Robert B. Edgerton as "City Core and Suburban Fringe: Distribution Patterns of Mental Illness"; the Macmillan Company, Inc. for Chapter 11, published in Anomie and Deviant Behavior, edited by Marshall B. Clinard as "Anomie and Mental Disorder"; and to the Wayne State University Press for Chapters 4 and 6, published in my book Community and Schizophrenia: An Epidemiological Analysis.

I thank Morton Miller, M.D. and Maurice Satin, Ph.D., colleagues in the Department of Psychiatry, State University of New York at Stony Brook for their help and support at various stages of this undertaking.

There are two colleagues and close friends who had given me always a very special understanding and support. They are the late Jacques S. Gottlieb, M.D. and the late Peter Beckett, M.D. I owe them much, very much.

My other colleagues in the Department of Psychiatry at Wayne State University also deserve my deep gratitude for their generous interest in my work. They are James Grisell, Ph.D., Elliot Luby, M.D., Calvin Shorer, M.D., and Garfield Tourney, M.D.

I am grateful to Mr. Colin Jones for his wise counsel with respect to bringing these papers together in one volume. Alex Richman, M.D. and George Fischer, Ph.D. were most supportive in the early planning stages of this work. I thank them.

I owe my special thanks to Mrs. Ruth Towers, secretary of Dr. Miller's division at the State University of New York at Stony Brook, for her skillful secretarial effort which she would squeeze into a very overburdened work schedule. Finally, my debt is great to Mrs. Edna Moritz, my long time secretary at Wayne State University. Her efforts in preparing the manuscript made it possible to meet the deadline.

H.W.D.

CONTENTS

SOCIAL SYSTEMS AND SCHIZOPHRENIA

PART ONE
INTRODUCTION

INTRODUCTION TO PART ONE

These selected papers represent an attempt to examine the linkage, often assumed, between a human social system and the incidence of schizophrenia. The establishment of such a linkage is suggested when the incidence of the disorder under examination is found to be in a significant excess in one population at risk as compared to another. The investigator then can approach the significant difference in the incidence rate from one of several bodies of theory in order to infer the agent that might account for one case of the disorder under examination. The validity of the inferred hypothesis then might be established through some clinical studies and/or by setting up a carefully designed epidemiological experiment. The value of the epidemiological method in the study of a given disease can be measured by its success in narrowing the available hypotheses that might account for the disease.

The above perspective is analyzed in the two chapters constituting Part I of this volume. In the first chapter an attempt is made to define the problem—the linkage of the social system to the incidence of schizophrenia—and to depict the value of the epidemiological method in exploring this relationship. This chapter also notes the several approaches that can be used in the interpretation of epidemiological findings. The genetic, biochemical, psychosomatic, and psychological approaches all have been used in the past to bring order into epidemiological findings. But only in the last half century has the sociological approach emerged to provide another theoretical framework for the interpretation of epidemiological findings. Since this approach offers the newest brand of theory to explain selected mental disorders, I have presented in Chapter 2 an analysis of the assumptions upon which this approach is grounded. One should note that this approach as compared to the others is more broadly gauged and does not conjure up immediately the specific social factors that might be causally related with the mental disorder under examination. The causal factors suggested by the sociological approach do not have the specificity that a defective gene, a toxic substance, a bacterial infection, or a repressed unhappy experience provides. The utility of the sociological approach to the study of mental disorder provides the foundation for the emergence of the social model to offset and challenge the more traditional medical model.

The well-established medical model provides a framework for a search for specific agents to account for the failure of the organism to function according to well-recognized physical and social standards of a particular society. In contrast, the social model provides a conceptualization that encompasses certain mental disorders, abnormal mental constructs, various mood swings, and erratic, bizarre behaviors. Each one of these forms can be compressed into a personality type that is rejected and isolated by others with whom the individual interacts.

An extreme application of this social model is represented by labeling theory. In this theory the mentally ill person is viewed as a product of social interaction where the others around him act toward him in such a fashion that defines him as different. His response is often of the kind that supports this difference. When he responds in the expected manner he is only helping to tighten the noose that defines for him that he is mentally ill. Thus the definition of the situation to the person who eventually defines himself as mentally ill is a product of social interaction.[1]

The increasing popularity of the social model for explaining schizophrenia results up to the present time from two research failures: the failure to discover a specific etiological agent for schizophrenia, and the failure to develop generally acceptable criteria for diagnosing the disease.

During the past century much effort and money have been spent in the attempt to discover the factor or factors that could provide a causal explanation for schizophrenia. Sometimes it seems that during this past century practically every conceivable factor has been examined as a possible cause for the disease. The factors examined run the gamut from hereditary tainting through focal and other infections to traumatic experiences in childhood. Perhaps the positive results of this search for causal factors are found in Kraepelin's monumental effort to describe and delimit clinically the various types of schizophrenic disorders in the twin studies, where concordance percentages of monozygotic twins range from 38 to 72 percent, and in the largely negative results from all other researches.[2] But even with the positive but uneven findings of the twin studies there are great difficulties; these percentages contain many hidden assumptions, including uncertainty as to the diagnosis, uncertainty as to the zygosity of the twin pairs, the differing criteria for identifying a case of schizophrenia, and the wide range of time from 1928 to 1972 in which the separate studies were conducted. During this extended research period there have been periodic reviews of the literature, notably by Lewis in 1933 and the several reviews by Bellak.[3] This failure to achieve any breakthrough of a conclusive character that would explain schizophrenia has only served to widen the net concerning the criteria for diagnosing the disorder.

The widening of the schizophrenic net brings one to the second failure. This net has extended the criteria for identifying a case of schizophrenia and has led to what I have called the "hard" and "soft" diagnoses. The hard diagnosis has the longest history. It is grounded in Kraepelin classical clinical studies of dementia praecox. This hard diagnosis emphasizes the basic organic processes as described by Bleuler and depends on the isolation of specific biological and neurological entities.[4] Consequently, much of this research is of a genetic or biochemical type that either attempts to isolate some characteristic of the genotype or to discover some ever present biochemical substance in the physiology. The chief aspect of the hard diagnosis is its foundation in carefully isolated and measured genetic, biochemical, and/or physiological factors that can provide an explanation for those organic processes typical of schizophrenia.

By contrast, the soft diagnosis has the shortest history and has gained its initial support from psychoanalysis. In medicine the roots of the soft diagnosis are found in psychoanalytic theory, in psychology in learning theory, in social psychology in socialization theory, and in sociology in anomie theory. When Bleuler suggested the term schizophrenia to emphasize the splitting of the intellectual from the affective state as the most significant aspect of the disease, he gave considerable push to the soft diagnosis. It soon acquired followers from psychology and the social sciences. The numerous reports of their schizophrenia studies revealed them as humanistic, sympathetic, imaginative, and very readable. They appeared to tap some of the deeper emotions of the universal human nature. While these investigators frequently give lip service to a genetic base, they quickly forget about it in their interest in describing the patient's psychic suffering and abstracting the sense from the nonsense with respect to the patient's verbal and behavioral productions. The soft diagnosis makes an interesting and sometimes plausible case, but does not provide as yet a satisfactory etiological explanation.[5] These research failures have provided the rationalization for the sociological approach that is examined in Part I.

NOTES

1. T. J. Scheff, Being Mentally Ill: A Sociological Theory (Chicago: Aldine, 1966); idem, "The Role of the Mentally Ill and the Dynamics of Mental Disorder: A Research Framework," Sociometry 26 (1963): 436-53; and W. I. Thomas, "The Behavior Pattern and the Situation," in Personality and the Social Group, ed. E. W. Burgess (Chicago: University of Chicago Press, 1929), pp. 1-15.

2. J. Shields, L. Heston, and I. Gottesman, "Schizophrenia and the Schizoid: The Problem for Genetic Analysis," in Genetic Research in Psychiatry, ed. R. D. Fieve, D. Rosenthal, and H. Brill (Baltimore: Johns Hopkins Press, 1975), pp. 167-98.

3. Nolan D. C. Lewis, Research in Dementia Praecox (Past Attainments, Present Trends and Future Possibilities) (New York: National Committee for Mental Hygiene, 1936); and L. Bellak, Dementia Praecox—The Past Decade's Work and Present Status: A Review and Evaluation (New York: Grune and Stratton, 1948).

4. E. Kraepelin, Dementia Praecox and Paraphenia, trans. R. M. Barclay (Edinburgh: E. and S. Livingstone, 1919); and E. Bleuler, Dementia Praecox or the Group of Schizophrenia (New York: International Universities Press, 1950).

5. This discussion of the hard and soft diagnoses of schizophrenia has been adapted from my paper, "Sociocultural Studies of Schizophrenia," Archives of General Psychiatry 24 (March 1971): 206-14.

1
SOCIAL SYSTEMS AND MENTAL DISORDERS: APPROACHES, METHODS, AND PROBLEMS

The chapters that constitute this volume represent an attempt to explore those relationships that are assumed to exist between human social systems and mental disorders that develop among some persons who, in their contacts and interactions, can be regarded as parts of its organization. This organization in any human social system is extremely complex. Its degree of complexity will vary with size and density of population and level of technology. The justification for any attempt to explore the relationship between a social system and mental pathology is found in every textbook of psychiatry, where some consideration is always given to the role of social factors with respect to each mental disorder.

In order to comprehend the totality of this relationship, it is necessary to conceptualize the nature of a human social system. First, a human social system implies that there exists a process of communication among the individual units of the system that enables meaningful actions to take place among them. The use of symbols or language makes this possible. Second, a human social system can be regarded as an emergent level resulting from millions of years of an evolutionary process, of which the lowest form would be the living cell. Third, the human social system can be viewed as a theoretical model of society. As such it represents an environment that can be studied scientifically to determine the development of malfunctions within the system. Such malfunctions as found might prove to have a significance for the emergence of psychological disturbances among some persons composing the system. While the emergence of a human social system from antecedent levels of organization has been well documented, there is still disagreement as to the patterns of organization that can be regarded as the structure of a social system.[1]

Currently, two theoretical models of a human social system are recognized as possible existing forms of organization. A commitment to one or the other model would influence the interpretation of the incidence of mental disorder as distributed throughout the system. One theoretical model can be designated as the rational type. This model implies an organizational structure of separate parts. Those researchers adhering to this model hold that each separate part can be manipulated and modified in such a fashion that an increased efficiency and morale will be achieved for the entire social system.

The other theoretical model is of the natural system type. In this model the social system is also made up of separate and different parts, but the emphasis is placed on their interdependence. This means that a change made in any one part will have a differential spreading effect throughout the system. Consequently, each separate part will be affected by a change that is introduced at any point in the system. Thus, intervening in the system by the introduction of a new structure for an element that has been found to be responsible for the malfunctioning of the system should bring about a change in functioning that, it is hoped, would reduce the stress on the individual units. With respect to mental disorders, a therapeutic intervention in the system would be one that reduced the incidence of total mental disorders or a specific mental disorder.

The adherence to either model can suggest hypotheses, guide the designing of empirical studies, point to inferences from empirical findings, and suggest the development of specific experiments. The author's own preference is for the natural system model.

The conceptualization of human society as an organized social system provides for any social scientist a more detailed view of what constitutes environmental factors. It provides new access to the causal chain linking social factors to the development of those mood, thought, and behavior patterns that prove unacceptable to a specific society. It can provide new ideas as to when, how, and where to intervene in a social system to decrease the influence of noxious factors upon the individuals composing the system. It also enables an investigator to view more clearly the mosaic provided by the interrelationship of geographical, interpersonal, biological, and cultural environments. Finally, it enables an investigator to select for detailed clinical study those persons who could provide essential data concerning a particular mental pathology.

The above considerations of the nature of social systems project a foundation for the evaluation of the empirical findings reported in this work. While the more general concern is the relationship between mental disorders and social systems, the author has been concerned here primarily with the possible ways that schizophrenia is related to social systems. Other functional mental disorders have been considered here, but mainly to the extent that they help to clarify the relationship between schizophrenia and social systems. Primary reliance has been placed upon epidemiology as a method of study. In the remainder of this chapter the following will be examined: epidemiology as a method of investigation, the various approaches to the evaluation of epidemiological findings, and some problems posed by the epidemiological investigation of mental disorders.

Epidemiology has been given a varied definition in the hands of different investigators. One of the first definitions considered epidemiology to be the sum total of existing knowledge about epidemics. Later, epidemiology was viewed as the study of the natural history of diseases. Still later, under the influence of John Gordon's work, epidemiology became medical ecology.[2] Medical ecology, in turn, provides a theoretical framework to account for both health and disease in terms of an interaction among agent, host, and environment that functions to maintain an equilibrium between human beings and their environment.

The above definitions give epidemiology a substantive character in the field of medicine. As substance it would refer to the sum total of current knowledge about the incidence and prevalence distribution of both physical and mental diseases in social systems.

Epidemiology also can be viewed as a method for the study of disease—merely another way to study disease alongside of the clinical and laboratory methods. However, the basic character of epidemiology consists in the distribution of the incidence of a given disease in several populations of risk broken down by any number of demographic characteristics that will enable an investigator to make some inferences about cause and prevention possibilities.[3] This final definition is a more pointed one and is the conception that has been utilized by the author as he pursued the epidemiological study of mental disorders.

Before considering the various aspects of epidemiological investigations it is essential that the student have a clear conception of the several measures that are essential for such investigations. The first measure is that of incidence of a disease. The incidence count of a disease refers to the number of new cases that are detected and diagnosed in a specified time period, for example, a month, six months, or a year. Incidence measures for schizophrenia in a delimited population at risk would be the number of new cases detected within a year in relation to the total adult population. It is expressed as follows:

$$I_s = \frac{\text{No. Cases (new)} \times 1{,}000}{\text{Population 15-64 years}}$$

The prevalence measure is divided into three types. First, there is point prevalence, which refers to the number of cases that are sick with the disease on any given day in relation to the total population on that day. Second, there is period prevalence, which refers to the number of persons who are sick with the disease during any one month, six months, or a year. Third, there is a measure known as lifetime prevalence, which refers to the number of persons who develop the disease at any time during their lives. This measure presents several difficulties and is seldom used because it has not been of research value.

Finally, there are age and sex specific rates that are merely reduced incidence measures and produce a rate of new cases for a specific age or sex group.

An age and sex specific rate would be computed as follows:

$$I_{(m-20-29)} = \frac{N_{(m-20-29)} \times 1,000}{P}$$

where

I(m-20-29) = Incidence measure for males, 20-29 years of age
N = number of new cases of males 20-29 years of age
Base = 1,000
P = Total male population 20-29 years of age in population at risk

These well-established measures in epidemiological investigations have had to confront a widespread skepticism when utilized to measure incidence and prevalence of mental disorders. The skepticism arises in the attempt to define a new case. For example, how is a new case of schizophrenia to be detected? Does a new case refer only to a person who has been admitted to a hospital, clinic, or psychiatrist's office and given a diagnosis of schizophrenia? Or should any count of new cases include persons who have schizophrenia but reside in the community and have not been admitted to a psychiatric facility at the time a count is taken?

At this point it is necessary to spell out as clearly as possible the several procedures that have been utilized to achieve a valid incidence count in a population at risk. These procedures will be enumerated and then briefly discussed. First, there is the case count of first admissions with specific diagnoses to hospitals, clinics, and private practitioners. Second, there is the house-to-house survey where a qualified psychiatrist makes inquiries at each dwelling and has an opportunity to make a diagnostic judgment about any person who says he is ill or whom other family members say is ill. Third, there is the community survey of a random drawn sample in a population of risk by utilizing an instrument that the researchers have developed that will select out those persons in a community who are sick. Such a count, when secured by such an instrument and extrapolated to the total population, can be utilized as an incidence count by itself or can be combined with a first admission count after case duplications have been eliminated. Fourth, there is a random sample drawn from a population of risk, and all first-degree relatives of the sample cases who are mentally sick are counted to secure an incidence rate. Finally, there is the birth-register cohort that draws a random sample from the birth register of 60 years ago and then checks clinic and hospital records to determine those cases who developed some type of mental illness during their lives.

The development of these several procedures gives some idea of the misgivings that various investigators have had concerning incidence counts of mental illness. While at first glance a complete count of first admissions to all public and private psychiatric facilities would seem to provide a valid incidence count, many investigators have argued that it misses those persons who never get caught in the care and treatment net. If this is so it mainly has to do with the count of total mental disorders in a population at risk. The author has taken the position that when persons in the community that have a mental disturbance are not counted, they are mainly those with minor mental disorders. In other words, those who have bona fide psychoses are eventually included in any first admission count. This would particularly be true for persons who have a schizophrenic disorder. Persons who develop this disorder and who live in urban populations get into the first admission count sooner or later. Here age and sex specific rates are likely to be less valid than a total rate of schizophrenia for a total population.

The house-to-house survey made by a psychiatrist would seem at first glance to be the best method of securing a valid incidence count. However, there are two difficult obstacles: it is a very expensive method, and it can only be carried out for relatively small, isolated populations. It would be almost impossible to use in an urban population.

The community survey of a random drawn population sample utilizes a previously constructed instrument that can detect the presence of a mental disorder but not a specific mental disorder. To date there have been several such instruments constructed that have the purpose of detecting persons who have a psychiatric disorder but are not receiving any form of treatment. These instruments are of two types: first, a self-administered questionnaire, which is a series of scales where a person judges himself along three-, five-, or seven-point scales, and a psychiatric interview-schedule administered by a skilled psychiatric interviewer. A new instrument is being developed that might provide specific diagnoses according to the 18 categories in the Diagnostic and Statistical Manual III.[4]

These instruments all have some method of scoring so that the score at one end of a continuum will indicate a person who has a mental disorder. All of them have demonstrated that they are useful in selecting persons who have a psychiatric disorder. Their reliability has been shown to be fairly high. However, none of them has been able to solve the problem represented by the selection of false positives and the neglect of false negatives. In other words, any instrument tends to give high scores to some persons who do not have a mental disorder—the false positives—and fails to detect other persons who have a disorder—the false negatives. If the investigator could be sure that false positives were equal to false negatives, then it would make no difference and the number of cases above the cutting point could provide the incidence measure. However, one can never be sure that this is a valid assumption. It often has been suggested that those cases that indicate mental pathology according to the instrument used might be subjected to a blind clinical study by a psychiatrist. It is generally held that an agreement between psychiatrist and the instrument would establish the validity of the instrument. But would it?

These difficulties mean that the number of cases uncovered would differ in any given survey according to the instrument used and the general attitude about mental illness held by members of the population at risk. Differences in survey results are depicted clearly when the prevalence rates for surveys made before 1940 are compared with surveys conducted after 1950. In four surveys conducted before 1940 the average rate was 41 per 1,000, while in four surveys after 1950 the average rate was 203 per 1,000.[5] There seems to be a clear tendency to view more persons as mentally ill today than a generation ago. These figures also support one other difficulty with the survey, namely, the claim that the survey is much more useful in giving support to a prevalence rate but cannot produce a valid incidence rate.

While most surveys of a population of risk provide a diagnosis for the cases uncovered, such diagnosis seldom results from the direct clinical confrontation between psychiatrist and patients as Hagnell was able to do for his Swedish parish.[6] Rather, diagnoses are made from the information about the patient collected by the survey or the degree of agreement among several more expert judges. In spite of this difficulty, an examination of the prevalence rates from eight surveys in different parts of the world showed that there was very close agreement on the prevalence rates for schizophrenia, much less agreement for the rate for total psychoses, and wide disagreement on the rate for total mental disorder. These data are depicted in Figure 1.1.

Generally, there are three levels of epidemiological study. First, there is the descriptive level. This level is primarily a statistical presentation that shows the distribution of a given disease broken down by sex, age, and race, distributed through time or geographical area. Other types of breakdowns also may be presented. The descriptive level provides information for administrators who are concerned with organization of programs for treatment and control of a disease, and for those scientists who are concerned with designing epidemiological investigations.

The second level of epidemiological study is analytic. Here the basic concern is to examine the distribution of the incidence of a specific disease in two or more populations of risk. If the incidence rate is several times larger in Population 1 than Population 2, the immediate question is, "How is this to be explained?"

At this point the investigator may infer some causal factor suggested by human genetics, the physical environment, the population structure, the socialization process, or the group culture. If he thinks such a factor has explanatory power, he may attempt to construct an index that would encompass the factor and then attempt to determine the degree of correlation existing between the factor and the distribution of the disease.

Findings on the analytic level lead naturally to the third level, that of experimental epidemiology. Here an investigator would attempt to design an experiment that would test the causal role of the factor that was suggested by the results obtained on the analytic level. For example, if he finds that a disease is heavily concentrated where the population density is high, will this relationship hold when the incidences of the disease in two selected populations with similar demographic characteristics but with contrasting densities are compared? If the result is positive, the investigator has succeeded in narrowing the dimensions of the problem.

While the author's approach to the epidemiological study of mental disorders is that of a sociologist, it is most essential that the student be aware that there are several other well-recognized approaches to the interpretation of epidemiological data. An approach to data constitutes a conceptual framework for investigators as they examine distributions of a disease in a population at risk. This conceptual framework suggests to the investigator some possible factor that might explain differential distribution patterns. However, he does have to determine, possibly by an experiment, if the data as organized give any support to the factor suggested by his conceptual framework.

FIGURE 1.1

Prevalence Rates for Total Mental Disorders, Total Psychoses, and Schizophrenia, in Eight Epidemiological Surveys
(rates per 1,000 general population)

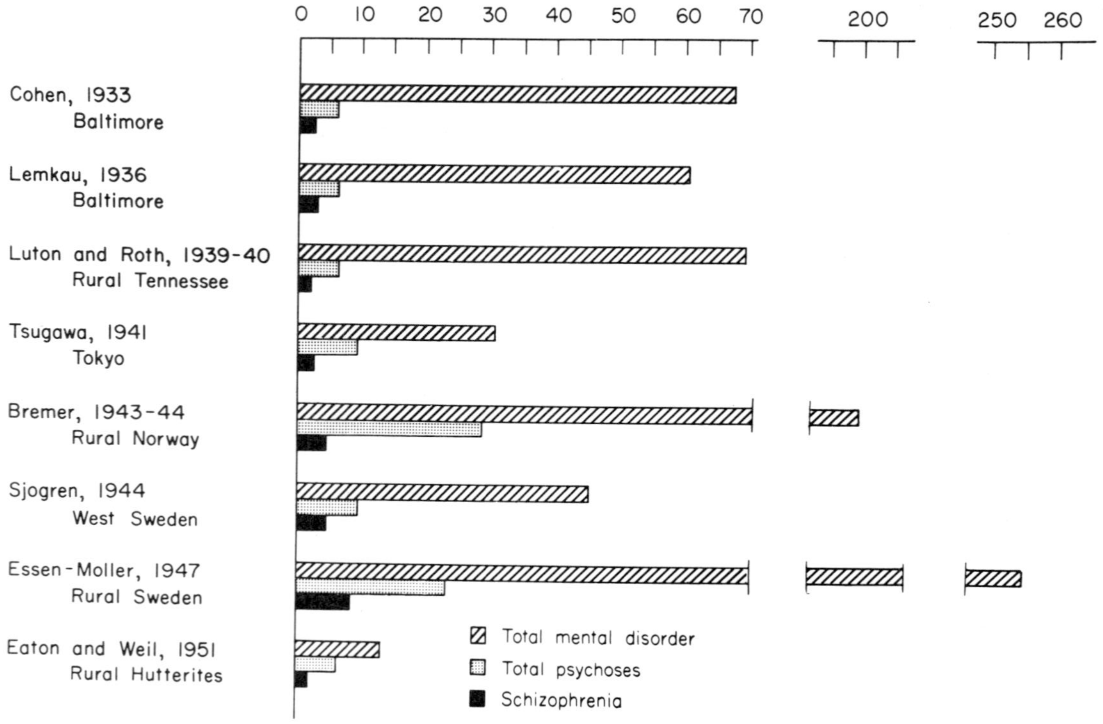

In addition to a sociological framework, there are other approaches useful for the interpretation of epidemiological findings of which every epidemiologist is aware. First, there is the biological approach. Here the investigator is likely to hold that a genetic factor, if not ruled out, always must be taken into account in examining the distribution of a disease in a population at risk. If the investigator observes that the disease seems to run in families and is absent in families with no history of the disease, he will take this into account when examining epidemiological distributions. Jan Böök's work in Sweden is a good illustration of the biological approach.[7]

Second, there is a demographic approach. Here the investigator is concerned with detecting any relationship between the incidence of the disease and certain characteristics of the population. Is the incidence of the disease highly concentrated in a sex, age, racial, or ethnic group? Does the disease vary significantly with population density or abnormal sex ratios in the population? Does it strike people living in cities more often than people living in rural areas? Does the disease appear to concentrate in certain occupational groups? There are many other questions that stem from the demographic approach. However, the suggestions for analysis should give the student some idea as to how this approach is valuable for narrowing down the dimensions of the task at hand. The studies of Benjamin Malzberg provide an excellent illustration of this approach to the analysis of mental disorders.[8]

Third, there is a psychological approach to the findings of epidemiological investigations. Here the investigator finds certain psychological concepts useful in interpreting epidemiological analysis. The work of S. Parker and R. Kleiner is an illustration of the utilization of psychological concepts to interpret epidemiological data collected from a survey of a sample of blacks in a large urban community. Goal striving, maladaptation, physiological reactions, and psychic stress equal mental disorder is the equation for which their data are intended to provide an adequate test.[9]

Finally, there is an environmental approach. This approach is well illustrated by the early public health physicians who sought in the physical environment those factors that might explain their areal distribution patterns of physical disease. Snow's classic epidemiological study of cholera in London illustrates well this environmental approach. Snow was able to establish the fact that the differential mortality rate for cholera in several districts of London was directly related to the different sources for the water supply. With this relationship established, Snow had not only a hypothesis concerning the source of the infection, but also he had explained the outbreak of the disease in certain districts and households and its absence in other districts and households.[10]

While Morris has identified seven uses of epidemiology, the present author, in his studies of psychiatric illnesses, emphasized only one use: that conception that enables one to make inferences concerning the etiology from the distribution of the incidence of a mental disorder in two or more populations of risk.[11] The epidemiological study of psychiatric disorders does present certain special problems that are less likely to be apparent with respect to physical diseases. Psychiatric medicine contains four main groups: the psychotics, the psychoneurotics, the psychopathics, and the mentally deficients.

While it is conventional to state that mental illness should be viewed and responded to like physical disease, the fact remains that there is one difference that makes it difficult to adhere to this position, namely, that mental illness frequently disrupts the process of communication so that the patient cannot explain himself to the physician. The physician must make his inferences on the basis of the patient's mental constructs and behavior forms. Consequently, the field of psychiatric medicine carries some special problems for epidemiological study that are less likely to be in evidence with respect to physical illness. It is not intended to state that these obstacles are never present with respect to physical disease, but rather that they become more complicated with respect to mental illnesses because of the ambiguity about and the uncertainty of present knowledge concerning psychiatric cases. Nevertheless, in spite of this quality, what some of these problems are will be outlined here.

The first problem that every investigator who studies mental disorder faces is what constitutes a case of mental disorder. With no established baseline that determines who is sick and who is not, how does the physician know when he is confronted with a bona fide psychiatric case? In a sense this is the problem of detection. For the most part, in Western society the case is selected out of the population by family members, employers, police, teachers, or friends and brought to a hospital or clinic with a statement from the person escorting him that he is behaving strangely, always getting into arguments, or the like. Consequently, when he finally faces the doctor the situation already has been defined in such a way that the doctor, on examining him, merely gives the patient a diagnostic label. While the doctor may bring in a finding of no mental disorder, the cards often have been stacked in such a way that such a finding is unlikely. The absence of a baseline supported by some objective test for determining a psychiatric diagnosis means that a case is defined by such factors as family members' judgments, social values and preferences, community toleration levels, or behavior unacceptable to the patient's community.

Second, there is a great variety of diagnostic types, often with obscure etiology, in the current psychiatric nomenclature. The examining psychiatrist frequently has difficulty separating out the bona fide psychoses from the cases of psychological adjustment problems and those of learned deviant behavior. This sometimes makes for the tendency not to separate out any of these specific types, but to consider mental illness as some type of generic entity.

The third obstacle is posed by the diagnostic problem and the lack of objective criteria for determining the diagnosis, particularly among the psychoses. The differential diagnosis is often difficult to make. Among the psychotics, approximately one quarter of the cases may end up with a different diagnosis at the end of the treatment period or a completely different diagnosis on entering treatment for the second time.

Fourth, there is the problem of coverage with respect to psychiatric cases. This has to do with the detection and identity of the case and whether or not all the persons who have symptoms of the disease in a given community can be located and identified. If, as some claim, the hospitals and clinics provide only about 50 percent of all psychiatric cases to be found in a given community, then there tends to be a question as to both the validity and reliability of any computed rates and, particularly, any computed specific rates by sex and/or age for any demographic or cultural category.

A fifth obstacle that in a sense is related very closely to the problem posed by coverage is the time gap that is supposed to exist between the onset of the disease and the recognition of the disease by a qualified psychiatrist. This gap is likely to be variable in different populations. Then it becomes almost impossible to make any comparative study of either incidence or prevalence rates. If this gap were constant among cases in the different demographic, temporal, and cultural segments of a population, then its significance would be minimized as far as making comparisons between rate distribution patterns.

A sixth problem, with respect to psychiatric epidemiology and to some extent for every disease condition, is the mobility of populations in the more technologically advanced societies. This becomes a problem because it denies the possibility of computing rates that are stable enough to make comparisons between societies or communities in relation to either incidence or prevalence of the disease. Frequently the epidemiologist finds that he has several populations in a given community that should be examined in order to obtain a complete epidemiological picture. These populations would include the following:

the population that was born in the community and continued to reside there up to the time of the epidemiological survey;
the population that was born in the community but moved out at various points in time before the survey began;
the population that was born outside of the community but moved into the community and resided there at the time of the survey; and
the population born in the community that moved outside and returned, and was present in the community at the time of the survey.

The problem presented by this population mobility has been an important factor in causing epidemiological investigators of psychiatric disorders to seek closed and stable populations where there is hardly any in- or out-migration, and where an increase or decrease in population is accounted for solely by a natural phenomenon, such as an excess of births over deaths or vice versa.

A seventh complexity is in the age span of the cases that develop some type of mental disturbance. This age span ranges from the childhood years to the years of senescence. It is possible that through a series of events or the lessening of social pressures that a person destined for some sort of psychological breakdown may postpone it, possibly for many years. The breakdown occurs only when the stress situation in his environment makes it impossible for him to cope any further. This again points to the desirability of carefully examining age and sex specific rates with reference to any mental illness.

Finally, there is the problem of the interpretation of epidemiological data. This problem is especially acute with respect to mental disorder because the causal chain is likely to be very complex, encompassing genetics, psychological, and sociological factors. An epidemiological investigator in this area should be knowledgeable about the various approaches so as not to overlook any factor that may operate in the chain of causality. The addition of the sociological perspective to the interpretation of epidemiological studies calls attention to a new set of factors that otherwise would be ignored. This new perspective includes both interpersonal and cultural environments, thereby enlarging the concept of environment that always has been viewed as significant in the causation of various mental disorders. Thus there is the possibility of the development of sociological hypotheses from epidemiological studies that can be tested by designing an experiment.

These problems that are reviewed here are central to the study of mental illness utilizing the epidemiological method. By confronting them, an investigator is in a better position to control them when planning his research. Those that cannot be controlled in designing his study must be taken into account as he interprets his findings and attempts to derive hypotheses for further study and testing.

Thus, from the beginning of his research, the author utilized a sociological approach to examining the distribution of mental disorders in populations of risk. He gradually became aware of the value of other approaches and the necessity to be knowledgeable about them in the interpretation of epidemiological findings. But as the sociological perspective was basic to his scientific education, the author deemed it essential to explore the basic postulates and assumptions that are fundamental to the sociological perspective, something which is attempted in Chapter 2.

NOTES

1. Here, social groups and societies are viewed as an extension of the evolutionary process. See Talcott Parsons, Action Theory and the Human Condition (New York: Free Press, 1978). See also the recent volume by James G. Miller, Living Systems (New York: McGraw-Hill, 1978).

2. J. E. Gordon, "Medical Ecology and the Problem Health," American Journal of Medical Science 3 (1958).

3. S. L. Kark, Epidemiology and Community Medicine (New York: Appleton-Century-Crofts, 1974), p. 2.

4. Lee N. Robins, "Psychiatric Diagnosis in the Community: How and Why," Rema Lapouse Lecture, American Public Health Association Meetings, New York City, November 7, 1979.

5. R. Plunkett and J. Gordon, Epidemiology and Mental Illness (New York: Basic Books, 1960), p. 90.

6. Olle Hagnell, A Prospective Study of the Incidence of Mental Disorder (Stockholm: Bonniers, 1966).

7. J. A. Böök, "A Genetic and Neuropsychiatric Investigation of a North-Swedish Population," Acta genetica et statistica medica 4 (1953).

8. B. Malzberg, Social and Biological Aspects of Mental Disease (Utica, N. Y.: State Hospital Press, 1940).

9. S. Parker and R. Kleiner, Mental Illness in the Urban Negro Community (New York: Free Press, 1966).

10. J. Snow, On the Mode of Communication of Cholera (1855), reproduced in Snow on Cholera, 2d ed. (New York: Hefner, 1965).

11. J. N. Morris, Uses of Epidemiology, 2d ed. (Baltimore: Williams and Wilkins, 1964).

2
METHODOLOGY OF SOCIOLOGICAL INVESTIGATIONS OF MENTAL DISORDERS

The purpose of this chapter is to make explicit certain methodological considerations in sociological investigations of mental disorder. Mental disorder includes not only different types of psychoses, but also a great variety of observable deviations in the mental, emotional, and behavioral spheres. Certain of these deviations, where etiology is still obscure, may prove to be grounded in the genetic structure, others in injuries or infection in the organism after birth, and still others in the nature of the ties that bind people to one another. Some mental deviations may be the result of certain social relationships acting upon specific kinds of biological organisms. The existence of this last possibility is of concern to the social scientist and emphasizes the need for a careful statement of his methodological position. Such a statement is also necessary to bring about a more meaningful communication on research in mental disorder between psychiatrists and psychologists on the one hand, and anthropologists and sociologists on the other. Their present difficulties in communication are mainly due to differing conceptions concerning the natures of human beings and society and the bond between them.

A recent controversy concerning the assumptions underlying the ecological approach to mental disorder has served further to point up the need for such a statement.[1] Clausen and Kohn have attempted to state what they consider to be the assumptions among research workers using the ecological approach to mental disorder.

Used with permission from the International Journal of Social Psychiatry 3 (Summer 1957): 1-11.

The authors imply that investigators using a method based on these assumptions, which are not derived from human ecological theory as they should be, have attempted to do something with the method that it is not designed for and cannot do. However, instead of making clear the value of the method in sociological investigations of mental disorder, they appear to challenge the sociologists who have used it because it seems to leave them "stranded in the middle of the stream," rather than bringing them close to the etiological issues.

To avoid such confusions in the future, to facilitate interdisciplinary communication, and to provide a theoretical basis for the areas of sociological concern will require the careful formulation of a methodology for sociological research into mental disorder. Such a statement should include the central standpoints, the underlying assumptions, the basic theoretical concepts, the various approaches with their interrelationships, and the unresolved central hypotheses.

The author has constructed this methodological statement from the following general standpoints:

The central objective in the sociological study of mental disorder is twofold: to isolate those social variables that are causative or predisposing in the etiology of the several types of mental disorder, and to isolate those complexes of social conditions that are associated with high incidence rates of the various mental disorders.

The achievement of this twofold objective necessitates the utilization and integration of clinical, ecological, and cultural approaches.

Empirically developed sociological generalizations eventually must square with validated theory stemming from biological, physiological, and psychological investigations of mental disorder in human society.

From these standpoints the assumptions behind sociological inquiry into the nature of mental disorder can be stated. These assumptions serve not only to underscore the essential concepts, but also to point up the approaches necessary for sociological inquiry. These assumptions are:

Symbolic communications and interpersonal relationships, which have a relevance in accounting for normal mentality and behavior, also must have some relevance in accounting for abnormal mentality and behavior.

The interconnectedness of external events and their internalization in the person encompass a set of factors that will account for greater variability in mood, mentality, and behavior.

The personality of a person and the culture of his society constitute interrelated systems that are in a constant process of change.

Both personality and culture in a given society will manifest greater stability at some historical periods than at others, but such stability as does occur will be temporary, never permanent.

Variations in the dynamics of any social system in time and space will make for significant differences in the feeling, thinking, and acting of persons in that system.[2]

These assumptions embody the sociological theory that accounts for variabilities in feeling, thought, and action of persons in human groups. These variabilities may or may not be found eventually to represent the incipient stages of recognizable types of mental disorder. But if it is assumed that they are, then the following hypotheses can be stated:

The bizarre, integrated, and organized distortion in varying degrees of feeling, thought, and conduct that can be observed in persons can be classified, systematized, and objectified sufficiently for the development of differential diagnoses. This hypothesis focuses attention on the need for clinical study of the case from biological, physiological, psychological, and sociological perspectives.

A given culture in the functioning of its social system through time will show significant correlations between its incidence rate of mental disorder and certain kinds of cultural change.

A given heterogeneous culture—one with two or more bodies of custom—will show significant differences in the incidence of mental disorders among its various subcultures.

Selected homogeneous cultures when compared will differ significantly in their incidence of mental disorder and will have either higher or lower incidence rates than will the subcultures of heterogeneous cultures. These above three hypotheses point to the utilization of the ecological approach.

The manner in which elements of the culture and events of the social situation make their ingression into the human organism, and the manner in which the human organism organizes, integrates, and utilizes these elements to form his ongoing experience, will produce certain emerging configurations of mentality and behavior that will not meet with acceptance by the social group. This hypothesis sets the stage for a cultural approach.

What follows is a discussion of the central concepts contained in the assumptions listed above. The concepts essential to the analysis are culture, socialization, cultural internalization, and social system.

When one speaks of culture, one is speaking of a thing that makes human beings unique among all other mammals, for they alone possess culture. This culture, which literally pervades every aspect of their existence, is an accumulated product that has been passed down through the generations and had its beginning at that point of time in the development of human beings when symbolic communication first appeared among interacting mammals, the human mind, the human self, and the early crude forms of culture also appeared. These crude forms were mutual expectancies that human beings developed with respect to physical things, social situations, and conceptual objects. Culture, then, is an accumulated body of mutual expectancies, ideas, and ideologies that human beings in any society "carry around in their heads." In short, it consists of the customs of the group. These customs become hardened into language, norms, rules, laws, and institutions that are observable and make for the tenacious quality of any culture. The nature and amount of these mutual expectancies, ideas, and ideologies will differ from one society to another and among the various status and role positions within the same society. The level of development in tools and technology is an important, objective, external aspect of any culture, but these things emerge as products of the heritage of the subjective elements and gain their significance for the society in the action patterns that human being develop in relation to them. A person is culturally at home when he shares with others these subjective elements and action patterns; he finds himself uncertain, insecure, and confused when placed in situations where he does not share them.

Socialization is the process by which the newborn child is molded into the culture of his group and hence becomes an acceptable person in that society.[3] The family provides the initial situation from which the human organism takes on the early rudiments of the culture. In any society there are numerous possibilities with respect to the completeness of socialization. Some persons may take over not enough of the culture to function properly, others may take over deviant versions that make their behavior unacceptable in the light of the norms of their respective groups, and still others may take over just enough of the culture to enable them to function in relation to others with a minimum of acceptance and effectiveness. There are still others—perhaps those designated as the well adjusted—whose absorption of the culture is so complete that they are able to maintain an extremely even balance between their mental life and conduct and the customs and conventions of their social groups. Finally, there are the creative individuals who internalize numerous and large segments of the total culture and then refashion these materials in such a way that new ideas and relationships emerge to be expressed in science, invention, and art and eventually become a part of the cultural heritage.

For the most part, human experience can be regarded as the internalization of culture. Human experience encompasses, of course, more than this. It is deeper and more complex, for it is also affected by the manner in which the person organizes the internalized cultural form with respect to both his own individuality and his previously acquired cultural values. The person internalizes the culture of his group by means of learning, both conscious and unconscious. Through intensive and extensive contacts with persons, things, and ideas, he has a high probability of internalizing enough of his culture to enable him to enter into a mutually satisfactory social existence with other human beings.

A social system is an organized structure of human beings that functions toward the ends of maintenance and survival. It also must satisfy certain needs of those humans composing it. It is held together through symbolic communication, which makes culture possible. If an increasing number of persons in the structure have difficulties in adaptation, it is said that the structure functions badly; if these numbers decrease markedly, the structure is seen as moving toward a greater maximum efficiency. (A more detailed consideration of social system is found in Chapter 1.)

In attempting to analyze the various theoretical approaches significant for sociological study of mental disorder, the author is operating within the assumptions that he has laid down. Of the approaches useful to sociological study, the clinical approach is the oldest because it lies closest to a commonsense level. It is the person with variant behavior and distorted mentality who is most easily observed, and such observation, to the trained and perceptive mind, points immediately to the need for some kind of systematic examination.

The concern here with the clinical approach is primarily in terms of its research value, although in psychiatry, as in other branches of medicine, its use is intimately tied up with the pressing need for therapy of any pathology that is demonstrated or inferred. The clinical method is naturally preferred in medicine because it brings the physician into firsthand contact with the patient who requires treatment.

Here the concern is with the clinical method as used in psychiatry and psychology, particularly to the extent that the method as used by these disciplines can be fused into an instrument that will be useful for the sociological study of mental disorder. The development of the clinical method in psychiatry has been both descriptive and analytical. It has been descriptive in the sense that careful case examinations have been used to build up various schemes of classification on the basis of symptoms that could be observed and at least partially objectified. It has been analytical in the sense that various investigators have attempted to make the data secured from examination support or fit into some etiological theory.

It is natural and expected that the clinical method, favored by medical research and practice, would prove useful in psychiatry. Kraepelin's work in psychiatry is a demonstration of the clinical method.[4] Through this method Kraepelin and others have attempted to build up a careful accounting of specific symptoms appearing in the various diseased conditions and to develop precise methods for their observation and examination. These methods constitute the core of the psychiatric examination and thus have been the essential framework for the practice of psychiatry. However, the examiner, acting in an objective spirit, has never succeeded in transcending the necessity for numerous subjective interpretations.

The static psychiatry that is still strong in state mental hospitals revealed its weakness in its atomistic conception of mental life, its methods of examination, and its failure to take account of the fact that people, wherever they are found, lead a group existence. The atomization of the emotional and mental life into such entities as mood, thought content, orientation, remote memory, recent memory, retention, recall, thinking capacity, general knowledge, intelligence, insight, and judgment did provide the basis for a psychiatric diagnosis, but did not provide much that could be turned to therapeutic use. Also, the methods for getting at these entities were simple and direct. They provided no check on their validity and gave no conception of the interrelationship of the entities in the total personality.

Freud's discoveries concerning the individual's mental life were eventually to challenge this static conception of psychiatry. In his psychoanalytic theory, Freud provided a closed psychological system wherein certain observable mental symptoms could be explained by the damage, restrictions, and pressures that Western culture placed in the way of the unfolding sexual instinct. These cultural harassments of sexual nature were described by careful clinical accounts of the playing out of the family drama where emotional growth would be either facilitated or arrested. This image of the individual and society proved not to have the universality ascribed to it, but it did furnish the means for breaking through the static quality of previous psychiatry by encompassing the total changing life of the individual as he moved from uninhibited infancy to controlled and responsible adulthood. Through its techniques of free association and dream analysis, it provided in one blow a method for both research and therapy.

Clinical psychology in its development has supported and paralleled the development of clinical psychiatry. The construction of the first mental tests by Binet during World War I not only gave an impetus to the emergence of clinical psychology but also, and more importantly, created an objective measure of one aspect of the mental life with which the psychiatrist was concerned in his examination. If intelligence could be determined objectively, it seemed only logical that many other mental and emotional characteristics could be eventually identified and described in objective terms. During the past half century certain psychologists have directed their energies toward the perfection of instruments to provide objective measurements for such clinical inferences as reaction time, attitudes, personality traits, aptitudes, perceptions, educational level, interests, values, neurotic tendency, and personality type.

Psychiatry, sensing some value in this work, turned increasingly to clinical psychology for objective measures of certain mental and emotional characteristics. As psychiatry moved from its early static conception to a dynamic view, clinical psychology attempted to keep pace by constructing instruments that would in an objective manner lay bare the richness, movement, content, and conflicts of the mental life. The development of such clinical instruments as the Rorschach, Thematic Apperception, and the Szondi tests emphasizes this change of pace. These tests have been regarded in some quarters as providing an objective check upon the psychiatric diagnosis.

In general, the clinical approach as used in psychiatry and psychology has the following purposes: first, to lay bare the intercorrelation of physiological and mental mechanisms in order to account for subjective outlook and behavior, and second, to develop measures for objectively determining certain discrete but subjective characteristics. From some perspectives in these disciplines, the assumption is made that the cause of the mental disorder is the interaction or combinations of those physiological and psychological elements found in the person.

The clinical approach also is found in sociology, but from quite an altered perspective concerning the nature of the individual and his relationship to society. Here, the clinical approach is best seen in the use made of the life-history document. The life-history method has two major functions. First, it is a technique for studying the process involved in the internalization of experience with its meaning to the person in terms of his self-conception and his orientation to the world. Second, it can be and has been used as a means for gaining insight into the organization and functioning of certain aspects of a given culture, as viewed through one human experience.

Fifty years ago when Dollard stated his criteria for judging the adequacy of the life-history document, he emphasized as one of them that "the person should be considered a specimen in a cultural series."[5] This criterion actually states the very essence of the differences between the clinical approach as it is described and as it is used by the social scientist. From this perspective the person does not stand in opposition to his culture, nor does he create the culture on the basis of his biopsychic endowment; rather, the person is both a creature of and a creator of culture. Thus it follows that the clinical approach in the study of mental disorder or any deviant behavior should aim at the examination of the case from different theoretical positions. Further, since it is a research technique for analyzing human personality and behavior, it should not be used to test or prove the correctness of any one theory. With every person who is identified as having distortions in the thinking, feeling, or acting spheres, the examiner should attempt in his clinical study to answer the following questions: Does the evidence secured by the clinical examination provide plausible support for a biological, psychological, or sociological explanation for the maladjustment in question? Does the burden of the evidence favor one type of explanation as against the other types? Are there elements from all three sources that form some integration to produce the complete clinical picture? What are the specific evidences that point to the selected alternative? The answers to these questions are all-important for they determine the next steps not only in research but also in treatment.

In discussing the ecological approach, the author is concerned with studies analyzing the distributions of various types of mental disorder in time and space.[6] In such studies the investigator is immediately faced with the question of whether or not any one distribution contains the same type of cases as another. If various bits of evidence can give him assurance on this point, then he can proceed to look for significant rate variations for a given type of case either in time or in social space.

Consider, for the moment, significant rate variations for schizophrenia in a community or social space. What do such rate variations signify? At present there are at least two possible explanations. First, local areas in the community where rates are high have a greater prevalence of social conditions and characteristics that are schizophrenically inducing than do areas where rates are low. Two assumptions are implicit here: (1) the social conditions and characteristics favorable to the disorder are relatively constant over a long period of time in the life of the community; (2) the persons who make up the rate in the local area have been subjected to these conditions rather consistently through their growth years. A second explanation states that certain areas have disproportionately high rates because the social conditions and characteristics of these areas are favorable for selecting and bringing to official attention numerous schizophrenic persons who in other communities, if they give no trouble, are left to the care of family or friends. This explanation implies that a societal judgment, in contrast to a psychiatric judgment, is crucial in determining who gets labeled as schizophrenic. In both explanations one is assuming an equal accessibility to hospital and clinical facilities. This is probably not the case in countries as large and as varied as the United States. The marked variation in first admission rates in the 50 states may be only a reflection of unequal facilities and not variations in true incidence. However, until more adequate checks are available, one cannot determine what the actual situation is. Unequal facilities may explain some rate variations, but it hardly can be said to constitute a theory.

One theory of social selection is found in the Hollingshead-Redlich hypothesis of differential treatment. Their findings support the hypothesis that "current prevalence is a measure of the responses patients in the several classes make to the treatment process," although they are quick to point out that this does not shed any light on why, from the beginning of treatment, schizophrenic patients are highly concentrated in the lower class.[7] An acceptance of this hypothesis requires assurance on two counts. Under the condition that no treatment was available, what would be the prevalence index by social class? What evidence is there that current treatment techniques available to upper class persons actually arrest the development of schizophrenia?

Look again at the two theoretical explanations outlined above. Significant rate differentials for areas within a community might be explained by either of these theories. But the ecological approach, even though skillfully used, is not likely to provide much of a basis for determining which theory is most valid.

These two theories also are relevant in examining those studies dealing with the distributions of new mental cases through time. Does the functioning of a social system have a greater pathic effect during some periods of time than at others, or is it merely that more cases come to be selected for psychotic designation in these pathic periods? Goldhamer and Marshall in their recent study present statistical evidence to the effect that there has been no marked increase in the psychoses of the central age groups over the past century. They believe their findings serve to refute the view current in some quarters that there has been a marked increase in mental disease during the twentieth century, and that such an increase is related to the killing pace of contemporary civilization.[8] If their findings are accepted, it means, as Goldhamer and Marshall point out, that the particular stress factors relevant to the production of psychosis have not increased over the past century or, if they have, they do not have the particular pathic effect that has been attributed to them. One also might infer that a short-term increase in rates, which they see as a possibility, means that in particular stress periods more persons are selected and defined as psychotic than in nonstress periods.

These inferences have a direct bearing upon the community and social class distribution studies, for there would seem to be no question but that stress and strain are distributed differentially in the various parts of any social structure. This reasoning leads one to the original explanations. Does maximal social stress in an area operate in the production of psychotics or merely in the selection and designation of more persons as psychotic than in areas where social stress is at a minimum?

It is this author's judgment that this issue will not be resolved very quickly or easily. To aid in its resolution three possible procedures are available. Here, schizophrenia will be used again because it is the number-one mental health problem. One procedure is to perfect clinically the diagnosis of schizophrenia. This may mean the eventual breaking up of this present diagnostic category into several entities.[9] It would be necessary here to develop objective procedures for determining a diagnosis for each of these new entities. Another alternative, if no headway can be made in this direction, is to assume that schizophrenia is socially induced. If persons in the family or neighborhood say a person is mentally unbalanced, then one may have to conclude after careful screening that the person is a schizophrenic. This means that the social definition of schizophrenia will vary in the different areas of a community structure, and thus one will have an understanding of the schizophrenic rate differentials in various communities. Schizophrenia, then, might be regarded as a joint product of social stress and social judgment.

Still a third procedure is to locate some community in Western culture that has been rather stable over a generation and influenced little by in- or out-migration. If such a community could be located, an investigator then could proceed to locate the areas of conflict, stress, and tension. After delimiting such areas within the community, he would proceed to examine the schizophrenic rate. If the rate was significantly higher in areas of high social stress than in those of low social stress, he might be in a stronger position for asserting the role of stress in the etiology of schizophrenia.

Ecological findings of distribution and correlation always face two questions: What theoretical principle provides the most valid explanation for the findings? How can such findings be most effectively utilized for the development of hypotheses about mental disorders that then must be studied by other methods?

The cultural approach is closely linked with the ecological. To the extent that the ecological area can be said to encompass a subculture, the two approaches have a close working affinity, since it is the elements of his subculture that a person internalizes and utilizes in coming to terms with other subcultures within the larger cultural framework. Some investigators have tended to concentrate on the observation and study of child-training techniques when working within a cultural approach.[10] Findings from these studies have been more eloquent in reporting differences than in showing the significance of child-training techniques for mental disturbances.

The significance of the cultural approach is not reflected adequately in these studies, but lies rather in cross-cultural observations and studies of mental disorder. The person who proposes to investigate mental disorder from a cross-cultural perspective would be concerned with seeking answers to the following questions:

Do the kinds of behavior and syndromes that constitute various abnormal mental states show incidence variations within a given cultural system?

Are there significant variations in the incidence of mental disorder between different cultural systems?

Does a given culture affect significantly both the form and content or only the content of abnormal mental states?

Are there marked variations between cultures in terms of the presence or absence of psychosis-inducing elements?

Are the strains and stresses or the general ethos of a given culture significant for the development of mental disorders?

The significance of these questions can be seen more clearly by making certain assumptions about culture and then attempting to point to certain logical consequences that follow from each assumption.

Because cultural relativism is still a prevailing doctrine among many anthropologists, one should start here. Cultural relativism as an intellectual position in anthropology asserts that the values and practices observed in any culture are to be understood and evaluated only in terms of the total framework of that particular culture. To be sure, there has been concern among certain anthropologists to find universal moral values, but while this problem may cross the mind of a cultural relativist, he seldom confronts it as a problem that can be solved.

Thus if one starts from a position of cultural relativism in attempting to explain functional mental disorder, one would expect the following propositions to have validity: First, both form and content of functional mental disorder will vary in different cultures. Second, certain cultures will have a greater incidence of their particular mental disorders than other cultures will have of their own. This is equivalent to saying that some cultures contain more psychosis-inducing elements than do others. Third, the incidence rate of mental disorder in a given culture will be relatively constant during periods of stability, but will rise or fall with swift and sharp changes in the cultural system.

The opposite assumption now will be made, namely, that there is a psychic unity of mankind that is independent of any particular cultural system. The following conclusions would logically follow: First, functional mental disorders will be found among people in every culture. Second, the content of a psychosis will vary from culture to culture, but its form will not. Third, variations in the incidence of mental disorder between different cultures will be accounted for by either a given culture providing acceptable roles for certain psychotics (that is, psychotics in Western diagnostic terms), or a given culture containing within it more psychosis-inducing elements than other cultures. If the former accounts for differential incidence, then by taking account of such cases one might expect to bring the rate of functional psychoses in that culture up to a rate parity with that in other cultures. If significant variations still exist between cultures, one would then be in a more confident position for asserting the validity of the latter alternative.

One final assumption will be made: the incidence of functional disorders among different cultures is approximately equal, but in any given culture sharp increases or decreases are observed. Where could one look for explanations for such occurrences? Current theory already suggests certain possibilities for inquiry, and so no more than brief mention will be made of them here. First, if a given culture develops sharply contradictory definitions in certain areas of behavior, one might expect such contra-indications to be registered in an increased rate of functional mental disorder. Second, if a culture is in the process of acculturation due to penetrating contacts with another culture, one might again expect an increase in rate. Third, if a culture shows sudden and quick social changes from within, one deals with another possibility for a rate increase. Finally, if a given culture is threatened in its peace and security from a force or forces outside of itself, one would expect the mental disorder rate to decrease significantly.

In dealing with these logical possibilities, the author is well aware of the empirical difficulties. Most cultural barriers may be swept away before the means can be developed to test the hypotheses. Two surveys of observations and investigations of mental disease among so-called primitives have served to focus attention either directly or indirectly on the issues raised in attempting to explore the possible relationships between culture and mental disease. Paul Benedict and Irving Jacks contend that while abnormal mental states peculiar to individual cultures have been reported, a more penetrating analysis of individual dynamics along with an awareness of the cultural context demonstrate the "underlying similarities of these mental disorders among primitive peoples to those seen in the West."[11] They call for more detailed and systematic investigations of mental disorders among non-Western societies. Their conclusion is much the same as that made by R. H. Felix and R. V. Bowers five years before, when they called for more intensive studies of the development and breakdown of personality in differing cultural milieus.[12]

In elaborating these various approaches, the author has been especially concerned with sharpening the issues that they raise and using theory to point to those areas where sociological investigations will be most rewarding. He has seen that the great obstacle to more fruitful sociological investigations revolves around the lack of agreement as to what constitutes a case of schizophrenia or any other functional disorder. It is possible that the present schizophrenic category contains many different entities with differing etiologies. If in the future ways can be found for breaking up the current schizophrenic grouping and for determining objectively a diagnosis of schizophrenia, psychiatric medicine will have achieved its greatest triumph. If this does not take place, then one will be thrown back upon social judgments in diverse cultural milieus for determining just exactly who is "crazy." Even so, while a disturbance may take similar forms in different cultural milieus, the level of tolerance of a culture then becomes relevant in determining who will be selected to fill the role of the psychotic person. A resolution of this issue will greatly help to determine the relevance of the various sociological approaches for shedding light on mental disorder.

This chapter has attempted to formulate a methodology for the sociological investigations of mental disorder. It has emphasized the necessity for such a methodology not only to guide subsequent sociological investigations in this area, but also to bring about more productive collaboration between the scientific disciplines concerned. It began by attempting to make clear the general standpoints of sociological investigation. From these it formulated the assumptions that give direction to sociological inquiry. This chapter further elaborated the basis for sociological investigation by a statement of some essential concepts—culture, socialization, cultural internalization, and social system—that are essential for understanding the individual's relationship with his fellows. It examined the theoretical approaches essential for sociological investigations of mental disorder and attempted to show the manner in which they can be integrated for a total attack from the sociological side. Finally, it showed how from these approaches certain specific hypotheses could be derived that might well serve as starting points for future sociological research into the problems posed by mental disorder in human society.

NOTES

1. See John A. Clausen and Melvin Kohn, "The Ecological Approach in Social Psychiatry," with "Comment" by H. Warren Dunham and "Rejoinder" by J. A. Clausen and M. Kohn, American Journal of Sociology 60 (September 1954): 140-51.

2. See my "Problems of Mental Health," in Analysis of Social Problems, ed. M. G. Caldwell and Lawrence Foster (Harrisburg, Penn.: Stackpole, 1954), p. 332, for another attempt at making these assumptions explicit.

3. In attempting to describe the process of socialization, I have included what has sometimes been referred to as the process of culturization. In making observations of child growth and development, it is extremely difficult to separate the two processes. Socialization may be more significant in the prelingual period, but after the child begins to use words the process of culturalization is in full swing. Socialization produces the social self and culturalization, the moral or cultural self, concepts comparable to Freud's ego and superego. The cultural self also is an extension of the social self and gives it content. For a good statement of this distinction, see J. S. Slotkin, Personality Development (New York: Harper Brothers, 1952), parts II and III.

4. See E. Kraepelin, Dementia Praecox and Paraphrenia, trans. R. Mary Barclay (Edinburgh: E. and S. Livingstone, 1919).

5. See J. Dollard, Criteria for the Life History (New Haven: Yale University Press, 1935).

6. See Robert E. L. Faris and H. Warren Dunham, Mental Disorders in Urban Areas (Chicago: University of Chicago Press, 1939); E. Mowrer, Disorganization—Personal and Social (New York: J. B. Lippincott, 1942), chaps. 15 and 16; C. W. Schroeder, "Mental Disorders in Cities," American Journal of Sociology 47 (July 1942): 40-47; Henry B. Elkind and M. Taylor, "The Alleged Increase in the Incidence of the Major Psychoses," American Journal of Psychiatry 92 (January 1936); B. Malzberg, Social and Biological Aspects of Mental Disease (Utica, N. Y.: State Hospital Press, 1940), chap. 1; and H. Goldhamer and A. Marshall, Psychosis and Civilization (Glencoe, Ill.: Free Press, 1953).

7. A. Hollingshead and F. Redlich, "Social Stratification and Schizophrenia," American Sociological Review 19 (June 1954): 302-06.

8. Goldhamer and Marshall, Psychosis, pp. 95-96.

9. L. Bellak's concluding comment after reviewing the research in schizophrenia is very pertinent in this connection: "We believe that it may be helpful to conceive of any given case [of schizophrenia] as actually occurring on some point of a continuum from a hypothetical

point of complete psychogenecity to a hypothetical point of complete organicity." See his Dementia Praecox: The Past Decade's Work and Present Status—A Review and Evaluation (New York: Grune and Stratton, 1948), p. 444.

10. See M. C. Ericson, "Child Rearing and Social Status," American Journal of Sociology 52 (November 1946): 190-92; A. W. Green, "The Middle Class Male Child and Neurosis," American Sociological Review 11 (February 1946): 31-41; and W. H. Sewell, "Infant Training and Personality Development," American Journal of Sociology 8 (September 1952): 130-39.

11. See N. J. Demerath, "Schizophrenia among Primitives," American Journal of Psychiatry 98 (1942): 703-07; and P. Benedict, and I. Jacks, "Mental Illness in Primitive Societies," Psychiatry 17 (November 1954): 377-89.

12. R. H. Felix and R. V. Bowers, "Mental Hygiene and Socio-Economic Factors," Milbank Memorial Fund Quarterly 26 (1948): 125-47.

PART TWO
THE COMMUNITY VARIABLE

INTRODUCTION TO PART TWO

The chapters in Part II are focused on examining the relationship between the nature of community organization and the incidence of schizophrenia. This relationship was not clear at the outset of this research, but was brought clearly into focus by the findings reported in Chapter 3. The distribution of schizophrenic rates showed a high concentration at the city's center, with rates declining in all directions toward the city's periphery. This means that the highest rates are found in the most economically impoverished subcommunities in the city. By contrast it should be noted that the distribution of manic-depressive psychoses' rates is random in character. This most unexpected finding suggested a number of hypotheses for investigation bearing on the relation between the sociocultural environment and the incidence of schizophrenia.

The findings hardly had been digested by other investigators before the criticisms began coming. The criticisms centered on two issues of coverage and interpretation. With respect to coverage, the critics were saying that the distribution picture is not valid because it is based only on first admissions to state and private hospitals. The case count is not complete because it does not include those persons who have schizophrenia and are living in the community but never get admitted to a psychiatric facility. With respect to the interpretation issue, the critics were asked if the distribution pattern meant what it seemed to mean. In other words, could a case be made for the apparent finding that a subcommunity at the city's center produced more cases of schizophrenia than a subcommunity at the city's periphery.

In speaking of one subcommunity producing more schizophrenic cases than another subcommunity, it is assumed that there are more aspects of the community organization of the high-rate community that are schizophrenic inducing than are found in the low-rate community. To argue against this proposition that a subcommunity at the city's center produced an excess of schizophrenic cases, the drift hypothesis was suggested as an alternative explanation. This hypothesis stated that high schizophrenic rates were a product of the drift of persons who had the disease into these areas that produced the highest rate.

A careful consideration of these two critical issues was uppermost in the designing of the research reported in Chapter 4. In this research the first step was to select from the distribution of schizophrenic first-admission rates to state hospitals two subcommunities in Detroit—one high-rate area at the city's center and a low-rate area at the periphery. An answer to the two central criticisms of the first study was to be made by building into the research design three types of data. First, it was proposed that the coverage for both subcommunities was to be as complete as possible. This was to be accomplished by exploring every psychiatric facility, both private and public, that had any contact with mentally disturbed persons. In analyzing all that was involved by coverage, it became clear that while there are probably some mentally disturbed persons who never get into a custodial or treatment facility, it seemed highly unlikely considering the nature of schizophrenic symptoms and the nature of city life that these persons would have schizophrenia. In other words, a person with schizophrenia living in a large city eventually gets to a psychiatric treatment facility.

Second, the design provided for a clinical examination by a qualified psychiatrist of every case of schizophrenia that was turned up by the total covering of facilities. Finally, the design also provided for each case uncovered that information be collected on place of birth, number of persons in household, length of time living in the subcommunity, and the number of times moved. It was argued that an analysis of these data would establish the validity of the subcommunity rates, determine if there really were significant rate differences between central city and periphery, and discover the extent to which schizophrenics are indigenous to the subcommunities where they are first picked up.

Chapter 5 reports on another crucial issue centering on the distribution pattern of schizophrenic rates. An attempt is made to show the manner in which the social changes affecting cities are reshaping the distribution patterns of schizophrenic rates as well as other psychoses.

3

THE ECOLOGY OF FUNCTIONAL PSYCHOSES IN CHICAGO

Studies of the geographical distribution of social data go back for over 100 years. This technique, as used by the modern social scientist, is hardly a new one. However, improved statistical methods, more adequate, basic population data, and improved statistical records enable the modern social scientist to get a more accurate picture, quantitatively speaking, of any social phenomenon that he may study. Many of those early studies were made by distributing a type of social data within the counties or provinces of a country or nation. Later studies attempted distributions within certain areas of modern nineteenth-century cities. In England, Mayhew attempted some early distribution studies with the city as a unit.[1] A generation later, Booth, who studied economic and social stratification in London, originated the idea of the natural, circular growth of the city.[2] This idea was later refined and improved by Burgess's attempt to delimit the natural areas of the city and make the scheme applicable to all U. S. cities.[3]

These nineteenth-century social scientists studied by the use of this method practically all of the social problems that are receiving attention by the modern students of social phenomena. However, there was no significant attempt to study insanity by this method, although there were some early statistical studies giving rates by areas or provinces within a country.[4] Otherwise, scientists of the nineteenth century were definitely concerned with this problem, for there is ample evidence in the literature to prove the scientific

---

Used with permission from the American Sociological Review 2 (December 1937): 467-79.

interest in the study of mental disorder.[5] The definite determination that spirochaeta pallida was the cause of general paralysis in about 1897 was the first great achievement in isolating a definite mental disease.[6] During practically the entire nineteenth century idiocy, alcoholism, moral insanity, melancholia, mania, dementia, and epilepsy constituted the chief diagnostic categories of mental disorder.[7]

While there were some attempts to compute insanity rates by areas within the countries, it is doubtful if much of this material was ever portrayed on maps. An early study of the geographical distribution of mental disorders was made by J. S. Sutherland in 1901.[8] At about the same time, W. A. White presented a paper on the geographical distribution of insanity in the United States.[9] While he presented no actual maps, he pointed out, on the basis of his statistics, that the older and longer-settled sections of the country had a much higher incidence of insanity than the newer and more-recently-settled sections. He also found that among the blacks in the southern states there was a much lower rate of insanity than among the blacks in the northern states. The fact that both men were concerned with all cases of insanity indicates the fact, even at this date, that any diagnostic category of mental disorder in use was hardly of significance for statistical manipulation.[10]

These scattered attempts at presenting and interpreting insanity rates for provinces within a geographical area were the only studies purporting to investigate insanity in relation to the social milieu in which it developed. In the evolving scientific division of labor the study of mental disease and abnormality had come to be the exclusive concern of the medical profession in both Europe and the United States. This resulted in the very definite tendency to study mental disease by the same methods as had been used in studying physical disease, and consequently this tended to hinder and restrict other approaches to this problem. Since 1930 at the University of Chicago, certain ecological, statistical, and case studies have been made of certain types of mental disorder. This chapter has for its purpose the presentation of the ecology of the two main functional psychoses in Chicago and a theoretical discussion of the implications of this ecological analysis.

As is well known, schizophrenia is the most frequently diagnosed mental disorder in the state hospitals throughout the country. This psychosis constitutes between 25 and 40 percent of the first admissions to hospitals for mental disorders. The percentage varies throughout the United States.[11] Between 1922 and 1931, 7,253 persons from Chicago were admitted to state hospitals for the first time and given a diagnosis of schizophrenia. Frequency rates for these cases were calculated for the local communities. For the population base of the rates, the estimated adult population of each community in

1927, the middle year, is used.[12] An ecological map of these rates indicates very definitely that schizophrenia shows a great variation in frequency in the different communities. The pattern formed by the rates is a regular and typical one and follows in the gradients of its rates Burgess's scheme of the circular growth of the city.[13] The distribution of rates range from 111 in community 1, at the extreme northeast end of the city, to 1,195 in community 32, the Loop or central business district. The average rate is 289 and the median rate is 322, and these figures indicate that the bulk of the community rates are clustered at the low end of a skewed frequency distribution. In other words, there are a few communities close to the center of the city that have extremely high rates, while the great bulk of the communities have much lower rates. The highest rates for schizophrenia are in the hobohemia, the rooming-house, and the foreign-born communities close to the center of the city. There are no glaring exceptions to this regular pattern. The noticeable rise of the rates in the south Chicago region is consistent with the regular pattern for Chicago, as these communities represent areas of some social disorganization due to their close approximation to the steel factories. In addition to the concentration of the rates in those communities close to the center of the city, it is significant to note the order of the rates in the south side black belt. The three black areas in this belt extending south of the Loop have rates of 662, 470, and 410 respectively. All of these rates are higher than the average and median rates and decline in a regular manner, similar to the rates on other radial lines from the city's center, and so tend to negate any theories in relation to race as a factor in schizophrenia. If race were a significant factor, there would seem to be no legitimate reason why there should be such wide variations in the rates in these communities in which 90 percent of the population are blacks.

Among these cases of schizophrenia the males are slightly more numerous than the females, the ratio being 117 males to 100 females.[14] This would indicate that the factor of sex has some significance in connection with schizophrenia. However, in a study of the distribution of the male and female schizophrenic rates separately, there appears to be no radical deviation in the expected pattern.

Of the 7,253 cases, 3,916 are males. The rates range from 79 in community 1, to 1,417 in community 32. These are the same communities that form the extremes in the distribution of total schizophrenia. The average rate is 396 and the median rate is 365. This indicates the same type of frequency distribution as was noted in the distribution of the total schizophrenic rates.

The distribution of female rates, based on 3,337 cases, also shows a similar wide range. The lowest rate is 130 in community 8A, the Gold Coast, and the highest rate is 932 in community 28A, a hobohemia community directly west of the central business district. The average rate is 367 and the median rate is 312, and so a similar skewed frequency distribution is in evidence. This distribution of the female schizophrenic rates is typical of the other two, with approximately three exceptions. These three exceptions in the regularity of the pattern are to be found in community 32, which has an extremely low rate, and in communities 17 and 56+, which have unexpectedly high rates. * It is difficult to explain away these exceptions. However, it can be noted that in community 32, the central business district, the hobohemia community contributes practically all of the male cases, and there are practically no desirable places for women to live in this community. The total number of women in the population is extremely low. There were 98 male schizophrenic cases found in this community and only three female schizophrenic cases. These female cases included a maid at an expensive club on Michigan Boulevard, a resident of a first-class hotel, and a resident of a cheap hotel of a disorderly character on Wabash Avenue. The position of these three exceptional communities tends to reduce the resulting coefficient of correlation between the male and female schizophrenic rates to $.59 \pm .07$. It is interesting to note that the sex ratio in the total schizophrenic group holds true for the high-rate schizophrenic areas as well as for the city as a whole. In the upper quartile of the 17 communities, the schizophrenic sex ratio is 143 to 100, while the sex ratio of the population in this area is only 130 males to 100 females.

Because of the limitations of space, the distribution of the rates for the separate types of schizophrenia are not discussed here. It is sufficient to point out that they all show heavy concentration in the disorganized areas of the city and present the familiar skewed frequency distribution, such as was noted in the distribution of the total schizophrenic cases.[15] The paranoid and hebephrenic distributions of rates are similar to the distribution of total schizophrenic rates. However, the catatonic distribution of rates does not follow the pattern of the other types, although it does show a definite concentration of rates in certain of the disorganized areas of the city, notably the foreign-born and black communities.

In addition to the distribution of the above schizophrenic rates, the case data that constitute these distributions, with the addition of three more years, have been distributed in the 120 subcommunities

---

*Local communities 56, 57, 62, 64, and 65 were combined to form one community, referred to as 56+.

of Chicago.[16] The distribution of the average yearly rate based on a total of 10,575 schizophrenic cases is shown in Map 3.1.* The range of rates in this distribution is from 14 in community 92, an apartment and two-flat area, to 150 in community 74, the central business district, with a median rate of 30.1 and an average rate of 34.6. The same skewed frequency distribution, as was noted in the previous distribution of schizophrenic rates, is also in evidence. Likewise, the same concentration of rates is noticed, with the high average rates falling at the center of the city and the low rates on the periphery. The highest rates are to be found in the hobohemia, rooming-house, foreign-born, and black communities.

The objective findings in connection with the ecology of schizophrenia can be stated as follows: (1) The high rates for total schizophrenia are concentrated in communities of marked social disorganization in Chicago. (2) The distribution of the male and female schizophrenic rates separately show the same concentration in the disorganized communities of the city. (3) The distribution of rates shows the same pattern and concentration by both local and sub-communities. (4) The high rates for paranoid and hebephrenic schizophrenia are concentrated also in these extremely socially disorganized communities in a similar fashion to the total group. The correlation coefficient between paranoid and hebephrenic schizophrenia is .75 ± .05. (5) The high rates for catatonic schizophrenia are concentrated mainly in the foreign-born and black communities. While this distribution is different from the other types because of the paucity of the catatonics in the rooming-house communities of the city, nevertheless, a definite concentration of rates is noted. (6) The rates for the three types of schizophrenics, as well as the rates for the total schizophrenic series, show a skewed frequency distribution, with the bulk of the communities having low rates and a few of the communities at the center of the city having high rates.

---

*It should be noted that the total case basis in these maps showing distributions by subcommunities includes private hospital cases as well as state hospital cases. In the schizophrenic distribution, the private hospital cases are negligible, amounting in all to 13.7 percent of the total, while in the following manic-depressive distribution, the private hospital cases amount to exactly 50 percent of the total, a large enough percentage to affect the character of the distribution pattern. However, while there is a difference in the distribution of manic-depressive rates, when the cases from state and private hospitals are distributed separately (Pearsonian $r = -.06 \pm .10$), this does not affect the conclusions set forth in this chapter.

MAP 3.1

Schizophrenia, All Types, Average Rate per 100,000
Based on 1930 Population, Aged 15-19
(based on data from 4 state and 8 private hospitals)

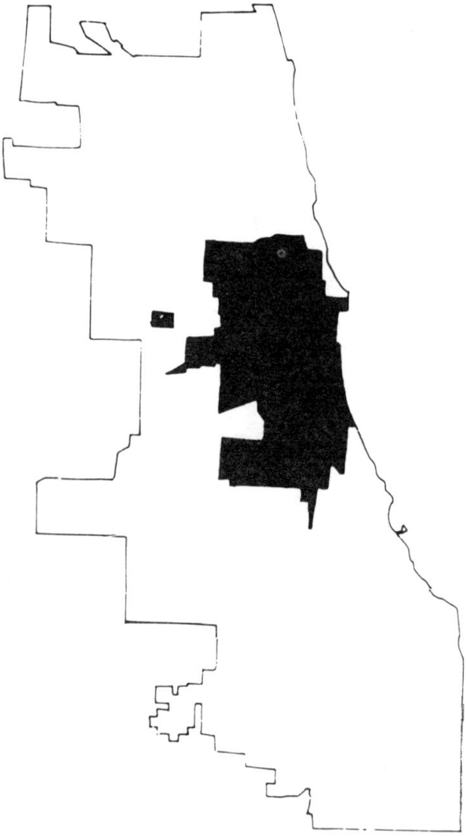

While these different distributions of schizophrenic rates present an interesting comparison within themselves, they attain an additional significance when compared with the other main functional psychosis, manic-depressive. Because the diagnostic problems in the functional disorders are so great, a study of the distribution of the manic-depressive group might be significant in ascertaining whether or not any real distinction between them has been made. A preliminary distribution of manic-depressive rates was computed from a base of 734 cases, of which 296 were males and 438 were females. The sex ratio of 68 males to 100 females is very different from the sex ratio in the schizophrenic group. The range of rates is low as compared to any of the schizophrenic distributions, the rates varying from eight in community 59, an area of second immigrant settlement, to 84 in community 28C, a foreign-born section.* The average rate is 37 and the median is 37, and this indicates that the characteristic skewness of the schizophrenic distributions is lacking. The distribution shows no marked concentration of the high rates close to the center of the city. In fact, far from being regular, the pattern of rates might be described as random. It is significant to note that while the highest rate is in a community near the center of the city, it is bordered by communities that have both low and median rates. This distribution, therefore, is different in many respects from the schizophrenic distributions that have been examined.

Because of the low case basis in the above distribution of manic-depressive rates, it seemed particularly desirable to study a distribution of rates based on a larger number of cases. The distribution of such rates in the subcommunities of Chicago is shown in Map 3.2, based on 2,311 cases. As might be expected from the preliminary distribution, there is an absence of the typical pattern. In this distribution, the rates range from 1.5 in community 70, a two-flat and single-home area, to 19.3 in community 74, the central business district. The median rate is 6.9 and the average rate is 7.2. The high rates show no semblance of a pattern in their distribution throughout the city. There are high rates at the center of the city and there are also some high rates on the periphery. This is very much at variance from any of the schizophrenic distributions where, as has been shown, there is a complete absence of high rates in the

---

*The female catatonic group with approximately the same number of cases (711) has a much greater range, varying from none in community 2, to 222 in community 24A. This indicates again the skewed distribution in any schizophrenic sample of the cases in the manic-depressive sample.

MAP 3.2

Manic-Depressive Psychoses, All Types, Average Rate per 100,000
Based on 1930 Population, Aged 15-64
(based on data from 4 state and 8 private hospitals)

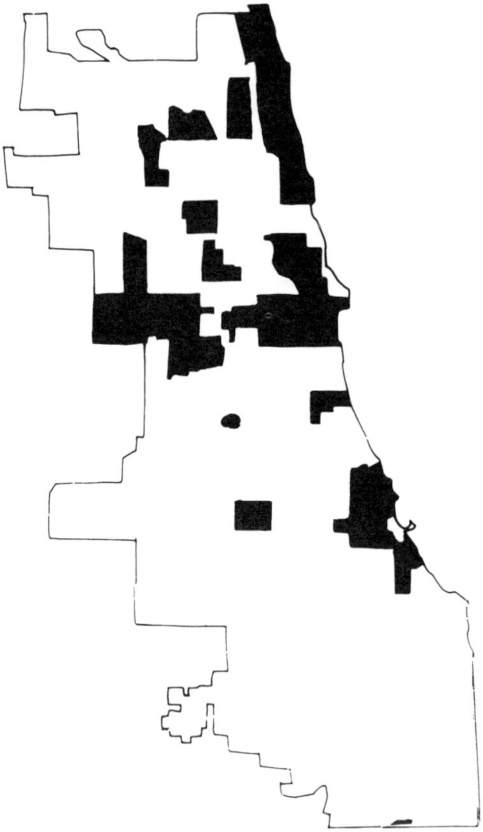

outlying communities of the city. Again, the very definite lack of skewness in the manic-depressive frequency distribution is to be noted.

When the rates for each sex of the manic-depressive group are distributed in the subcommunities, the same random pattern is in evidence. The patterns also are random to each other as evidenced by a coefficient of correlation of $.33 \pm .08$. This contrasts quite sharply with the relatively high correlation figure obtained when the schizophrenic rates by sex are considered together.

When the manic-depressive cases are separated into their respective types of manic and depressed, and are distributed among the 120 subcommunities, the distribution of the rates in each type still forms a random pattern, although somewhat dissimilar to the random pattern formed when the types are combined together. In other words, not only is there a random pattern formed by the total case basis of the manic-depressive rates, but the pattern also is random when either one of the two chief types in this diagnostic category are considered separately. The distribution of rates for each type is not only random in itself, but also is random when compared with the other type. In fact, the coefficient of correlation between them is $.104 \pm .10$. This figure still remains low when the rates by sex, for each type, are correlated together, the coefficient being $.15 \pm .09$, when the male manic rates are considered with the male depressed rates, and $.30 \pm .08$ when the female manic rates are correlated with the female depressed rates.[17] These low correlation figures tell a story in themselves when compared with the correlation figures presented for schizophrenia, by sex and type, where high correlations are in evidence.

The objective findings in connection with the ecology of the manic-depressive psychoses can be stated as follows: (1) The pattern formed by the rates is a random one. Both high and low rates are distributed in no systematic fashion throughout the city. (2) The distribution for male and female manic-depressive rates separately show the same random and unsystematic distribution. (3) The distribution of rates shows the same random pattern for both local and subcommunities. (4) The rates for the separate types of manic and depressed also are extremely random in their distribution. (5) While the addition of the private hospital cases tends to change the distribution of the rates in the city, the elimination of these cases does not change the random pattern of the distribution. (6) All of the distribution of manic-depressive rates show an absence of skewness in their frequency distribution, with approximately the same number of communities having high rates as low rates.

That there is a vast difference between the distribution of rates in these two main functional psychoses is to be seen again when they are correlated together. The distribution of the rates for these two mental disorders in the 68 local communities of Chicago has a correlation of .37 ± .10. When the rates of these two psychoses in the 120 subcommunities are correlated, the coefficient figure is .24 ± .08. In other words, it appears that when any sample of schizophrenic cases is distributed, there is a definite pattern that follows the ecological structure of the city, while when any sample of manic-depressive cases is distributed, there is no pattern formed that fits into this ecological scheme of the city.

Further evidence on this point can be seen when the rates of these two mental disorders are correlated with certain indexes of social life. In the second set of distribution of these two functional disorders, a correlation was effected between the respective rates and a housing index for the subcommunities. For this index the percentage ratio of hotels, apartments, and apartment hotels to the total number of dwellings in the subcommunities was used. The manic-depressive distribution correlated with this index .50 ± .07. When the manic-depressive cases from private hospitals are eliminated, and this index is correlated with the rates based upon a distribution of only manic-depressive state hospital cases, the correlation figure drops to .08 ± .10. The distribution of schizophrenic rates in the subcommunities of the city correlate with this housing index -.12 ± .09.

Other indexes tend to bring out the differences in the distribution in these two functional psychoses. If one takes as an index of cultural level the median school grade reached by the population in any subcommunity and correlates it with the manic-depressive rates, the resulting coefficient is .44 ± .07. When this index is correlated with the schizophrenic rates, the resulting coefficient figure is -.47 ± .07. This would seem to indicate a tendency for manic-depressive cases to come from those urban areas with a fairly high cultural level. The negative correlation in connection with schizophrenia indicates exactly the opposite. The same situation is noted when correlating these rates with an index of economic level in the subcommunities. For such an index, the median monthly rental paid by families for housing in the community was taken. This index correlates with the manic-depressive rates at .41 ± .08, and with the schizophrenic rates at -.51 ± .07.

It was pointed out above that in the second sample of manic-depressive cases, exactly 50 percent were admitted to public hospitals and 50 percent were admitted to private hospitals. This high percentage of private hospital cases in the manic-depressive group stands in sharp contrast to the low percentage of schizophrenic cases admitted to private hospitals. This high percentage of private hospital cases in the former group might be explained by either one of two conditions. First, there is a tendency for the private hospital to give the most hopeful diagnosis for the benefit of relatives, which means, according to traditional psychiatry, a manic-depressive diagnosis.* Second, it is possible that there may be a real selection of manic-depressive cases by the private hospitals. Some psychiatrists in the Chicago area feel that the former condition is the true one. However, there is some evidence in this study to indicate that the second condition is somewhat more than a remote possibility. While the pattern of manic-depressive rates in any distribution of such cases does appear to be extremely random, the correlation coefficients, with certain selective indexes, do indicate the tendency of manic-depressive cases to come from a higher social and economic level in contrast with the schizophrenic cases. Some additional evidence on this point, similar to that presented above, is obtained by contrasting the manic-depressive patients with the schizophrenic patients in terms of median rentals paid in the subcommunities. Over half of all the manic-depressive cases corrected for the population factor come from communities in the city that pay a median rental of $61.68 or above, while half of the schizophrenic cases, corrected for the population factor, come from communities that pay a median rental of $33.45 or above. There is no doubt that the excessive numbers of private hospital cases in the manic-depressive group tend to increase markedly this median rental figure. When the private hospital cases are eliminated, however, it is found that the remaining manic-depressive cases that are now entirely state hospital cases come from communities where the median rental is $43.44 or above. This rental figure is still considerably higher than the rental figure of half the schizophrenic cases, where the private hospital cases were not eliminated. There is, then, apparently a definite tendency for manic-depressive patients to come from a higher income group than the schizophrenic patients.

From this comparative study of the distribution of these two main functional psychoses and their relation to certain indexes of social life, the following conclusions might be briefly stated: (1) A comparison of the distribution of the rates of the schizophrenic and manic-depressive psychoses shows them to be unlike each other in almost every respect. (2) The schizophrenic rates show the typical ecological pattern and are concentrated in the disorganized areas of

---

*It may be of some significance to note that in the psychoneurotic series that also was part of this research, 67 percent of the cases were admitted to private hospitals and only 33 percent to state hospitals.

the city, while the manic-depressive rates do not show a typical pattern nor any definite concentration in the disorganized and poverty-stricken areas of the city. (3) There is a tendency, although not clearly defined, for manic-depressive cases to come from a higher cultural and economic level as compared with the schizophrenic cases. (4) The schizophrenic rates show a skewed frequency distribution, while the manic-depressive rates show no such skewness in their distribution.

While this ecological and statistical evidence may not be conclusive, it does appear that there is some real distinction in the distribution of these two functional disorders in Chicago. How far this will hold true of other U.S. cities is problematical. Every psychiatrist realizes that the diagnostic problems in the functional disorders are great, and the question can be raised as to whether anything is gained by making distributions of cases falling in these two categories when the percent of diagnostic error is so high. The percent of error in the present data probably ranges from 30 to 40 percent, according to estimates given by the psychiatrists themselves. Even with this high percentage of error, the number of cases is large enough in each sample to assert that the pattern of rates in these two psychoses is a fairly reliable one.

While it is necessary to be cautious about interpreting these data, certain implications can, with some justification, be pointed out. The random pattern in the manic-depressive distribution, in juxtaposition to the typical pattern in the schizophrenic distribution, would seem to imply that some valid distinction has been made in classification. From this implication, others follow. Chief of these might be the implication that the environment is a very potent factor in the etiology of the schizophrenic disorder, but that it plays no part in the manic-depressive disorder. It then would follow that if environmental factors are not significant in manic-depressive psychosis, time is a certain justification for asserting the priority of hereditary and constitutional factors. This would be in line with the statistical studies of heredity in the functional psychoses that universally show that biological inheritance is more significant in manic-depressive than in schizophrenia. Even though there is a great difference between the pattern of rates of the two psychoses, it does not necessarily follow that the schizophrenic psychosis bears a definite relation to the environment and the manic-depressive psychosis does not. Both may be connected with different types of social processes. It is only in the case of the schizophrenic pattern that this connection appears to be more definitely established.

A possible sociological explanation of the manic-depressive pattern might be found in the suggestion that precipitating factors are causal ones in relation to these psychoses.[18] Such precipitating factors occur in all social and economic levels of life and, consequently, are not so likely to have a definite connection with the community situation, but rather with the interplay of personality and psychological factors of family relationships and intimate personal contacts. An explanation of the high rates of schizophrenia in the extremely disorganized areas of the city has been made by stating that persons with schizophrenic tendencies or predispositions drift down into these areas. If this hypothesis is a correct one, the implication would seem to follow from the evidence presented that manic-depressives do not drift at all or at least show no tendency to drift into the disorganized areas of city life. These suggested implications are only intended to point the way toward additional research. First, however, it will be necessary to establish beyond a shadow of a doubt that there is a difference in the distribution of these two functional disorders as outlined in this chapter. Diagnostic problems still make this thesis somewhat uncertain. The study of the distribution of these two functional disorders in other U. S. cities would appear to be the next step in this ecological research.

NOTES

1. H. Mayhew and J. Benny, The Criminal Prisons in London (London: Charles Griffin, 1862).

2. C. Booth, Life and Labor of the People of London (London: Williams and Margate, 1891).

3. R. E. Park and E. W. Burgess, The City (Chicago: University of Chicago Press, 1925), p. 50.

4. Journal of the Statistical Society of London (1851): 49-62; ibid. (1852): 250-56.

5. In this connection it is interesting to note the establishment of numerous journals in the European countries devoted to scientific inquiry into insanity. The Journal of Mental Science (London) was founded in 1855; the Annales d'hygiene publique et de médicine légale (Paris) in 1829; the Journal of Nervous and Mental Disease (United States) about 1873.

6. See A. Rosanoff, Manual of Psychiatry, 6th ed. (New York: Wiley, 1926), p. 270.

7. J. C. Buchnill and D. H. Tuke, A Manual of Psychological Medicine (Philadelphia: Blanchard and Lea, 1858), pp. 88-100.

8. J. S. Sutherland, "Growth and Geographical Distribution of Lunacy in Scotland," in Report of the Seventy-first Meeting of the British Association for the Advancement of Science (Glasgow) (1901): 742-43. See also W. R. MacDermott, "The Topographical Distribution

of Insanity," letter in the British Medical Journal 2 (September 26, 1908): 950.

9. W. A. White, "Geographical Distribution of Insanity in the United States," Journal of Nervous and Mental Disease 30 (1903): 257-79. Also see A. O. Wright, "The Increase of Insanity," Conference of Charities and Corrections (1884), pp. 228-36.

10. Some statistics on the incidence of insanity by types are to be found in an article by P. Garnier, "La Folie a Paris," Annales d'hygiene publique et de medicine legale 23 (1890): 5-44.

11. Mental Patients in State Hospitals (Washington, D. C.: Bureau of the Census, 1928).

12. The local communities, as worked out by the Local Community Research Council at the University of Chicago, were used as a basis for these rates. Some of the communities that contained populations too small to be used as a basis for reliable rates were combined with adjoining areas, and three of the communities near the center of the city were subdivided. The city was divided in this manner so that each community contains reasonably homogeneous characteristics and yet has a sufficiently large population to make possible reliable rates. Rates on the maps presented in this chapter are distributed in the 120 subcommunities of Chicago, which are merely a further refinement of the census tracts. The use of these subcommunities makes possible a somewhat finer discrimination of the differences to be found in the various parts of the city.

The use of the adult population is not a perfect adjustment for age, but since there are few persons under 21 years of age in the schizophrenic group, the adjustment is probably adequate for the purpose. It should be noted that in those maps showing the distribution of cases in the 120 subcommunities of the city, there has been a closer refinement for age, and these rates are based on the population 15 years and over. It also should be noted that the rates in the more detailed 120 subcommunities are average rates as contrasted to total rates in the local communities.

13. The phrase "a regular and typical pattern" as used in this chapter means a pattern in which the high rates for given phenomena are to be found at the center of the city, with the rates declining in every direction as one approaches the periphery. For a good example of such a pattern, see C. R. Shaw, Delinquency Areas (Chicago: University of Chicago Press, 1929).

14. The sex ratio in the estimated adult population used as the basis for the rates is 105 males to 100 females. There is, then, a real excess of schizophrenics among the males, a fact that also is true of the total number of schizophrenics in the United States. See Mental Patients in State Hospitals, p. 12. See also H. M. Pollock, "Frequency of Schizophrenia in Relation to Sex, Age, Environment,

Nativity and Race," in Schizophrenia—An Investigation of the Most Recent Advances, reported by the Association for Research in Nervous and Mental Diseases, vol. V (New York: Paul B. Hoeber, 1928).

15. See H. W. Dunham, "A Study of the Distribution of Six Major Psychoses in the Local Community Areas of Chicago" (Master's diss., University of Chicago, 1935).

16. The opportunity to distribute these data in the 120 subcommunities was provided by the setting up of a WPA project to study the trend of mental disease during the depression years. This project was sponsored by the State Psychopathic Institute of the Department of Public Welfare, State of Illinois. Dr. H. D. Singer of the Psycopathic Institute and Professors Wirth and Burgess of the University of Chicago served as advisers for the project.

17. The scantiness of the cases in the manic-depressive group throws some question on the reliability of the rates by sex and by type. See Frank A. Ross, "Ecology and the Statistical Method," American Journal of Sociology 38 (January 1933): 507-22. Also see the reply to this criticism by C. C. Peters, "Note on a Misconception of Statistical Significance," American Journal of Sociology 39 (September 1933): 231-36. Ross examined Faris's insanity rates for the city of Chicago and pointed out that the number of cases used in the study was too small and that the distribution pattern might be due to chance. However, when he combined areas and made a test with an error formula for determining the significance or nonsignificance of rates between different communities, he concluded that the pattern could not be due to chance alone. In the schizophrenic series the case basis has been so increased that it would seem that criticism on this point has been sufficiently answered. In the manic-depressive series, while the case basis is still rather low and the same criticism might be made as to this pattern, it would seem from the other statistical evidence that there is a marked difference between this pattern of rates and the schizophrenic pattern.

18. On this point see C. A. Bonner, "Psychogenic Factors as Causation Agents in Manic-Depressive Psychoses," in Manic-Depressive Psychosis—An Investigation of the Most Recent Advances, reported by the Association for Research in Nervous and Mental Diseases, vol. XI (Baltimore: Williams and Wilkins, 1931), pp. 121-30; M. J. Brew, "Precipitating Factors in the Manic-Depressive Psychoses," Psychiatric Quarterly 7 (July 1933): 401-10; and J. H. Travis, "Precipitating Factors in the Manic-Depressive Psychoses," Psychiatric Quarterly 7 (July 1933): 411-18.

4
COMMUNITY ORGANIZATION AND SCHIZOPHRENIA

The central purpose of this chapter is twofold: to determine if the character of a subcommunity's social organization can account for significant rate differentials in the incidence of schizophrenia, and to discover any elements within it that might function as etiological agents in the development or precipitation of schizophrenia. This statement of purpose is intended to point up the confusion in thinking so often apparent among sociologists in their evaluation of the findings of epidemiological studies of mental disease. Their confusion arises from the fact that they are confronting two levels of analysis that they fail to recognize as two and often try to treat as one. By this it is meant that they are quick to move from the finding of significant rate variations in different social structures to explanations emphasizing a specific sociocultural factor in the etiology of the disease that they are studying from an epidemiological perspective. Consequently, their interpretations frequently shuttle back and forth between the social system level and the social-psychological level.

This chapter centers mainly on questions derived from the social system level of analysis. Toward this end five questions have been raised:

Does schizophrenia show significant differential incidence rates in different types of communities?

Used with permission from my book Community and Schizophrenia—An Epidemiological Analysis (Detroit: Wayne State University Press, 1965), pp. 133-71.

To what extent can one have confidence that all cases that should enter into a rate have been uncovered within a given population?

To what extent can it be shown that the cases that make up the rate for a given community are indigenous to the community?

Do significant rate differentials between contrasting types of communities give one any basis for inferring a psychosis-inducing quality for a given community organization?

Is the presence of certain stress factors related in any manner to the incidence of schizophrenia in a given community?

These questions appear to be crucial in any attempt to pin down the more precise role of community organization in affecting the incidence of schizophrenia.

The previous epidemiological studies of Faris and Dunham in Chicago, Hare in Bristol, England, Lin in Formosa, Jaco in Texas, and Hollingshead and Redlich in New Haven have amassed a certain amount of evidence that suggests, as Jaco puts it, that mental disorder is not randomly distributed in a population; rather, it shows tendencies to concentrate in one part of a population in contrast to another.[1] This finding also has been demonstrated for the schizophrenic psychosis. While there have been other studies that have questioned this finding, the issue never has been resolved with any high degree of confidence. This is precisely one of the issues that this study has been designed to test.

ANALYSIS OF INCIDENCE RATES

This chapter is concerned only with the analysis of the psychiatric cases for 1956, 1957, and 1958 that have turned up by screening 176 psychiatric facilities in southeastern Michigan. The procedure will be to present some findings from the other studies and then examine the evidence from this intensive study to see if the previous findings can be supported or rejected. This will be done by examining the rate differences for schizophrenia between high- and low-rate areas, as reported by these other studies. In general, the ratio of cases between high- and low-rate areas runs approximately three to one, making a difference that in all cases is statistically significant. The concern is to find out if the rates in these two subcommunities will maintain the same ratio. The ratios for selected previous studies are presented in Table 4. 1.

Next the two subcommunities will be compared with respect to the incidence of schizophrenia, as well as that of other mental disorders. Four sets of data are presented: various estimates for schizophrenia in a given population; the case count by diagnostic

TABLE 4.1

Ratio between High- and Low-Rate Areas Based on Incidence Rates of Schizophrenia Computed from Known Cases as Reported by Various Studies

Investigators	Place	Data		Number	Population	Rate per 1,000	Ratio
Faris and Dunham	Chicago	state hospital 1st. adm.	high	155	240,796	.64	
		1922-31	low	199	383,241	.20	3:1
Faris and Dunham	Chicago	state and private hospital	high	1,483	206,662	7.3	
		1st. Adm. 1922-34	low	250	159,887	1.6	4.5:1
Dunham	Detroit	state hospital 1st. adm.	high	411	300,474	1.4	
		1958	low	61	179,974	.33	4:1
Jaco	Texas	public and private	high	—	—	.84*	
		1950-51	low	—	—	.35	2.5:1
Lin	Formosa	house-to-house survey	high	29	5,572	5.21	3:1
			low	14	7,984	1.75	

*All functional disorders.

group at different points in time in the screening process; the final rates for schizophrenia and the other two diagnostic groups in 1958 as a result of intensive and nonintensive screening; and a comparison of incidence rates for schizophrenia for the years 1956 and 1957 with the base year, 1958.

Estimates for a Given Population

In Table 4.2 are presented several estimates of the number of schizophrenics that would be expected to appear in the subcommunities in Detroit, using percentages suggested in the literature. These estimates are then compared with the actual number of schizophrenic cases that were turned up in the subcommunities. The assumption is that the amount of schizophrenia occurring in any population during any one year is about the same, and any differences found are largely due to chance. It is interesting to note that the estimate based on the .0005 level, using the 15-64 age group population as a base, is actually equal to the number of cases found in one of the subcommunities, but that the number of cases found in the other subcommunity far exceeds the estimate. Reinterpreted as a rate for Conner-Burbank, this gives a figure of .5 per 1,000 population 15-64 years of age, or 1.0 per 2,000 population in this age group.

Case Count at Different Time Points

Table 4.3 presents a case count in the subcommunities by diagnostic groups at different points in time during the screening process. It is of interest to note that after 31 facilities had been screened, the case count for the three diagnostic groups, and in both subcommunities, was equal to the final count and, in some instances, in excess of the final count. In any instance where the cases tended to decrease, the smaller number of cases is due to careful screening to ascertain the date of first contact with a facility. The failure of the cases to increase with the addition of more facilities is related to the fact that many duplications of cases were involved.

A picture supporting these data can perhaps be seen when one examines Maps 4.1 and 4.2, which are based on state hospital cases only, and show a distribution of schizophrenic cases found in the two subcommunities. These distributions of schizophrenic cases as first admissions to state hospitals can now be compared with the distribution of schizophrenic cases in the two subcommunities after the screening process was completed. These distributions are shown in

TABLE 4.2

Ratios of Several Estimates of Incidence to Number of Observed First Contact Schizophrenics in Two Detroit Subcommunities, 1958

Percent	Over 15 Years	Ratio E/O	15-64 Years	Ratio E/O	Total Population	Ratio E/O
			<u>Cass</u>			
.0005	19/46	0.41	16/46	0.35	25/46	0.54
.00075	30/46	0.65	24/46	0.52	37/46	0.80
.001	37/46	0.80	32/46	0.10	50/46	1.09
.002	75/46	1.63	65/46	1.41	99/46	2.15
.008	297/46	6.46	259/46	5.63	398/46	8.65
			<u>Conner-Burbank</u>			
.005	27/24	1.13	24/24	1.00	36/24	1.50
.00075	40/24	1.67	36/24	1.50	54/24	2.25
.001	54/24	2.25	47/24	1.96	71/24	2.96
.002	107/24	4.46	95/24	3.96	143/24	5.96
.008	428/24	17.83	378/24	15.75	571/24	23.79

TABLE 4.3

Case Count by Number of Facilities Screened and Diagnostic Group in Two Subcommunities on Specified Dates

Date	Number of Psychiatric Facilities	Cass			Conner-Burbank		
		Schizophrenic	Nonschizophrenic	Additional	Schizophrenic	Nonschizophrenic	Additional
10/13/59	4	27	28	—	11	11	—
3/ 1/60	30	37	201	—	16	30	—
5/18/60	31	46	78	271	19	52	43
6/29/60	44	46	72	271	18	51	43
12/23/60	44	46	67	245	21	51	34
2/ 7/61	45	42	64	246	21	51	34
3/29/61	45	45	52	244	22	39	31
6/ 2/61	151	44	62	241	25	50	34
7/ 6/61	164	45	62	242	24	47	34
			Final Count				
4/ 1/62	176	46	63	238	24	48	35

MAP 4.1

Incidence of Schizophrenia in Cass Subcommunity, Detroit, 1958 (based on first admissions to state hospitals)

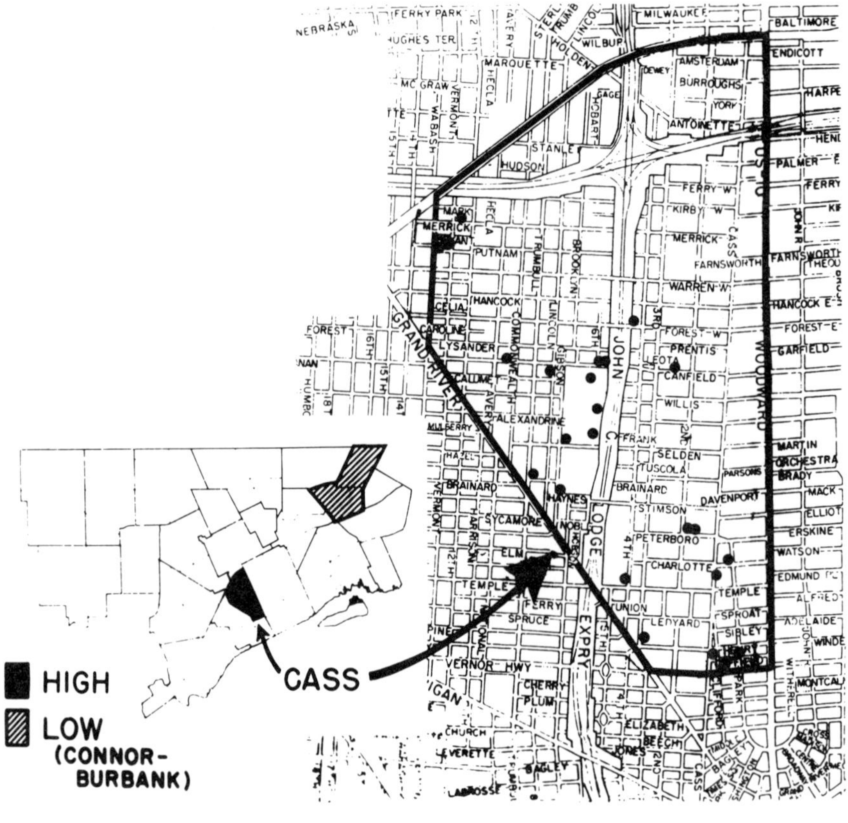

MAP 4.2

Incidence of Schizophrenia in Conner-Burbank Subcommunity, Detroit, 1958 (based on first admissions to state hospitals)

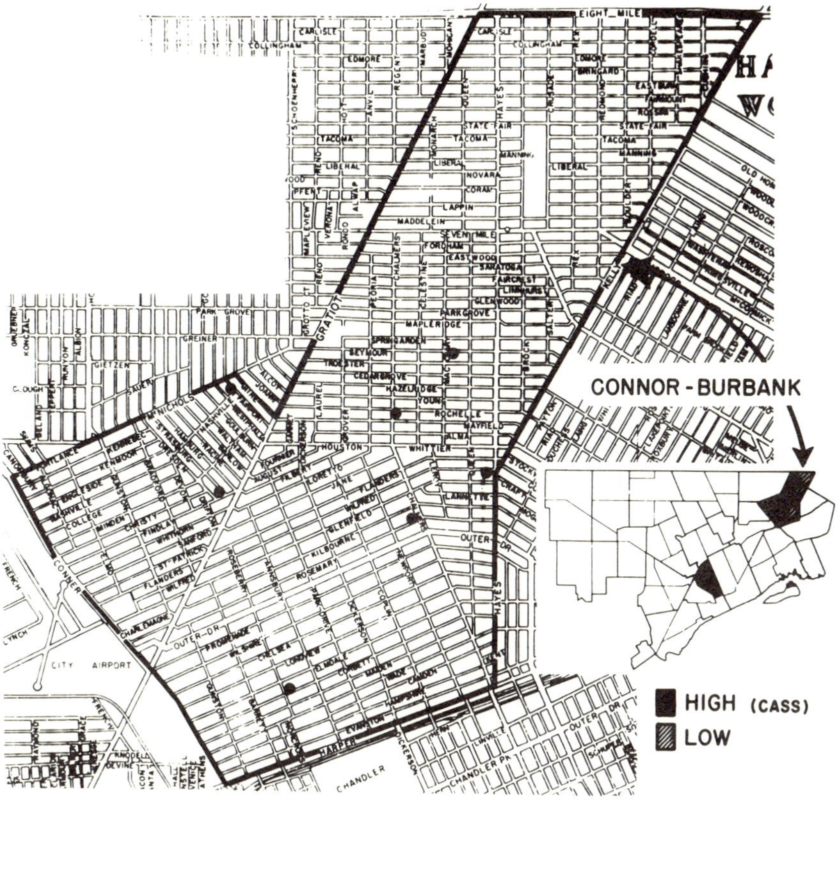

MAP 4.3

Incidence of Schizophrenia in Cass Subcommunity, Detroit, 1958 (N = 46)

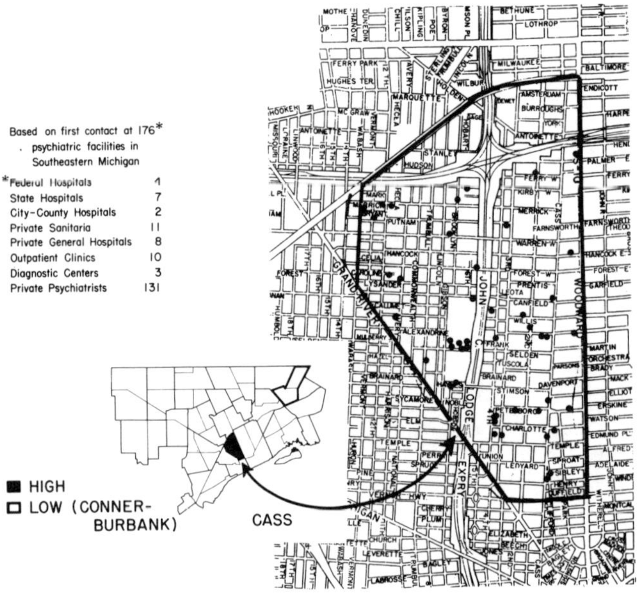

MAP 4.4

Incidence of Schizophrenia in Conner-Burbank Subcommunity, Detroit, 1958 (N = 24)

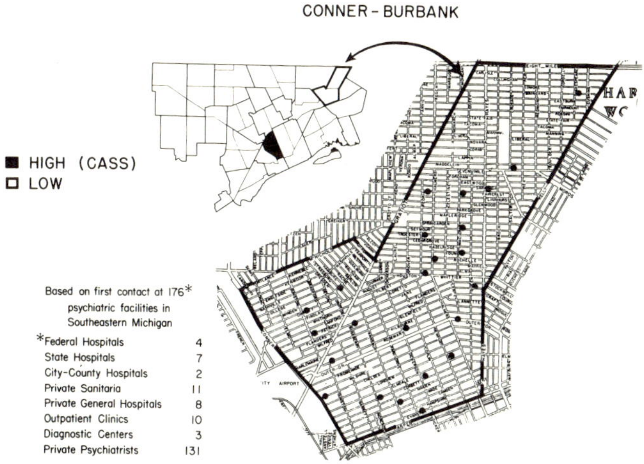

MAP 4.5

Incidence of Nonschizophrenic Cases in Cass Subcommunity, Detroit, 1958 (N = 63)

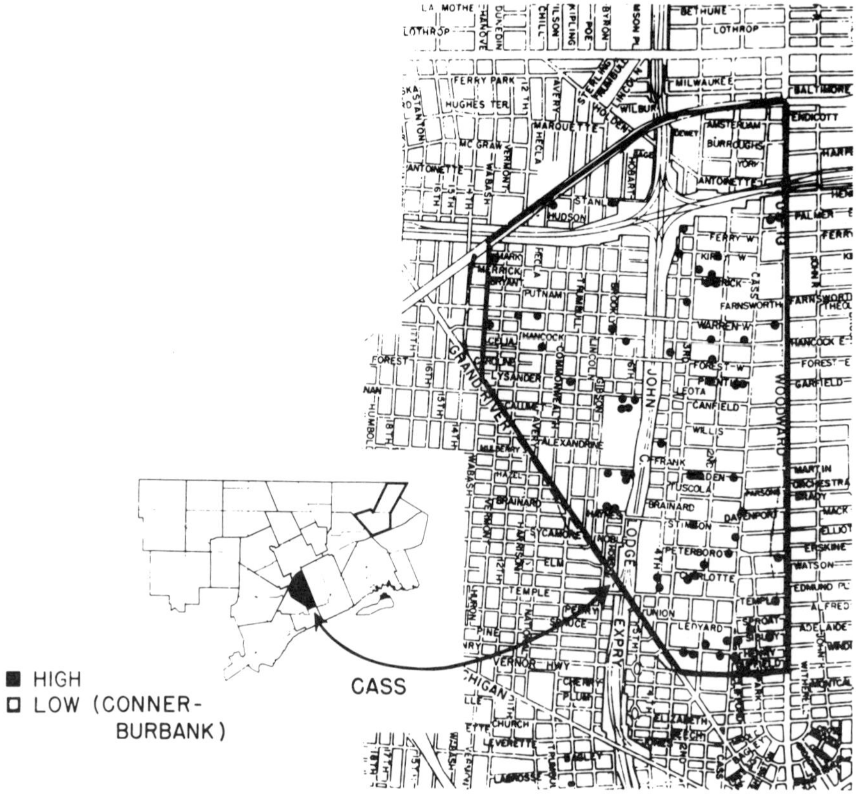

Includes:

Involutional Reactions
Paranoid Reactions
Other Psychotic Reactions
Psychoneurotic Reactions
Personality Disorders
Character Disorders or Neuroses
Compulsive Personality
Psychophysiologic Disorders

Based on first contact at 176* psychiatric facilities in southeastern Michigan

*Federal Hospitals	4
State Hospitals	7
City-County Hospitals	2
Private Sanitaria	11
Private General Hospitals	8
Outpatient Clinics	10
Diagnostic Centers	3
Private Psychiatrists	131

MAP 4.6

Incidence of Nonschizophrenic Cases in Conner-Burbank Subcommunity, Detroit, 1958 (N = 48)

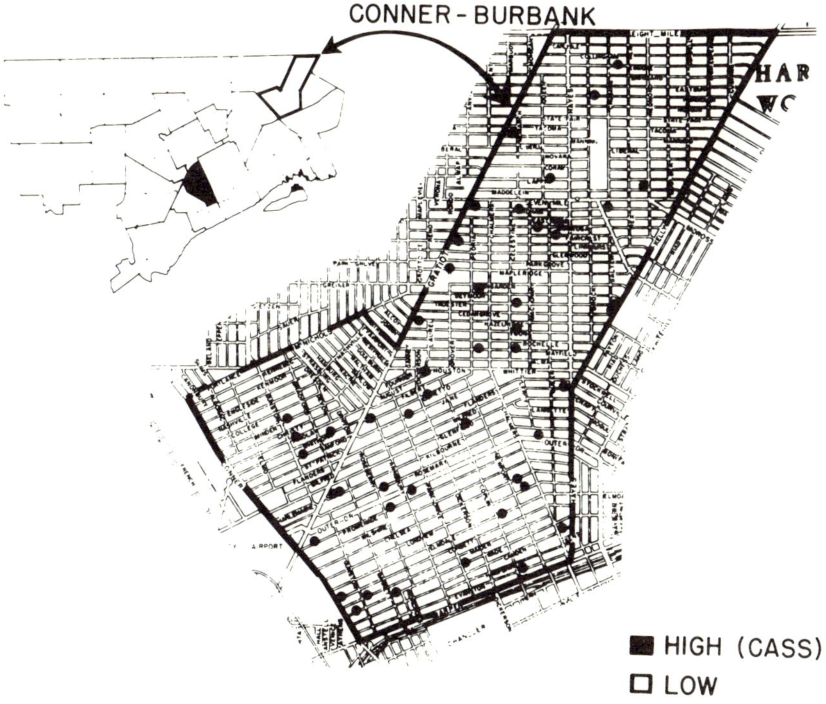

Includes:

Involutional Reactions
Paranoid Reactions
Other Psychotic Reactions
Psychoneurotic Reactions

Personality Disorders
Character Disorders or Neuroses
Compulsive Personality
Psychophysiologic Disorders

Based on first contact at 176* psychiatric facilities in southeastern Michigan

*Federal Hospitals	4
State Hospitals	7
City-County Hospitals	2
Private Sanitaria	11
Private General Hospitals	8
Outpatient Clinics	10
Diagnostic Centers	3
Private Psychiatrists	131

MAP 4.7

Incidence of Additional Cases in Cass Subcommunity, Detroit, 1958 (N = 238)

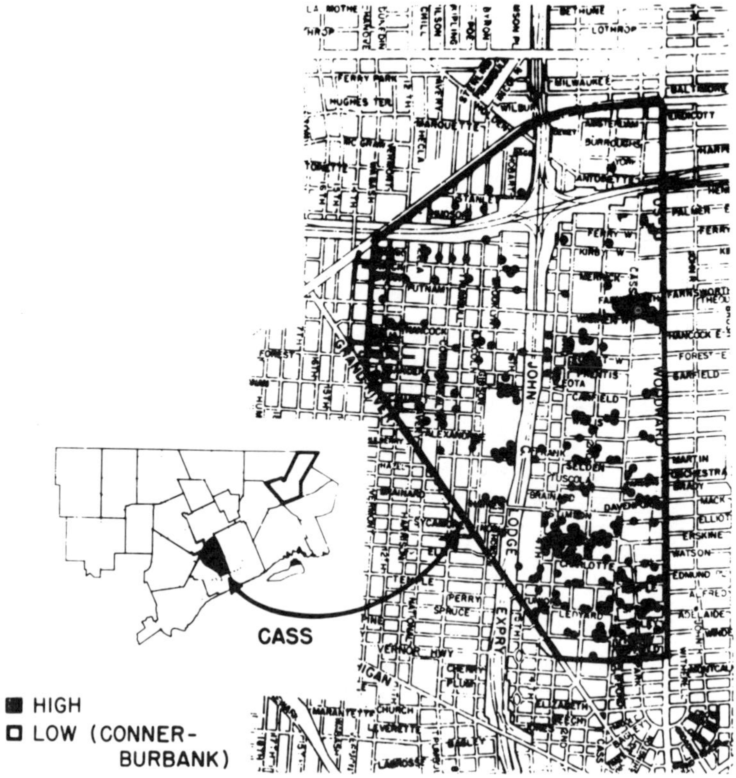

Includes:

Inadequate Personality
Sociopathic Personality Disturbance
Acute Brain Syndrome
Personality Trait Disturbance
Special Symptom Reaction
Transitional Situational Personality Disturbance
Chronic Brain Syndrome (Alcohol and Drug)

Based on first contact at 176* psychiatric facilities in southeastern Michigan

*Federal Hospitals	4
State Hospitals	7
City-County Hospitals	2
Private Sanitaria	11
Private General Hospitals	8
Outpatient Clinics	10
Diagnostic Centers	3
Private Psychiatrists	131

MAP 4.8

Incidence of Additional Cases in Conner-Burbank Subcommunity, Detroit, 1958 (N = 35)

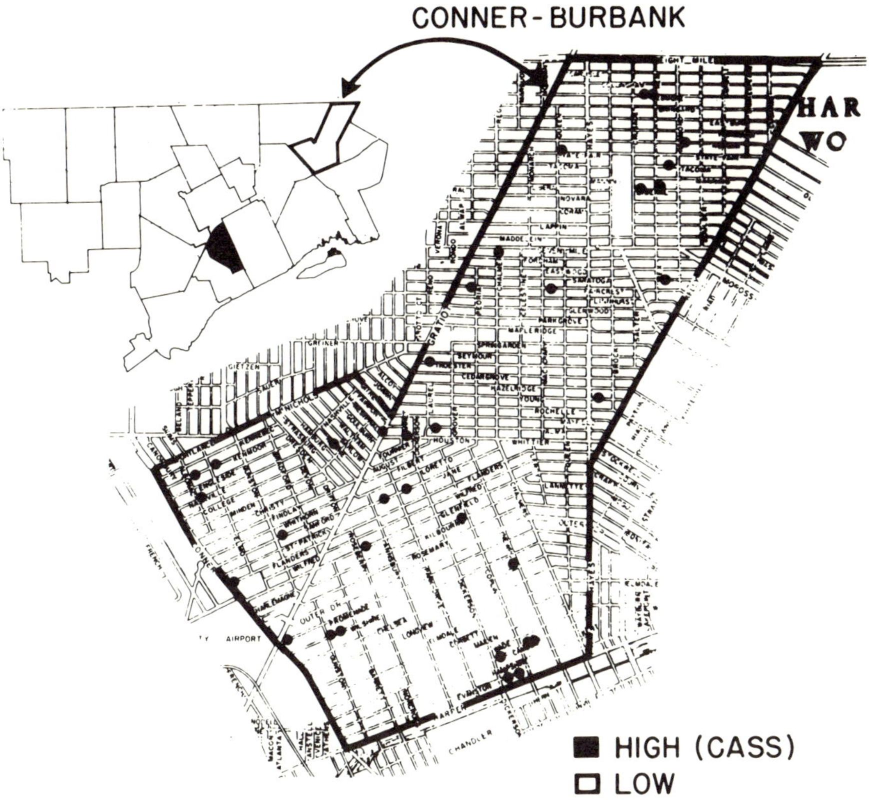

Includes:

Inadequate Personality
Sociopathic Personality Disturbance
Acute Brain Syndrome
Personality Trait Disturbance

Special Symptom Reaction
Transitional Situational Personality Disturbance
Chronic Brain Syndrome (Alcohol and Drug)

Based on first contact at 176* psychiatric facilities in southeastern Michigan

*Federal Hospitals	4
State Hospitals	7
City-County Hospitals	2
Private Sanitaria	11
Private General Hospitals	8
Outpatient Clinics	10
Diagnostic Centers	3
Private Psychiatrists	131

TABLE 4.4

Number and Incidence Rates[a] for Three Diagnostic Groups Resulting from Intensive Screening in Two Subcommunities of Detroit, 1958

Diagnostic Group	Cass			Conner-Burbank				Ratios	
	Number	Rate	σ_{r_1}	Number	Rate	σ_{r_2}	$\sigma_{r_1=r_2}$	C/C-B	C/C-B[b]
Schizophrenic	46	1.24	.18	24	.45	.09	.20	2.8:1	2.7:1
Nonschizophrenic	63	1.69	.21	48	.90	.13	.25	1.9:1	1.9:1
Additional	238	6.39	.41	35	.65	.11	.43	9.8:1	9.8:1
Total	347			107					

[a]All rates per 1,000 estimated population, 15 years and over, 1958.
[b]Ratio based on rates from estimated total population, 1958.

Maps 4.3 and 4.4. A careful examination of these four maps shows that by intensive screening the number of schizophrenic cases found in Cass was doubled, or increased by 100 percent, while the number found in Conner-Burbank increased by 323 percent.

For comparative purposes, the distributions of the nonschizophrenic and additional cases also are presented for both subcommunities. These are shown in Maps 4.5, 4.6, 4.7, and 4.8. It is noted immediately that as far as numbers of cases are concerned, the difference between the two subcommunities is less marked for the nonschizophrenics as compared to the schizophrenics, but that the distributions of the additional cases between the two subcommunities differ sharply from the distributions of the two other diagnostic groups. The additional cases include, in the main, the acting-out disorders; the distributions indicate that such disturbances are likely to be much more characteristic of the people in Cass than of the people in Conner-Burbank. This finding closely parallels that of Leighton and associates for the small villages that they surveyed in Nova Scotia.[2]

Final Count

The following is an examination of the rates as compiled from these final counts of cases at the end of the intensive screening process. First are presented the rates for schizophrenia and the other two diagnostic groups in the two subcommunities for 1958. These rates are based upon the population 15 years of age and over, along with ratios from rates based on the total population. These data, shown in Table 4.4, point to the following findings: in all three diagnostic groups the rates differ significantly between Cass and Conner-Burbank; the ratio of cases between the two subcommunities is approximately the same in each diagnostic group regardless of the population base; the ratio of schizophrenic cases between the two subcommunities is approximately of the same size as found in previous studies; and the ratios between the two subcommunities for the additional group are much larger than the other two ratios.

Incidence Rates Compared

The comparable statistically significant data now will be examined for the years 1956, 1957, and 1958, which do not represent intensive screening but rather represent case counts as they came from the psychiatric facilities after initial screening. These data are shown in Table 4.5. Perhaps the most marked finding that

TABLE 4.5

Number and Incidence Rates* for Three Diagnostic Groups without Intensive Screening for 1956, 1957, and 1958 in Two Subcommunities of Detroit

Diagnostic Group	Cass			Conner-Burbank		
	Number	Rate	σ_{r_1}	Number	Rate	σ_{r_2}
		1956				
Schizophrenic	33	0.81	.14	18	.34	.08
Nonschizophrenic	55	1.35	.18	24	.45	.09
Additional	353	8.64	.46	62	1.16	.15
Totals	444			104		
		1957				
Schizophrenic	41	1.05	.16	20	.38	.08
Nonschizophrenic	58	1.49	.20	44	.83	.13
Additional	321	8.22	.46	76	1.42	.16
Totals	420			140		
		1958				
Schizophrenic	30	0.81	.15	16	.30	.08
Nonschizophrenic	56	1.50	.20	43	.80	.12
Additional	269	7.22	.44	51	.95	.13
Totals	355			110		

Ratios: Cass/Conner-Burbank

	1956	1957	1958
Schizophrenic	2.5:1	2.7:1	2.7:1
Nonschizophrenic	3.0:1	1.8:1	1.9:1
Additional	7.4:1	5.8:1	7.6:1

*Population base 15 years and over.

stands out is that the ratio of cases in each one of the diagnostic groups is about the same with or without intensive screening. The only one that seems seriously out of line is the nonschizophrenic ratio for 1956. From these data it appears that the efforts at intensive screening for rate computation were pointless, inasmuch as the same ratio is obtained as when no intensive screening was done. In addition, there is a general consistency of the rates from year to year in three diagnostic groups and the two subcommunities.

Up to this point the data largely have supported the previous ratios between high- and low-rate areas found to exist in other studies. As one can see by referring to Table 4. 4, the schizophrenic ratio between high- and low-rate communities is approximately three to one, the same ratio that was found by both nonintensive and intensive screening processes. One other finding with respect to the rates for schizophrenia that are found in both subcommunities is that they are as high as, and in fact higher than, most of the rates for schizophrenia that have been examined. It is noted that the rate for schizophrenia in the lower-middle-class area (Conner-Burbank) is somewhat higher than the rate that Hollingshead and Redlich found in Class V; the rate in Cass is quite in line with the rates reported from other studies and is in general somewhat higher.

This analysis leads to the following conclusions: significant differential incidence rates for schizophrenia have been found to exist between two markedly contrasting types of subcommunities in Detroit; the three-to-one ratio is maintained, which is comparable to the ratio from other studies; this ratio is maintained irrespective of intensive screening; the ratio for two other years, 1956 and 1957, is the same as for the base year of 1958.

Distribution by Age and Marital Status

Examined next were the cases in the two subcommunities in terms of their age distribution. The distribution of cases by age and age-specific rates is shown in Table 4. 6. The data appear to be quite comparable to other age distributions of psychiatric cases. It is perhaps worthy of note that the trend of rates of schizophrenia in both subcommunities is approximately the same, with the highest rate in each instance falling in the 30-39 age group. In the other two diagnostic groups there is some difference to be noted with respect to the trend of rates in the two subcommunities. In Cass in both of these diagnostic groups, the rate is highest in the 15-19 age groups and from there on the trend is downward. In Conner-Burbank these trends are not in evidence; in fact, in the additional groups most of the cases are in the 30-39 age group while in the nonschizophrenic

TABLE 4.6

Number and Age-Specific Rates According to Diagnostic Group in Two Subcommunities of Detroit, 1958

Age	Population	Schizophrenic		Nonschizophrenic		Additional	
		Number*	Rate	Number*	Rate	Number*	Rate
		Cass					
15-19	2,360	3	1.27	8	3.39	19	8.05
20-29	7,816	17	2.18	22	2.82	41	5.25
30-39	7,043	18	2.56	15	2.13	35	4.97
40-49	6,618	5	.76	12	1.81	21	3.17
50-59	6,271	1	.16	4	.64	12	1.91
60 and over	7,404	1	.14	2	.27	9	1.22
Total	37,512	45	.90	63	1.27	137	2.74
		Conner-Burbank					
15-19	5,276	2	.38	2	.38	4	.76
20-29	8,597	7	.81	13	1.51	7	.81
30-39	9,127	11	1.21	8	.88	2	.22
40-49	10,779	3	.28	10	.93	13	1.21
50-59	9,652			12	1.24	4	.41
60 and over	10,075	1	.10	3	.30	4	.40
Total	53,506	24	.34	48	.67	34	.48

*Includes total cases uncovered irrespective of obtaining contact with them.

TABLE 4.7

Number and Rates for Schizophrenic, Nonschizophrenic, and Additional Cases According to Marital Status in Two Subcommunities of Detroit, 1958

		Total		Schizophrenic*		Nonschizophrenic*		Additional*	
Status	Base Population	Number	Rate	Number	Rate	Number	Rate	Number	Rate
Single	21,278	69	3.24	23	1.08	19	.89	27	1.27
Married	53,218	113	2.12	26	.49	54	1.01	33	.62
Widowed, divorced, separated	14,364	41	2.85	14	.97	18	1.25	9	.63
Total	88,860	223		63		91		69	

*$\chi^2 = 9.3433$ df = 4 $p < .05$

age group the highest rates are in the 20-29 and the 50-59 age groups respectively. This difference may be partially a function of the fewer cases in Conner-Burbank in these diagnostic groups as compared to Cass; but if so, the small number of cases in the schizophrenic group does not change the trend in Conner-Burbank as compared to Cass. The age spread in other schizophrenic cases was quite surprising, for it was expected that with intensive screening the range and the average would be reduced markedly. No reduction was found, as the data show.

Next are examined the cases in the two subcommunities and diagnostic groups by marital status. The case basis in certain of the marital status groups was too small to compute reliable rates; consequently, the data of both subcommunities were combined in order to determine if there were any significant differences, as often has been suggested, between marital status groups. These data are shown in Table 4. 7. Interestingly enough, these rates point to only one significant difference, and this is in line with what previously has been known. This difference is between the single and married status categories for the schizophrenics where the critical ratio between them is at the 4. 9 level. The other two differences are nonsignificant. Two possible explanations have been made for such data: the presence of schizophrenia makes it more difficult for persons to marry, or marriage becomes a protection against a schizophrenic breakdown. Which alternative is the correct one cannot be determined from these data.

COMPLETENESS OF CASE COUNT

The second question examined dealt with whether all cases that should enter into the rate actually have been uncovered. On this point there is a high degree of confidence, as evidenced by the fact that after screening two thirds of the facilities it was found, at least for the schizophrenics, that the count was approximately the same as after all the facilities had been screened. One also notes that the final count for schizophrenics in both subcommunities was approximately three times the number found by screening only the admissions to state hospitals. This is somewhat a reverse of the statistical picture presented by the U. S. census, which shows that approximately three fourths of first admissions enter state hospitals. This kind of evidence makes one think that the coverage has been well-nigh complete. While one might argue that the persons who entered mental hospitals outside of Michigan have not been covered, one can only say that seeking aid from out-of-state hospitals is not a practice among the families in these communities. If a person did enter

TABLE 4.8

Case Count of First Contacts from Screening 176 Psychiatric Facilities in Southeastern Michigan by Diagnostic Group and Patient Contact*

	Cass			Conner-Burbank		
	Schizophrenic	Nonschizophrenic	Additional	Schizophrenic	Nonschizophrenic	Additional
Contacted	37	48	37	24	42	29
Not located	6	5	187		1	3
Moved out of city	3	6	12		2	
Refused		4	1		3	1
Deceased			1			2
Total	46	63	238	24	48	35

*Federal Hospitals	4	Private General	8
State Hospitals	7	Out-Patient Clinics	10
City and County Hospitals	2	Diagnostic Centers	3
Private Sanitariums	11	Private Psychiatrists	131

TABLE 4.9

Case Count of First Contacts by Diagnostic Group According to Status of Schedules

	Cass				Conner-Burbank			
	Schizophrenic		Nonschizophrenic	Additional	Schizophrenic		Nonschizophrenic	Additional
Status of Schedules	01	03	01	01	01	03	01	01
Completed	39	35	48	38	24	22	44	30
Not completed	7	11	15	200		2	4	5
Total	46	46	63	238	24	24	48	35

a mental hospital in another state it would occur only after he had moved from the subcommunities being studied here. While he could have resided in one or the other of the subcommunities for part of 1958, this possibility is remote.

One central procedure in this study was to locate and interview each case uncovered in the two subcommunities and in each diagnostic group for 1958. In the schizophrenic and nonschizophrenic groups, an attempt was made to have the psychiatrist examine each case in order to render his diagnostic judgment as to whether schizophrenia was present or absent. The only group that was not traced as intensively as the others was the additional diagnostic group in Cass. Most of these cases could not be located. The final count, with the status of each case with respect to contact, can be seen in Table 4. 8. Table 4. 9 shows the schedules completed and not completed. The discrepancy in the figures of the two tables is due to the fact that six cases had schedules filled out as a result of parents or spouse being interviewed while the patient himself was not seen. Schedule 03 was filled out by the psychiatrist for the schizophrenic cases only; all of these cases were seen and examined by him. While the author would have liked very much to have located all of the cases in Cass, and actually did locate all but six in Conner-Burbank for the schizophrenic and nonschizophrenic groups, he has no reason to think that the missing cases would change the picture of the findings or the analysis that has been presented.

THE MOBILITY FACTOR

The more intriguing question of to what extent the cases that make up these rates are indigenous to the two subcommunities now will be examined. This question touches on mobility, and means that one must examine the evidence at one's disposal in order to determine the length of time that these cases have been residents of the two subcommunities. The issue of mobility has for some time been investigated as a factor associated with mental illness. Ever since Ødegaard[3] published a study in which he made the interpretation that people who emigrate are more prone to a mental breakdown, the mobility of the mentally ill has been examined in numerous investigations. There has been some question that mobility of the mentally ill was a symptom of maladjustment;[4] at the same time mobility per se has been regarded as bringing about mental disturbances.[5] Freeman, Simmons, and Bergen report that the families of former mental patients appear to move for the same reasons that other families in certain neighborhoods of Philadelphia do.[6] The immediate concern here is to examine the extent to which mobility may account for the rate differentials in the two subcommunities.

Length of Residence in Subcommunity

Schedule 01 contains five questions that aim to throw light on the mobility patterns of these cases. Each patient contacted was asked for the length of time he had lived at his present address, the length of time that he had lived in the subcommunity, the address from which he came when he moved into the subcommunity, the number of times that he had moved during the past four years, and his place of birth. The cases that fall into each one of the diagnostic groups present a comparable picture with respect to their length of residence in the community. In general, the larger number in each diagnostic group have lived in the same house as long as they have lived in the subcommunity, while a much smaller number in each instance have lived in the subcommunity longer than they have lived in the same house. In other words, the movement within the community apparently bears no relationship to a given diagnostic group but rather, if significant at all, is a consequence of the general stability of life in the subcommunity. Thus it is noted that residential stability, as expected, is more marked in Conner-Burbank than it is in Cass, as shown in Table 4.10.

The real concern, however, is to look at the cases indigenous to the two subcommunities to determine if the ratio of the rates will change significantly in such an analysis. The central purpose in this research always has been to determine if these two contrasting types of subcommunities actually produce significantly different rates of schizophrenia. To get at this picture the cases in the two subcommunities were divided into two groups: those under and those over five years in residence. Rates were then calculated for both categories in each of the diagnostic groups. These data for the two subcommunities are shown in Table 4.11. When cases resident in the community for five years and over are counted, the rates for schizophrenia prove to be identical, while the rates in the other two diagnostic groups actually are higher in the more homogeneous subcommunity. It also is worthy of note that for those schizophrenic cases that have been in the community for only five years or less, the ratio remains approximately the same, namely, about three to one. These facts raise much doubt as to whether in two such contrasting subcommunities one can make a good case for significant differential rates.

It should be noted that these rates have been computed on the basis of the estimated population, 15 years and over, for 1958. A rationale can be constructed for this procedure by arguing that even

TABLE 4.10

Comparison between Length of Residence at Present Address and Length of Residence in the Community for Two Subcommunities of Detroit

	Schizophrenic	Nonschizo-phrenic	Additional	Total	Total Percent
		Cass			
Same	29	27	31	87	69.0
Longer	7	9	4	20	16.0
Unknown	3	12	4	19	15.0
Total	39	48	39	126	100.0
		Conner-Burbank			
Same	21	34	27	82	81.1
Longer	3	8	3	14	14.0
Unknown	0	4	1	5	4.9
Total	24	46	31	101	100.0

though, for example, two thirds of the population of Cass are mobile, the total number in the population was relatively constant for every year in the decade and consequently represented the whole environment for those schizophrenic cases that had been in the subcommunity five years or longer, as well as for those who had been there under five years. However, the correct procedure is to base these rates upon a population that was in the subcommunity for at least as long as the patients composing the three diagnostic groups. Therefore these same rates were computed based on a population that had been in residence in each of the two subcommunities less and more than five years according to the 1960 census. For those in residence five or more years (based on the population in residence for five or more years), the ratios between the two subcommunities for the three diagnostic groups become 2.5:1, 1.6:1, and 2.2:1, respectively. The ratios for those in residence under five years are 1.6:1, 1.8:1, and 1.8:1. While the rate differences between the two subcommunities are now not significant for the schizophrenic and nonschizophrenic groups because of the reduction in the case base, the ratios between the two subcommunities, while reduced slightly, are still in the same

TABLE 4.11

Number and Rates* by Length of Residence and Diagnostic Group in Two Subcommunities of Detroit, 1958

Length of Residence	Schizophrenic		Nonschizophrenic		Additional		Total	
	Number	Rate	Number	Rate	Number	Rate	Number	Rate
Cass								
Under 5 years	28	.75	27	.73	20	.54	75	2.01
Over 5 years	8	.22	15	.40	15	.40	38	1.02
Subtotal	36	.97	42	1.13	35	.94	113	3.03
Unknown	3	.08	6	.16	4	.10	13	.35
Total	39	1.05	48	1.29	39	1.04	126	3.38
Conner-Burbank								
Under 5 years	13	.24	11	.21	6	.11	30	.06
Over 5 years	11	.21	33	.62	24	.45	68	1.02
Subtotal	24	.45	44	.83	30	.56	98	1.08
Unknown	0	.0	2	.03	1	.02	3	.0
Total	24	.45	46	.86	31	.58	101	1.08

*Based on estimated population for 1958, 15 years and over: Cass, 37,229; Conner-Burbank, 53,504.

TABLE 4.12

Number and Rates* by Length of Residence and Diagnostic Group in Two Subcommunities of Detroit, 1958

Length of Residence	Schizophrenic		Nonschizophrenic		Additional		Total	
	Number	Rate	Number	Rate	Number	Rate	Number	Rate
Cass								
Under 5 years	28	1.00	27	.95	20	.71	75	2.65
Over 5 years	8	.63	15	1.18	15	1.18	38	2.99
Subtotal	36	.87	42	1.02	35	.85	113	2.76
Unknown	3	.07	6	.14	4	.10	13	.32
Total	39	.94	48	1.16	39	.95	126	3.08
	$\chi^2 = 3.5201$		df = 2		$p < .05$			
Conner-Burbank								
Under 5 years	13	.63	11	.53	6	.39	30	1.45
Over 5 years	11	.25	33	.73	24	.54	68	1.52
Subtotal	24	.37	44	.67	30	.46	98	1.50
Unknown	0	—	2	.03	1	.01	3	.04
Total	24	.37	46	.70	31	.47	101	1.54
	$\chi^2 = 41.41$		df = 2		$p < .001$			

*Based on (1) population in residence 5 years and under, 1960: Cass, 23,316; Conner-Burbank, 20,739; and (2) population in residence 5 years and over, 1960: Cass, 12,696; Conner-Burbank, 44,762.

TABLE 4.13

Schizophrenic Cases, Resident for 20 or More Years in Two Subcommunities of Detroit, 1958

Case No.	Sex	Age	Race	Class
		Cass		
0011	M	21	W	V
0022	F	32	B	V
0056	F	31	W	V
		Conner-Burbank		
0035	M	44	W	V
0040	M	22	W	I
0052	M	23	W	III
0064	F	32	W	III
0179	M	33	W	IV

direction for both categories of residence as in the combined cases. Here the trend, and not the absence of statistical significance between the rates, is important. Only in the additional diagnosis group does the rate difference stand up with a critical ratio of 4.5. These data are shown in Table 4.12.

It is interesting to examine those few cases that have been residents of the two subcommunities practically from birth. While little can be made of the data, it is worth noting that three cases were found resident in Cass for 20 years or more, and five cases resident in Conner-Burbank for that length of time. These cases by sex, age, race, and social class are shown in Table 4.13. With one exception (No. 0035), all of the remaining seven cases spent their childhood years in these two subcommunities. When one remembers that the population of Cass was 37,229 and that of Conner-Burbank 53,504 (aged 15 years and over for 1958), these two subcommunities would emerge with almost identical rates in terms of their nearly lifetime residents who developed schizophrenia.

Next is examined the mobility of the cases in the two subcommunities by the three diagnostic groups on the basis of the number of moves of residence that they had made during the four years prior to 1958. For those cases that had no moves of residence during this four-year period the rates, based on the estimated population for 1958 aged 15 years and over, provided ratios of 0.6:1, 0.5:1, and

TABLE 4.14

Number and Rate* by Moves of Residence Prior to 1958 and Diagnostic Group in Two Subcommunities of Detroit

No. of Moves in Four Years Prior to 1958	Schizophrenic		Nonschizophrenic		Additional		Total	
	Number	Rate	Number	Rate	Number	Rate	Number	Rate
			Cass					
No moves	5	.13	11	.30	13	.35	29	.78
One move	11	.30	11	.30	11	.30	33	.89
Two or three moves	13	.35	8	.21	9	.24	30	.81
Four or more moves	6	.16	5	.13	2	.06	13	.35
Subtotal	35	.94	35	.94	35	.94	105	2.83
Unknown	4	.11	13	.35	4	.11	21	.55
Total	39	1.05	48	1.29	39	1.05	126	3.38
			Conner-Burbank					
No moves	12	.22	32	.59	22	.41	66	1.23
One move	5	.10	3	.06	4	.09	12	.22
Two or three moves	5	.10	7	.13	1	.02	13	.24
Four or more moves	2	.03	1	.02	2	.03	5	.10
Subtotal	24	.45	43	.80	29	.55	96	1.79
Unknown	0	.0	3	.06	2	.03	5	.10
Total	24	.45	46	.86	31	.58	101	1.89

*Based on estimated population for 1958, 15 years and over: Cass, 37,239; Conner-Burbank, 53,504.

TABLE 4.15

Number and Percent of First Contact Psychiatric Cases by Diagnostic Group and Location of Previous Residence from Two Subcommunities of Detroit, 1958

Location of Previous Residence	Cass						Conner-Burbank					
	Schizophrenic		Nonschizo-phrenic		Additional		Schizophrenic		Nonschizo-phrenic		Additional	
	No.	Percent	No.	Percent	No.	Percent	No.	Percent	No.	Percent	No.	Percent
Inner city	25	78.1	23	74.2	21	60.0	15	62.5	14	35.9	12	44.4
Outer city	2	6.3	2	7.4	5	14.3	5	20.8	17	43.6	10	37.0
Other U.S. and foreign	5	15.6	6	19.4	9	25.7	4	16.7	8	20.5	5	18.6
Subtotal	32	100.0	31	100.0	35	100.0	24	100.0	39	100.0	27	100.0
Unknown	7		17		4		0		7		4	
Total	39		48		39		24		46		31	

0.9:1 respectively, which place the highest rates for all three diagnostic groups in the Conner-Burbank community. These data are shown in Table 4.14.

Previous Location of Residence within City

Perhaps the most telling and crucial finding with respect to the mobility of these cases results from an examination of the areas of the city from which these cases came before moving into the subcommunities. These data are shown in Table 4.15, where the cases have been distributed in accordance with the following procedure. First, the subcommunities were grouped into quartiles based upon the distribution of schizophrenic cases entering state hospitals from Detroit. The first two quartiles were regarded as representing the inner city, and the third and fourth quartiles and the suburbs as representing the outer city. Cases from other areas of the United States and from foreign countries were placed in a third category. It can be seen immediately that in the schizophrenic grouping 78.1 percent of the cases recorded for Cass and 62.5 percent of the cases recorded for Conner-Burbank came from the inner city. Using a test of significance for the difference between two proportions and assuming that the cases come from the same universe, the null hypothesis of no difference on the basis of a critical ratio of 1:3 is accepted. In the nonschizophrenic group the difference is markedly significant, with a critical ratio of 3:6; hence, one is able to reject the null hypothesis and infer that the origin of the Conner-Burbank cases, in contrast to the cases from Cass, was quite different for the nonschizophrenic group. This difference is reminiscent of those found between the distribution of schizophrenia and manic-depressive psychosis in an earlier epidemiological study in Chicago.[7] However, when one turns to the additional group one has a contrast comparable to the schizophrenic group. That is, one is forced to accept the null hypothesis on the basis of a critical ratio of 1:2. This is not entirely unexpected when one considers the behavioral types found in this diagnostic group.

Birthplace in Relation to Subcommunity and Family Status

Another finding with respect to mobility shows the relationship between birthplace and the subcommunity of residence for each diagnostic group. These data are shown in Table 4.16 and point to the fact that it is only in the schizophrenic group that one seems to get a difference in the type of birthplace of the respective cases in the two subcommunities. In the case of the schizophrenic group, when

TABLE 4.16

Distribution of First Contacts by Diagnostic Group, Birthplace, and Subcommunity, Detroit, 1958

Birthplace	Cass	Conner-Burbank	Total
Schizophrenic			
Other than large city	24	7	31
Large city	13	16	29
Total	37	23	60
$\chi^2 = 6.7328$	df = 1	$p < .01$	
Nonschizophrenic			
Other than large city	19	16	35
Large city	14	25	39
Total	33	41	74
$\chi^2 = 2.524$	df = 1	$p < .10$	
Additional			
Other than large city	19	14	33
Large city	15	14	29
Total	34	28	62
$\chi^2 = 0.213$	df = 1	$p < .50$	
Nonschizophrenic and Additional			
Other than large city	38	30	68
Large city	29	39	68
Total	67	69	136
$\chi^2 = 2.383$	df = 1	$p < .10$	

the two subcommunities are compared the chi-square test shows a significant difference at the 1 percent level, while in the other two diagnostic groups there is no significant difference. This finding demonstrated that the schizophrenic cases in Conner-Burbank are more indigenous to urban life, while a large majority of those schizophrenic cases picked up in Cass began their lives in smaller places, eventually drifted to the city, and found residence in the anonymity provided by life in Cass. Conversely, the finding that the origin of the cases in the other two diagnostic groups is similar for both sub-

TABLE 4.17

Comparison of Father's Occupational Status with Birthplace of Patient by Diagnostic Group for Both Subcommunities

	Father's Occupational Status		
Birthplace	High	Medium	Low
Schizophrenic			
Other than large city	2	3	26
Large city	4	6	12
Total	6	9	38
$\chi^2 = 5.44$*	df = 1	$p < .01$	
Nonschizophrenic			
Other than large city	8	10	14
Large city	6	19	11
Total	14	29	25
$\chi^2 = 1.27$	df = 1	$p < .20$	
Additional			
Other than large city	5	7	20
Large city	4	14	12
Total	9	21	32
$\chi^2 = 3.13$	df = 1	$p < .05$	

*For computation of chi-square, high and medium statuses are combined.

communities reinforces the notion that a certain percentage of schizophrenic cases seems to drift into Cass, thus inflating the rate in that subcommunity.

This finding also suggested the possibility that there might be a definite relationship between the status of the family and the birthplace of the patient. It was reasoned that if, among the schizophrenic patients, a majority in Conner-Burbank were born in a large city while the reverse appeared to be true for Cass, then one would pre-

TABLE 4.18

Comparison of Father's Occupational Status with Birthplace of Patient by Subcommunity and in Both Subcommunities Combined

	Father's Occupational Status			
Birthplace	High	Medium	Low	Total
	Cass			
Other than large city	6	12	40	58
Large city	8	8	21	37
Total	14	20	61	95
	$\chi^2 = 2.4865$	df = 2	$p < .20$	
	Conner-Burbank			
Other than large city	9	8	20	37
Large city	6	31	14	51
Total	15	39	34	88
	$\chi^2 = 13.326$	df = 2	$p < .001$	
	Both Subcommunities			
Other than large city	15	20	60	95
Large city	14	39	35	88
Total	29	59	95	183
	$\chi^2 = 12.413$	df = 2	$p < .01$	

dict that those persons born in a large city would come from higher status families. The father's occupation was taken as a measurement of status and related to the birthplace of the patient. When these data were broken down by diagnostic groups and combined from both subcommunities, a significant difference was found between father's occupational status and the birthplace of the patient among the schizophrenics, but the relationship in the other diagnostic groups was nonsignificant (see Table 4.17). This served to reinforce the above finding that those schizophrenics born in smaller places leave home to seek new opportunities precisely because the family occupies a

TABLE 4.19

Comparisons of Living Arrangements by Diagnostic Group in Two Subcommunities of Detroit, 1958

	Schizophrenic		Nonschizophrenic		Additional		Total*	
	Cass	Conner-Burbank	Cass	Conner-Burbank	Cass	Conner-Burbank	Cass	Conner-Burbank
Living alone	8	1	9	1	7	1	24	3
Living with others	29	23	27	41	27	29	83	93
Subtotal	37	24	36	42	34	30	107	96
N.A.	2	0	12	4	4	1	18	5
Total	39	24	48	46	38	31	125	101

*$\chi^2 = 16.36$ df = 1 $p < .001$

low status position. Subsequently, they fail in their search, and with their mental and personality disturbance serving as an additional obstacle, they eventually drift into Cass or some other similar type of urban community.

However, when diagnoses are ignored, no significant difference is found between the father's occupational status and the birthplace of a patient in Cass, but a significant difference was found in Conner-Burbank. These data with their chi-squares are shown in Table 4.18 with respect to residence mobility. Note the same significant difference in this comparison when the cases for both subcommunities are combined. This finding again supports the observation that patients born in smaller places and foreign countries tend to come from lower status families. However, this finding appears to apply less to the cases found in Cass and more clearly to the cases found in Conner-Burbank.

One final bit of evidence has helped to pinpoint the different situations, both past and present, of those schizophrenics that were picked up in Cass. It was reasoned that because schizophrenics in Cass are more likely to be born in places other than large cities and are more likely to come from lower status families, that many more will be found living alone in Cass as compared to Conner-Burbank. The results of this analysis are found in Table 4.19. The evidence is clear. All of the cases in each diagnostic category that are living alone, with the exception of three, are found in Cass. This reflects the possible anonymity of Cass, and with respect to the schizophrenic cases shows that those without families will be found almost entirely in Cass.

CONCLUSIONS AND INTERPRETATIONS

From the above analysis it would seem that five general conclusions can be drawn. (1) The two subcommunities with sharply contrasting sociocultural organizations will show rate differences for schizophrenia that are reduced to a nonsignificant level when length of residence in the community is considered. This finding apparently holds true also for the nonschizophrenic group but not for the additional diagnostic group. (2) The bulk of the schizophrenic cases and the bulk of the additional cases in both subcommunities lived in the inner belt of the city before establishing residence in the two subcommunities. (3) The birthplace of those schizophrenics picked up in Cass is most likely to have been in places other than a large city. (4) Those schizophrenics picked up in Cass are more likely to come from lower status families when their birthplaces were other than large cities. (5) Psychiatric cases of all types, when separated from their families, largely will be found in urban communities like Cass.

The main problem here is that of the most plausible interpretation of these findings. Perhaps the first point that should be made is that the accumulative evidence throws into question any significant rate differential in any geographical distribution of schizophrenic cases. The residential mobility so characteristic of large cities makes infeasible any attempt to assess rate differentials with respect to areas separated by geographical space. The findings of Clausen and Kohn with respect to the distribution of schizophrenia in Hagerstown, Maryland, now receive a certain validation.[8] It is possible that in the smaller city, where mobility may not be as prevalent, rate differentials of a significant degree do not show up. While the data here show that rate differentials between the two subcommunities are considerably reduced when length of residence is taken into account, the data at the same time point to the fact that many schizophrenics in the city of Detroit get some start in their life careers from the more deprived areas of the city. Thus the conclusion would be that community rate differences are most likely explained on the basis of the mobility of the cases rather than by any conditions that characterize the social organization of a given community within a large city.

If the mobility of schizophrenics explains rate differences in a geographical distribution, the question becomes why is it that some schizophrenics appear to move out into the outlying areas of the city and others do not. While this question has not been conclusively answered from the present data, the following hypothesis is suggested: the differential distribution of schizophrenic rates in a large urban community is caused by the fact that potential schizophrenics are born into families with differing life-chances. * In other words, if a schizophrenic is born into a family where the life-chances are better than average, he will improve his general condition to the extent that his family does; but if he is born into a family where the life-chances are poor, he will find himself surrounded by the same inadequate conditions of living that encompass his family. This is the factor that

---

*The life-chance concept has appeared in the literature of sociology for several decades. By life-chance is meant that a set of parents starting out with a high-level education and high income potential will provide opportunities for their children that are better in terms of education, health, socialized personalities, and housing environment as against families where education and income potential is on a low level.

accounts for some schizophrenics being picked up from the better organized middle-class communities in the city while other schizophrenics tend to remain in the more disadvantaged economic areas. The predominance of the schizophrenic cases in Cass that came from other areas than the large cities is supportive, but not conclusive evidence for this hypothesis. One would expect that if a sample of schizophrenic cases from a slum area were selected and compared with a sample of cases from a middle-class area with respect to the life-chances of their families at their beginnings, the evidence would show that the unfavorable life-chances would concentrate in the first sample.

The evidence appears to indicate that the population of risk in a relatively deprived community produces no more schizophrenics than does a more homogeneous middle-class community. Thus this research has served to shift the focus from one type of question to another. What accounts for the fact that the rate of schizophrenia in Cass is two-and-one-half times that of Conner-Burbank? Or putting the question in another form, why is it that from the total pool of potential schizophrenics two-and-one-half times as many cases in relation to the population end up in Cass instead of Conner-Burbank? Is it because more potential schizophrenics are born into families where the life-chances are poor? The author does not think so. Rather, it appears that coming from a lower-status family and leaving home early to improve one's educational or economic situation, combined with the toll that the incipient stages of the disease will take, will bring about the excess of schizophrenics in types of urban communities similar to Cass. Conversely, one would contend that the best chance that a potential schizophrenic has for ending up in an urban community like Conner-Burbank is to stick closely to his nuclear family.

Certain geneticists have been giving consideration to the mobility of persons with defective genetic makeup in relation to the general characteristics of the society.[9] They argue that in a relatively free, open, and democratic society mobility will tend to be excessive and more persons with defective genetic makeup are likely to be found at the bottom of the social scale; in a society with a more caste-like structure persons with defective genes are more likely to be evenly distributed throughout the society. Therefore, if it is granted that the necessary condition for schizophrenia is a defective genetic makeup, it would be likely that both voluntary and involuntary mobility processes would operate to bring about a significant excess of these persons in the more deprived residential areas and in the lowest social class, rather than even distribution in all the subcommunities comprising the city. Those who are found in the more adequately organized communities and the other social classes are found there because the life-chances of their families, to whom they continued to cling, were better for them from birth onward than were the life-chances of those schizophrenics whose families are found in the more deprived communities.

STRESS FACTORS

Consider now some of the possible stresses that might be operating with respect to schizophrenics in the two subcommunities. It frequently is hypothesized that stresses in the social environment will be more prevalent at the lower socioeconomic levels than at the higher ones. Consequently, one well might suspect that the stresses in Cass will be sharper than those operating in Conner-Burbank. It is well recognized that if stresses are defined in a purely objective manner it is impossible to catch the meaningful quality of the stress to the person. It also is well recognized that the same external stress possibly has different meanings for different persons, the meaning being dependent upon the past experiences and the immediate social situation to which the person is responsive. Stress has been viewed both in terms of a central etiological factor and as a precipitant of various psychotic reactions in persons either genetically or psychologically vulnerable. While in no position to resolve the issue through this research, a look can be taken at the two factors that have been regarded as being stressful and examine their consequences in the two subcommunities.

Nativity Discrepancy

The first stress factor defined was the presence or absence of a discrepancy between the nativity of the father and the nativity of the patient. It was reasoned that such a discrepancy would imply the presence of a cultural conflict in the family during the period in which the patient was growing up. The results of this analysis appear in Table 4. 20.

In this table two findings can be immediately noted. First, the schizophrenics in the Cass subcommunity show a little less stress as measured by nativity discrepancy than do the patients in the other diagnostic groups; second, the difference between the nativity of the father and that of the patient is more significantly marked for all three diagnostic groups in Conner-Burbank than in Cass. This finding is unexpected but fits in rather neatly with the previous hypothesis suggested to account for the rate differences between the two subcommunities. The most plausible interpretation would seem to be

TABLE 4.20

Number and Percent by Diagnostic Group According to Whether the Nativity of the Patient Was the Same as or Different from the Nativity of the Father in Two Subcommunities of Detroit, 1958

	Cass						Conner-Burbank					
Nativity of Fathers versus	Schizophrenic		Nonschizo-phrenic		Additional		Schizophrenic		Nonschizo-phrenic		Additional	
Nativity of Patients	No.	Percent	No.	Percent	No.	Percent	No.	Percent	No.	Percent	No.	Percent
Same	32	82.05	25	52.08	27	71.05	11	45.83	19	41.30	17	54.84
Different	7	17.95	8	16.66	10	23.68	12	50.00	24	52.17	12	38.71
Nonascertainable	—	—	15	31.26	2	5.27	1	4.17	3	6.53	2	6.45
Total	39	100.00	48	100.00	39	100.00	24	100.00	46	100.00	31	100.00

that stress by this measure is not significant in relation to the development of schizophrenia, and that the difference that can be found between the two subcommunities is a reflection of their ethnic composition and the possibility that schizophrenics in Conner-Burbank came from families where the life-chances were considerably superior to those of schizophrenics in Cass. Thus the fact that in all three diagnostic groups in Conner-Burbank a large percentage of the patients show a discrepancy between the nativity of the father and that of the patient merely reflects, on the part of the families from which these patients came, a more intense striving to improve their economic lot. This finding would seem to suggest the following hypothesis: persons who experience a schizophrenic breakdown are comparable with respect to the demographic characteristics, practices, and values of the communities with which they are identified prior to breakdown. These demographic characteristics, practices, and values vary with position in the social structure and are not likely to be related to the development of schizophrenia. That they may still contain within them certain factors or elements that may precipitate a schizophrenic breakdown can be determined only by getting at the meaning that the factors have for the potential schizophrenic.

In order to test the possibility that the schizophrenics found in the subcommunity merely reflect the ethnic composition of their respective populations, a comparison was made of their percentage distribution by nativity with that of the population. These data are shown in Table 4.21. The most surprising result here is that the total psychiatric cases show nativity distribution that is identical with the population in both subcommunities. The same occurs also for the schizophrenic cases, although the native-born schizophrenics in Conner-Burbank are in excess of the population by 11 percentage points. The case would seem to be clear that the ethnic composition of the schizophrenic group, far from pointing to a condition of strain in the life of the schizophrenic, is merely a reflection of the nativity composition of the population from which the schizophrenic came.

Along this same line the psychiatric cases will be compared with the populations of the two subcommunities with respect to length of residence. If the above hypothesis has any validity, one would confidently expect that with respect to mobility the psychiatric cases would reflect the general moving practice as found in the subcommunity. The distribution of these data is shown in Table 4. 22. The results for the most part justify the expectation. While the schizophrenic cases in both subcommunities show much less stability than does the population, the difference is not so great that it could not be accounted for by chance. While there is great variation between the schizophrenics and the other diagnoses as measured by chi-square,

TABLE 4.21

Number and Percent of Schizophrenics, Total Psychiatric Cases, and Population According to Nativity in Two Subcommunities of Detroit

	Schizophrenic		Total Psychiatric		1960 Population	
Nativity	Number	Percent	Number	Percent	Number	Percent
			Cass			
Native born	33	84.6	97	83.6	38,203	81.4
Native born-foreign	4	10.3	12	10.4	4,599	9.8
Foreign born	2	5.1	7	6.0	4,135	8.8
Total	39	100.0	116[a]	100.0	46,937	100.0
			Conner-Burbank			
Native born	15	62.5	49	50.5	36,830	51.4
Native born-foreign	7	29.2	31	32.0	22,552	31.5
Foreign born	2	8.3	17	17.5	12,258	17.1
Total	24	100.0	97[b]	100.0	71,640	100.0

[a]Unknown = 10 cases.
[b]Unknown = 4 cases.

TABLE 4.22

Number and Percent of Schizophrenic Cases, Other Diagnoses, and Population, 15 Years and Over, According to Length of Residence and Subcommunity, 1958

Length of Residence	Schizophrenic		Other Diagnoses		1960 Population	
	Number	Percent	Number	Percent	Number	Percent
Cass[a]						
Under 5 years	28	77.8[b]	47	62.3	28,316	69.1[b]
Over 5 years	8	22.2	30	37.7	12,696	30.9
Total	36	100.0	77	100.0	41,012	100.0
Conner-Burbank[c]						
Under 5 years	13	54.2[c]	17	22.9	20,734	31.6[d]
Over 5 years	11	45.8	57	77.1	44,762	68.4
Total	24	100.0	74	100.0	65,496	100.0

[a] $\chi^2 = 3.07$, $p < .05$, $df = 1$
[b] $\chi^2 = 8.29$, $p < .001$, $df = 1$
[c] Critical Ratio = 1
[d] Critical Ratio = 1.8

TABLE 4.23

Number and Percent by Diagnostic Group According to Religious Preference in Two Subcommunities of Detroit, 1958

Religious Preference	Schizophrenic		Nonschizophrenic		Additional		Total	
	Number	Percent	Number	Percent	Number	Percent	Number	Percent
				Cass				
Protestant	30	76.92	31	86.11	18	47.65	79	70.53
Catholic	7	17.95	4	11.11	13	36.13	24	21.43
Other	2	5.13	1	2.78	6	16.22	9	8.04
Subtotal	39	100.00	36	100.00	37	100.00	112	100.00
N.A.	0		11		1		12	
Total	39		47		38		124	
				Conner-Burbank				
Protestant	4	16.67	20	46.51	10	34.48	34	35.42
Catholic	19	79.16	23	53.49	18	62.07	60	62.50
Other	1	4.17	0	—	1	3.45	2	2.08
Subtotal	24	100.00	43	100.00	29	100.00	96	100.00
N.A.	0		3		2		5	
Total	24		46		31		101	

the other diagnoses have a distribution that more closely follows the population.

One further bit of evidence serves to support the contention that a group of psychiatric patients, and particularly schizophrenics, reflect the demographic characteristics, practices, and values of the populations from which they come. Such evidence is seen in the distribution of the religious preferences of the patients in the two subcommunities. The religious preferences of the patients in all three diagnostic groups reflect the religious composition of the subcommunity. These data are seen in Table 4. 23. While sufficient data are not available on the religious preferences of the population in the two subcommunities, enough information is available to know that Conner-Burbank is more than 50 percent Catholic, while Cass is overwhelmingly Protestant.

Overcrowdedness

Another factor that has been considered stressful in certain instances is overcrowdedness. From the data it was possible to calculate the average number of persons per room in each diagnostic group for the two subcommunities. One would expect that if this factor was a stressful one for potential schizophrenics, then in both subcommunities they would be disadvantaged as compared to the patients in other diagnostic groups. The number of cases and means per persons per room are shown in Table 4. 24. While the schizophrenics in both subcommunities appear to be at a disadvantage in comparison with the patients in the other two diagnostic groups, the

TABLE 4.24

Means of Persons per Room by Diagnostic Group in Two Subcommunities of Detroit, 1958

	Cass		Conner-Burbank	
Diagnostic Group	$\bar{X}$	Number	$\bar{X}$	Number
Schizophrenic	1.16	37	.82	23
Nonschizophrenic	1.00	33	.65	42
Additional	1.05	34	.63	29

difference between the means was in no case significant. This is true whether one compares the means of the diagnostic groups in each subcommunity separately or whether one compares the means of the diagnostic groups between the two subcommunities. While the patients in each diagnostic group in Conner-Burbank are in a better position using this measurement, it does not prove to be a significant difference in any case; it is merely a reflection of the better economic position enjoyed by the persons in Conner-Burbank. Again, the finding is a negative one and suggests that if overcrowding is a stress factor it apparently does not have much significance with respect to the schizophrenic disorder.

In this attempt to specify the exact role that the character of community organization plays in relation to schizophrenia, the issue has been broken down to two problems. First, when incidence rates for schizophrenia are not distributed at random in a given geographical area containing a risk population, but rather show marked concentration in one part of the area in contrast to another, what would be the best explanation for such a concentration of incidence rates? Second, does the nonrandom distribution of incidence rates for schizophrenia provide any basis for inferring that the nature of the sociocultural life in the area where the high rates are concentrated is a significant factor in the development of schizophrenia? These are two problems that significant, valid rate differences of schizophrenia pose.

SUMMARY

The relevant findings are summarized here with respect to the distribution of schizophrenia in two contrasting subcommunities within the city of Detroit.

The first-contact schizophrenic cases uncovered in the two subcommunities provide rate differences that show that the schizophrenic cases are in a ratio of 2.8:1 between the Cass and Conner-Burbank subcommunities. This finding is in line with the 3:1 ratio reported by other studies that have examined the geographical distribution of schizophrenia.

This same ratio was found to exist for schizophrenia for these two subcommunities for the years 1956 and 1957, as well as 1958.

This ratio also was the same in 1958 for both intensive and nonintensive screening of groups.

When one took account of those schizophrenia cases that had been in the subcommunity for five years or more, the incidence rates based on the 1958 population for the two subcommunities equaled one another. The ratio of those cases that had been in the community less than five years was still maintained at the 3:1 level.

There was little difference between the two subcommunities when length of residence at a given address was contrasted with length of residence in the community.

When incidence rates for schizophrenia in the two subcommunities for those who had been in residence five years or more were computed on the basis of the population that had been in residence five years or more, the ratio of cases between the two subcommunities dropped to 2.5:1, only slightly below the original ratio.

When cases in the two subcommunities were compared with respect to their previous address before moving into the subcommunity, it was found that 78.1 percent of the schizophrenic patients in Cass and 62.5 percent of the cases in Conner-Burbank had previous addresses within the inner city.

When rates for the two subcommunities were computed on the basis of those cases that had not had a move of residence for four years, it was found that the rates in Conner-Burbank for all diagnostic categories exceeded the rates in Cass.

When the birthplaces of schizophrenic patients in the two subcommunities were compared, there proved to be a significant difference between the cases in the two areas; that is, those cases in Cass tended to be born in smaller places, while those schizophrenic cases in Conner-Burbank tended to be born in the large cities.

The cases in the schizophrenic group that were born in places other than large cities tended to come from lower-status families.

In all diagnostic groups all patients found living alone were picked up in Cass with the exception of three found in Conner-Burbank, one in each diagnostic group.

Using as a measure of stress the discrepancy between the nativity of the father and the nativity of the patient, it was found that this had no significance with respect to schizophrenia in the two subcommunities.

Using a measure of overcrowdedness as a possible stress factor in schizophrenia, it was found that there was no significant difference between both the various diagnostic groups and the two subcommunities for each diagnostic group with respect to this factor.

Look again at the two initial problems that were raised at the beginning of this chapter. It was discovered that incidence-rate differences for schizophrenia, as found between two different types of subcommunities within the city, would appear to be more spurious than real. The hypothesis that best seemed to fit the evidence gathered is that rate differences found within the confines of a large, urban, industrial city of the Western world are to be explained in terms of the differing initial life-chances present in families that produce persons destined for schizophrenia. In other words, when a person who is later to develop this disorder is born into a family where the life-chances are good, he will reap certain benefits with respect to education, health, income, and residence, provided he stays with the family. When a family with good life-chances that contains a schizophrenic changes its residence, the potential schizophrenic changes his residence also. While this may account for the fact that a fair number of schizophrenics are found in Conner-Burbank, making for an incidence rate comparable to most schizophrenic incidence rates, it does not account for the excess number of schizophrenics found in Cass. It is hypothesized here that it is the break with the lower status nuclear family that produces the excess of schizophrenics in urban communities of the Cass type. As a corollary to these hypotheses, it is suggested that the schizophrenics drawn from any subcommunity within the city are likely to be similar to the population from which they are drawn and to reflect certain characteristics, practices, and values of that population.

Turning now to the second problem, one is forced to the conclusion that this epidemiological analysis with the data encompassed in it provides no basis for attaching any significance to the sociocultural organization of a community as a factor in the development of the schizophrenic disorder. On the contrary, the evidence shows that schizophrenia is found in every population group. While these cases may provide significant rate differentials, these differentials are to be accounted for mainly by the residential changes typical of urban communities under present conditions. One should remember the significant remark of Freeman, Simmons, and Bergen that "families containing schizophrenic patients move for the same reasons as do other families in the community."[10] Thus it would seem that the geographical mobility both of families containing potential schizophrenics and of potential schizophrenics themselves accounts for the differential spread of cases in a given metropolitan area.

The answer to the problem of why some cases fan out in the area and others do not can only be inferred and not answered conclusively by the data. While it has been suggested that certain characteristics of the family at its beginning provide differential life-chances for its offspring, this is not the only factor. Certain needs of the person—health, job, family housing, schooling for the children, location of friends, residence of family of orientation, avoidance of certain social and ethnic groups, and the like—all operate as positive pressures to distribute persons over the metropolitan area regardless of whether such persons are potential schizophrenics or non-schizophrenic types. The age at which the first symptoms of schizophrenia appear also is an additional factor that will determine the degree to which geographic mobility is likely to be limited. Consequently, it can be concluded that significant rate variations in the incidence of schizophrenia in a given geopolitical unit in the kind of society that characterizes the United States, are caused by a selection process operating through a social necessity for the maintenance of a balance between the needs of the persons and the characteristics of the social organization in that unit.

NOTES

1. R. E. L. Faris and H. W. Dunham, Mental Disorders in Urban Areas (Chicago: University of Chicago Press, 1939); E. H. Hare, "Mental Illness and Social Conditions in Bristol," Journal of Medical Science 102 (April 1956): 349-57; Tsung Yi Lin, "A Study of the Incidence of Mental Disorder in Chinese and Other Culture," Psychiatry 16 (November 1953): 313-36; E. Gartley Jaco, "Social Factors in Mental Disorder in Texas," Social Problems 4 (April 1957): 322-28; and A. Hollingshead and F. Redlich, Social Class and Mental Illness (New York: Wiley, 1958).

2. C. C. Hughes, M. A. Tremblay, R. N. Rapoport, and A. H. Leighton, People of Cove and Woodlot, vol. 2: The Sterling County Study of Psychiatric Disorder and Socio-Cultural Environment (New York: Basic Books, 1960).

3. Ø. Ødegaard, "Emigration and Mental Health," Mental Hygiene 20 (October 1936): 546-53; also Dorothy S. Thomas, Migration and Mental Disease (Social Science Research Council, 1956).

4. C. Tietze, P. Lemkau, and M. Cooper, "Personality Disorder and Spatial Mobility," American Journal of Sociology 48 (July 1948): 29-37.

5. For this implication, see the writings of B. Malzberg, especially Social and Biological Aspects of Mental Disease (Utica, N. Y.: State Hospital Press, 1940), chap. 6.

6. H. E. Freeman, O. G. Simmons, and B. J. Bergen, "Residential Mobility Inclinations among Families of Mental Patients," Social Forces 38 (May 1960): 320-24.

7. See Chapter 3.

8. J. A. Clausen and M. L. Kohn, "Relation of Schizophrenia to the Social Structure of a Small City," in Epidemiology of Mental Disorder, ed. B. Pasamanick, Publication no. 60 (Washington, D. C.: The American Association for the Advancement of Science, 1959).

9. Curt Stern, Principles of Human Genetics, 2d ed. (San Francisco and London: W. H. Freeman, 1960), pp. 645-46.

10. Freeman, Simmons, and Bergen, "Residential Mobility."

5

CITY CORE AND SUBURBAN FRINGE: CHANGING DISTRIBUTION PATTERNS

This chapter examines the distribution patterns of mental illness in the city in order to assess them within the context of the social changes that have taken place in U. S. cities over the past three decades. It also inquires whether or not the changes in city life that have taken place have produced any radical shift in the types of community milieus where the different types of mental illness are to be found. These concerns are of fundamental significance for certain theoretical positions that have evolved from correlations between types of urban milieus and selected types of mental illness. However, in order to assess the distribution patterns of mental illness in relation to the social changes in the cities, it is necessary to compare contemporary distribution patterns with those of an earlier period.[1]

Those studies that purported to examine the distribution of mental illness in the 1930s were quite definite in asserting that all types of mental illness, including most of the individual psychoses with the exception of the manic-depressive group, showed a concentration of high rates at the center of the city with rates declining in all directions toward the city's periphery. While there were certain variations in the distribution patterns of the individual psychoses, there seemed to be no doubt that all were highly concentrated in those local areas of the city that were marked by impoverishment, below-standard housing, ethnic conflicts, unstable families, and mobile populations, by virtue of which the people appeared to be isolated

---

Used with permission from Changing Perspectives in Mental Illness, ed. Stanley C. Plog and Robert B. Edgerton (New York: Holt, Rinehart and Winston, 1969), pp. 337-63.

from the mainstream of life. In fact, Schroeder asserted categorically, "There are insanity areas comparable to the delinquency areas of Chicago which Shaw discovered more than a decade ago."[2]

These earlier findings point up two questions: What evidence can be gathered showing that the distribution patterns of mental illness and specific psychoses within the city have shifted in form, thus disturbing the older reported concentration of cases of mental disorder at the city's core? Can it still be demonstrated that Schroeder's earlier contention stands up today or, in other words, can it still be established that there are valid differential rates between local area populations in a large city, and that a population in one area produces more mental illness than a population in another area? In this chapter these two basic questions will be examined.

ARE RATE PATTERNS CHANGING IN FORM?

The first issue is quite complicated, especially because of the variety of types among the mentally ill. However, there seems to be every reason to believe that the distribution patterns of mental illness will undergo sharp shifts because of the influence of certain factors that emerged during the past 25 years. These factors that have been at work and should bring about shifts in the distribution pattern of mental illness in large cities would include the following: accelerated social change set in motion by automotive technology, urban renewal, new educational programs, and the civil rights movement; the widening definition of mental illness; changing attitudes in the cities toward the mentally ill; and the multiplication of psychiatric facilities for care, treatment, rehabilitation, and research. It is submitted that these are the chief factors that are at work to bring about shifts in the distribution patterns of mental illness in the large cities of the country.

Social Change

Today as never before in human history, the process of social change becomes increasingly evident to larger numbers of people everywhere. For two or three decades it has been commonplace among intellectuals to recognize the significance of urbanization and industrialization as twin stimuli for bringing about social change. In recent years these phenomena, discussed openly on editorial pages and via radio and television, have acquainted more and more people with the processes of change all over the world. Further, there is the increasing awareness of the role that the new technology is playing with respect to changing the character of manufacturing and transportation, and even of office work. In the world of 100 years ago, in the technologically advanced countries, social change was hardly perceptible except over a generation. Today social change is measured in decades and, in some cases, two- or three-year periods; sometimes it almost seems to take place before one's very eyes. In fact, it comes so rapidly that people's patterns of thinking and behavior hardly catch up with the new change before further changes take place.[3]

The consequences of change apply not only to thought processes and behavior patterns, but also to the necessity to adapt institutional structures. It has been only in the last decade that communities all across the country have awakened to the defects and inadequacies of the school systems. High-school dropouts, who were of little concern to communities 35 years ago because they would be absorbed into the work force, now become a problem of major proportions because they are without the skills that are required to fit them into the work force. A recent conference in Michigan estimated that approximately 2 million young people literally had retired before the age of 20 because they could not find work. Such a group can and may still become a tremendous explosive force in the society unless some means is discovered, and discovered quickly, to locate these persons and incorporate them into various training programs that will equip them with new working skills appropriate to a changing economy.[4]

In another framework, the vast urban renewal program that has developed, as stimulated by the federal government during the past decade, has taken the bulldozer quickly through urban slums in an unselective fashion, disrupting old stable neighborhoods and scattering the inhabitants to new neighborhoods within the city where old friends are lacking and old contacts lost.[5] Within the cities this activity has been carried on by city-planning groups that, while giving lip service to the psychic and social needs of people, actually ignore these needs in their zest to erect new physical structures and build new bands of greenbelt near old city cores.[6] The development of high-rent apartments and expensive private houses near the city's core as in Detroit—the suburb at the center—will be a crucial factor in changing old ecological patterns.

The awakening of black citizens to the possibility of achieving full citizenship as guaranteed by the Constitution, resulting in part from the Supreme Court's decision that segregated schools are unconstitutional, represents still another factor in bringing about changes in urban ecological organization. Their pressure exerted on the schools, business organizations, courts, and voting patterns has been tremendous. It not only has activated the political right to oppose, but also activated large segments of lower- and middle-class society to support the civil rights movement. While there is marked dispute about some gains that have been achieved, there seems to be no doubt that in the white-collar areas more and more positions have become open to blacks, and business organizations that had never given a thought to the hiring of blacks are hiring them today.

Thus the new technology, the cultural lag in the schools, planned urban renewal, and the civil rights movement are the major forces that are changing the face of cities and their institutions in the United States. In a very definite sense it might be said that the recent war on poverty, as outlined by the federal government, represents a realization of an age-old promise of science and technology. That is, through science and the new resulting technology, it really becomes possible to eradicate those ancient scourges of mankind: war, disease, ignorance, and poverty.

The Widening Definition of Mental Disease

Perhaps the widening definition of mental illness more than any other factor is crucial in changing the perception of distribution patterns of mental illness. This factor highlights the perennial problem in psychiatric circles as to what constitutes a case.[7] This issue, while not settled, was much easier to cope with a quarter of a century ago, when practically the only available facilities for psychiatric help were the state and private mental hospitals. At that time it was clear that for the most part the "violent and furious" were hospitalized and the minor disturbances generally were neglected. But with the mounting frustration over the treatment and cure of persons with major psychoses, particularly schizophrenia, there gradually resulted a turning away of psychiatric efforts from the real psychoses and toward persons with minor psychiatric symptoms who seemed to be the best risks for therapy. This widening definition of mental illness is not noticeable with respect to the hard-core psychoses; its impact is registered in the minor emotional disturbances as reflected in such concepts as neurotic tendencies, withdrawal symptoms, mild depressions, character disturbances, passive-aggressive personalities, and the like. The old saw that anybody who goes to a psychiatrist ought to have his head examined contains perhaps more than a grain of truth. For when the person does go, the examining psychiatrist literally has a host of labels to apply, even though he may not force the patient into one of the diagnostic groups as listed and coded by the official psychiatric manual.

This state of affairs was well documented by two recent and carefully designed epidemiological studies of mental illness. Srole et al. report that 80 percent of a sample population of 1,660 were found to have some form of psychiatric symptoms.[8] Along the same line, Leighton and his associates, in their epidemiological study in Sterling County, conclude from all their available information, "that at least half of the adults in Sterling County are currently suffering from some psychiatric disorder defined in the APA Diagnostic and Statistical Manual."[9] The significant question here is what percentage of cases found to be psychiatrically impaired in these two studies are actually impaired by minor emotional disturbances.

A comparison of the community epidemiological surveys of mental illness in the 1930s with comparable surveys in the 1950s supplies the same kind of evidence. In making this comparison, one is struck with the fact that four to five times more cases of all kinds of mental disorder are reported in the more recent surveys than in those of the 1930s.[10] The only thing that can account for such a discrepancy is the widening definition in recent years of what constitutes a case of mental disorder.

The net also has been widened by the recent attempt to place into the psychiatrically sick role all those persons who might be regarded as failures in social adaptation. Consequently delinquents, sex offenders, alcoholics, drug addicts, homosexuals, prostitutes, beatniks, communists, and the racially prejudiced have all been, from time to time and in different clinical settings, fitted into one or another psychiatric diagnostic category, some of which have the APA official stamp and some of which do not. This is not to say that none of the persons found in these categories is mentally sick; indeed, some are. But any diagnostic category is likely to lose its significance unless carefully worked out criteria are rigidly applied. It also means that many of the persons who are forced into some psychiatric slot are likely to be regarded as normal and acceptable in their various subcultural milieus. In fact, much of their behavior also will be found acceptable in the more conventional areas of social life.

One other factor that has contributed to this widening definition has been the extensive and intensive education of psychiatrists in psychoanalytic theory and the use of psychoanalytic technique. This is not to say that psychoanalytic treatment should not be used with the clinically neurotic or the mild psychotic reaction types, but only to point out that it is used and extended to those professionals in the community, excluding the psychiatrists in training, who are functioning at some acceptable level of adequacy in their occupations and families and at the same time are earning $15,000 to $40,000 per year. The problem becomes complicated when such persons are considered to be psychiatrically sick and in need of treatment. Thus any epidemiological survey of all kinds of mental disorders, which includes cases seen by private psychiatrists, is likely to be weighted by such cases, producing a distorted picture of the incidence of valid psychiatric illness in the community.

All of these bits of evidence go to support the contention that what currently is defined as mental illness is a result of the widening definition of mental illness over the past two decades. This makes for tremendous difficulty in epidemiological studies for, with respect to total mental illness, there is no basis for the comparison of contemporary rates with earlier rates. Epidemiological study of mental illness also is hampered by policy differences in the various clinics relative to those cases that will be accepted for treatment and those that will not. Consequently, it is almost impossible to have any basis for establishing a true count of mental illness in the community; the line that separates the sick from the well is a variable and confusing one.

CHANGING ATTITUDES TOWARD THE MENTALLY ILL

A certain amount of evidence has accumulated over the past two decades that would indicate a marked shift in the attitudes of people toward the mentally ill in the various communities across the United States. That is, while the stigma attached to mental illness still lingers on in certain quarters, the irrational fear of the mentally ill that used to be manifested is gradually disappearing. For example, in his survey of a sample of the Louisville population in 1950, Woodward showed that a great majority of the people who were questioned held a naturalistic view of the development of mental illness.[11] Gurin's study in 1959 took much the same point of view and indicated a marked willingness of people to take their troubles voluntarily to those experts whom they thought might help them.[12] An attempt to tap the public opinion toward psychiatric home care indicated a definite sympathetic and helpful attitude toward the mentally ill in over three fourths of the persons in the sample. For example, to a statement, "The best way to handle people in mental hospitals is to keep them behind locked doors," 77 percent of 1,737 people gave a negative response. To the statement, "Almost all persons who have mental illness are dangerous," 74 percent gave a negative response. It is responses of this character that serve to point to the new attitude about mental illness that has been developing recently.[13]

Then too, the bombardment of various communities over the past decade via the media concerning the problem of mental illness has helped to spread this sympathetic and more tolerant attitude. In fact, it has reached the point in some communities that it seems that people have been promised more than psychiatrists can deliver. Now they often come voluntarily to the various outpatient clinics in the urban centers. This ground swell of persons who seem willing to be identified as psychiatric cases contributes, when they enter official counts, to the changing rate patterns of mental illness in the community.

Increase in Psychiatric Facilities

Since World War II many developments have taken place that helped to do away with the apathy about mental illness that seemed prevalent during the first half of the century. The psychiatric experience accumulated in the war effort, the entrance of the federal government into the mental health field, the discovery of the new tranquilizing and energizing pharmaceuticals, the increase of foundation money for mental health research, and the various sociological studies of mental health facilities all contributed to creating a climate of optimism relative to the care and treatment of the mentally ill. This new optimism was reflected in an increase in the number of psychiatrists, the development of new treatment facilities, and new research efforts to evaluate psychiatric facilities and therapeutic results. *

The frustrations over the older, more chronic cases have been reflected in the widening definition of what constitutes mental illness, which, in turn, helped to contribute to the idea that much was being accomplished, even with respect to the chronic cases who often had been long-time residents of mental hospitals. The application of the new drugs appeared to be moving them to some level of recovery, thus making it possible for more of them to return to their families in the community. This led to new projects geared toward rehabilitation and caring for any remissions occurring in their home settings. Thus day hospitals, night hospitals, halfway houses, and convalescent homes began to put in their appearance, first in England and then in the United States, as treatment centers that would encourage and support the mentally ill for living in the community. These new projects were further abetted by an increase in the number of public and private outpatient clinics in order to keep the patient out of the hospital as long as possible.

The changed attitudes on the part of people toward mental illness have helped to encourage two new developments. If people who are sick in their minds are to be regarded and acted toward in much the

---

*According to the American Psychiatric Association, from 1940 to 1965 the number of psychiatrists in the country increased by 477 percent, or from 2,403 in 1940 to 13,880 in 1965.

same way as are persons who are physically ill, then it also follows that such persons should have access to the general hospitals. This produced the development of psychiatric wards in general hospitals, often made possible because of the inclusion of provisions for mental illness in various health insurance plans. While it is true that most plans only cover approximately a month's illness, nevertheless, it was enough to help encourage the general hospitals to include facilities for the mentally ill. As a further development along this line, it was interesting to note that the new auto contracts signed in Detroit in 1964 carry certain provisions for the treatment of any mental illness that may arise among the workers.

The second development has been in terms of the techniques aimed at the rehabilitation of the person who has been mentally ill. The empirical experience that developed after World War II in connection with the rehabilitation of handicapped veterans obviously precipitated the notion that such procedures might work also with persons who are apparently recovering from their mental illnesses. These techniques are directed toward creating a more satisfactory self-image and equipping the person with skills that enable him to function in the community, if not at his previous level, at least at a level where he feels necessary and accepted. Rehabilitation is behind such therapeutic facilities as day hospitals, convalescent homes, halfway houses, and the like, which are used both to prevent prolonged hospitalization and to help fit back into the community those people who are recovering from a mental illness.

The latest development in this increasing number of psychiatric facilities has been the proposal for community mental health centers throughout the country. The purpose of these centers is to bring together the total psychiatric facilities of the community in one location so that treatment potentialities can be maximized. It is visualized that these centers would serve populations from 50,000 to 200,000 persons and would combine in one location all of the facilities necessary for diagnosis, treatment, prevention, and research, thus insuring continuity of care.

SOME EVIDENCE OF CHANGING RATE PATTERNS

In the account above, it was attempted to make a logical analysis of those factors observable in cities in the past two decades that should contribute significantly to changing the rate patterns of mental illness that have been reported for urban communities in the United States. In the earlier Faris and Dunham study, this author often was struck by the fact that the great bulk of the subcommunities in Chicago had, for the most part, rates for total mental disorder that were

FIGURE 5.1

Frequency Polygon of Subcommunity Rates for All Mental Disorders of First Admissions to State and Private Hospitals, Chicago, 1922-34 (N = 120 subcommunities)

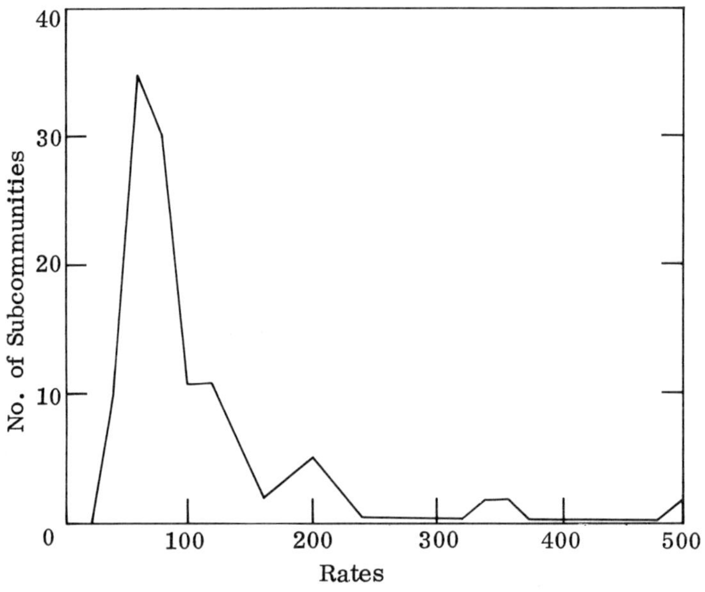

relatively low, while only about ten or 12 subcommunities had rates that might be regarded as high. The frequency distributions of the subcommunities in Chicago by size of rates for total mental disorders are shown in Figure 5.1. One notes in this distribution the small number of subcommunities with high rates.

If this analysis of the factors at work in the urban community has any validity, one would predict that the distributions of the rates for subcommunities in any large city would approximate a normal distribution. The first test of this prediction is provided by the distribution pattern of schizophrenic rates for Detroit. The distribution pattern for 1936-38 is contrasted with the distribution pattern for 1956-58. These data are presented as frequency polygons in Figure 5.2. One notes immediately that the rates for 1956-58 show a wider spread when contrasted with the rates for 1936-38. While the distribution of schizophrenic rates for 1956-58 is hardly a normal curve, it should be noted that within this time period 17 subcommunities have rates larger than 100 as compared to six in the 1936-38 time period.

This same difference also stands out when the distribution of schizophrenic rates in Detroit in these two time periods is broken down by sex. In the distribution of male first admission schizophrenic rates in the 1936-38 period, one notes that only seven subcommunities have rates above 100, but in the 1956-58 period 19 subcommunities had rates above 100, indicating that schizophrenia is distributed through the city much more widely in the recent period. The pattern formed by the female rates almost approaches a normal curve in the more recent period. Again, one notes that for the earlier period there were only

FIGURE 5.2

Frequency Polygons of Subcommunity Rates for Schizophrenia Based on First Admissions to State Hospitals, Detroit, 1936-38 and 1956-58
(N = 51 subcommunities)

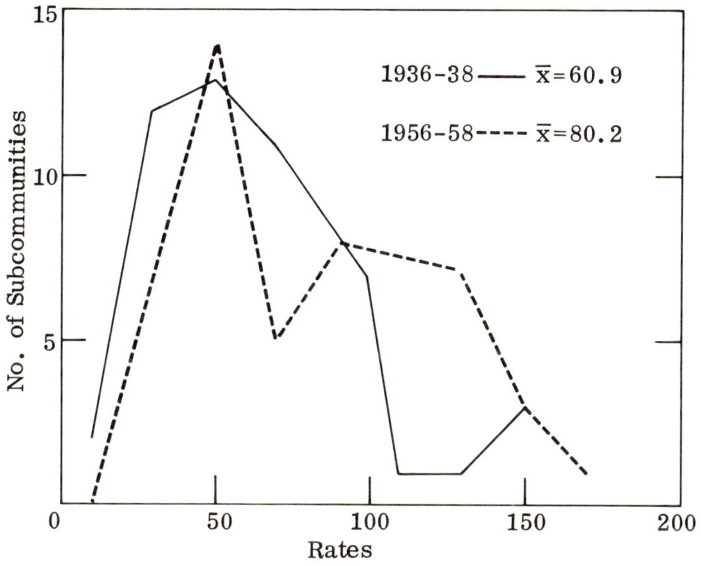

FIGURE 5. 3

Frequency Polygons of Subcommunity Rates for Schizophrenic Males Based on First Admissions to State Hospitals, Detroit, 1936-38 and 1956-58
(N = 51 subcommunities)

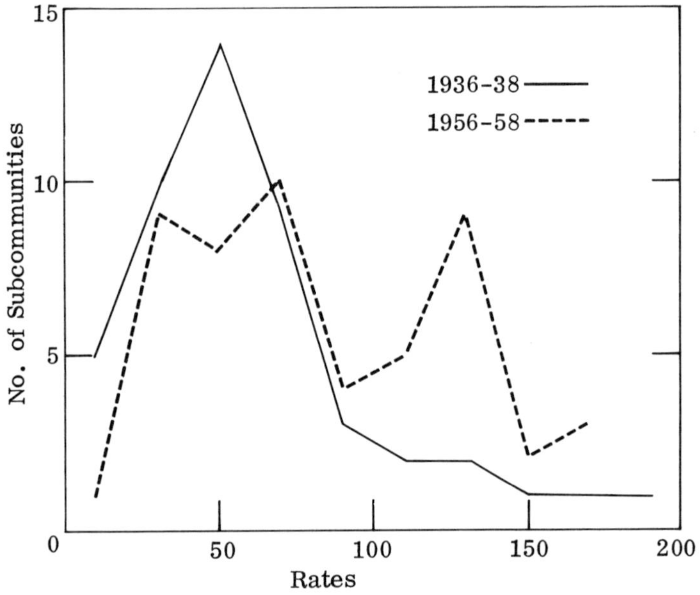

seven subcommunities with rates above 100. These distributions are shown in Figures 5. 3 and 5. 4.

A more definitive test for the prediction is provided by Levy and Rowitz's study in the 1960s, which was an attempt to replicate the Faris and Dunham study of the 1930s.[14] A comparison of the frequency distribution of schizophrenic rates for 1922-31 is contrasted with the frequency distribution of the schizophrenic rates for 1961 for Chicago as reported by Levy and Rowitz. Here one notes that the more recent data approximate a normal distribution curve, as contrasted with the very skewed curve for the results obtained 30 years earlier. This comparison is depicted in Figure 5. 5.

This evidence, scanty as it may be, serves to document the contention that the rate patterns of mental illness in large urban communities are changing. These changing patterns appear to follow both population and income shifts. That is, the city core has been continually losing population, some pushing out to the suburbs and others settling in those subcommunities beyond the city's core. In a like manner, the tendency of the income distribution to approach a normal curve for those incomes under $10,000 is associated with this shift in the rate patterns of mental illness.[15]

The factors that were analyzed in the above discussion can be regarded as social pressures of varying strengths that are effective in changing the distribution patterns of rates for total mental disorder as well as specific psychoses in cities. Thus it can be predicted that future studies that attempt to examine the distribution of mental disorders in large metropolitan centers may come up with rate patterns

FIGURE 5.4

Frequency Polygons of Subcommunity Rates for Schizophrenic Females Based on First Admissions to State Hospitals, Detroit, 1936-38 and 1956-58
(N = 51 subcommunities)

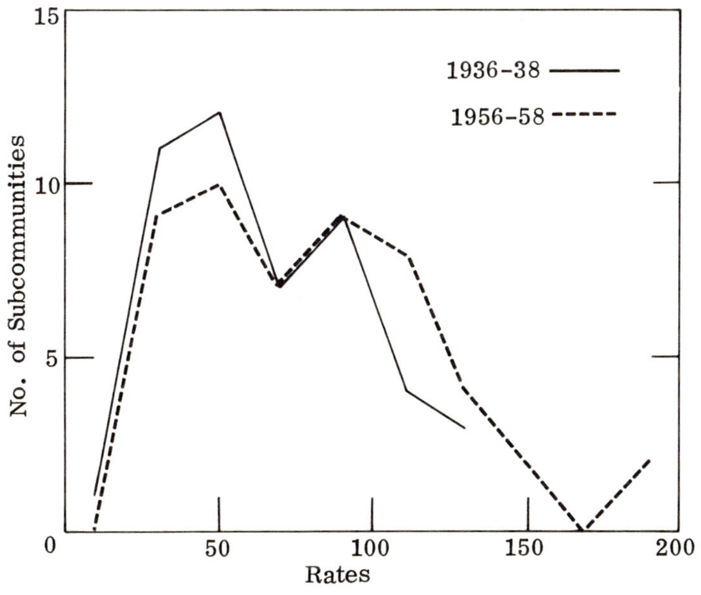

FIGURE 5.5

Frequency Polygons of Subcommunity Rates for Schizophrenia Based on First Admissions, Chicago, 1922-31 and 1961 (N = 75 subcommunities)

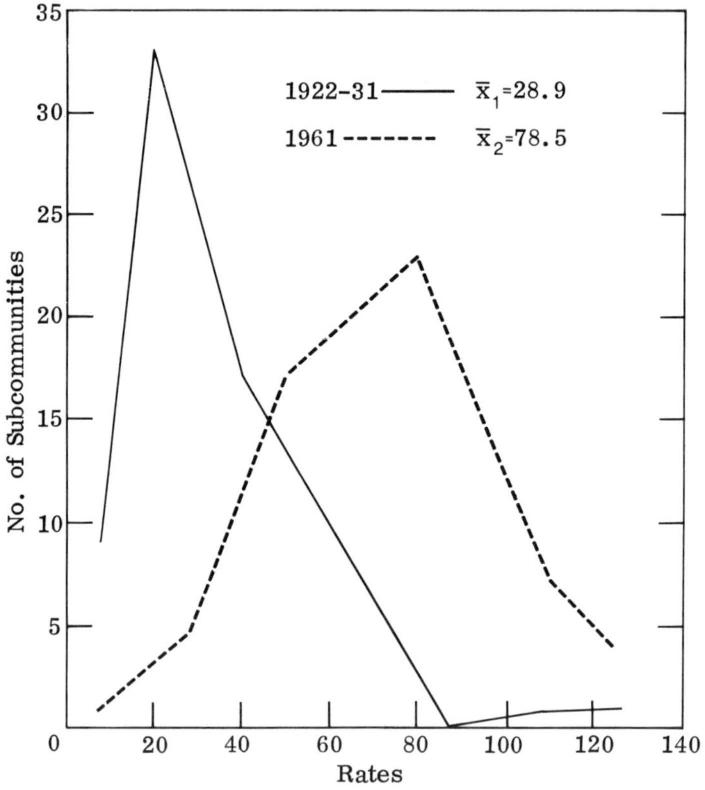

that, while still pointing to differential areal rates, will tend to show concentration of medium high rates in certain areas beyond the city's core. Further, as cities attain a more marked social and economic equilibrium, it would be expected that rates by local areas for total mental disorders, and especially for schizophrenia, would approximate a normal curve.

DO DIFFERENTIAL RATES MEAN WHAT THEY SEEM?

What follows is an examination of the second question, that is, Do significant differential rates between local areas of the city signify that the population in one area actually breeds more of one type of mental disorder than does the population in another area?

In order to effect such an analysis, the following questions will be analyzed: To what extent do the original findings of the Faris and Dunham study stand up today? What has been the character of the criticism of the Faris and Dunham study? To what extent did the findings of recent studies support those of Faris and Dunham? What is the most plausible explanation of differential rate patterns of mental disorders and, particularly, schizophrenia within the city?

Previous Epidemiological Findings

In any attempt to examine differences or similarities that exist between city core and suburban fringe, it is appropriate to recall the issues raised by the Faris and Dunham findings concerning the distribution of different psychoses in Chicago. The central finding of that study established that the high rates of schizophrenia were concentrated at the center of the city, with the rates declining in all directions toward the periphery, while the distribution of manic-depressive rates appeared to be randomly scattered throughout the city (see Chapter 3). This difference in the distribution rate pattern of these two psychoses in the city did not receive much attention in subsequent discussions of the study, for the critics concentrated on the schizophrenic distributions to discover if they really meant what they seemed to indicate, namely, that one kind of an urban population seemed to produce a significantly larger number of schizophrenics than another type of population. Yet the failure of the manic-depressive rates to form a pattern similar to the schizophrenic rates might be interpreted as meaning that the manic-depressive reaction enabled the person to relate to his immediate environment in a much more effective fashion than could the person who developed schizophrenia. In contrast, the schizophrenic reaction was of the type that prevented a meaningful relationship with family and peer group members, and so the person withdrew from these relationships and selected an environment where he would more likely be left alone. Thus he was isolated from becoming involved in close interpersonal relationships.

In this earlier study of the various distributions of schizophrenic rates, while the ratio between the high- and low-rate areas was approximately 3.5:1, a difference that was statistically significant, the problem of the interpretation of this difference was constantly present. Myerson sounded the alarm when he reviewed the study and pointed to the drift hypothesis as explaining the concentration of cases that made up the high-rate areas.[16] A decade or so later, Gerard and Houston tried to explain the concentration of schizophrenic cases at the center of the city by showing that they were to be accounted for primarily by schizophrenics living alone, and that

TABLE 5.1

Number and Percent[a] of General Paresis and CNS Syphilis First Admission to All Facilities[b] by Sex, 1923-62

Year	Males		Females		Total	
	Number	Percent	Number	Percent	Number	Percent
1922	5678	8.10	1474	2.10	7152	10.20
1938	6092	5.85	2125	2.04	8217	7.89
1948	3565	2.56	1499	1.08	5064	3.64
1962	312	.19	127	.08	439	.27

[a]Refers to percentage of total first admissions.

[b]Includes all state, city, county, and private facilities, excluding Veterans' hospitals.

Source: U.S. Department of Health, Education, and Welfare Publications, "Patients in Mental Institutions," 1923, 1938, 1948, 1960, and 1962 (Washington, D.C.: Government Printing Office).

if one looked at the distribution of schizophrenics coming from a family base, the differences between high- and low-rate areas tended to disappear.[17] Clausen and Kohn, in a study of the distribution of first admission schizophrenic rates in Hagerstown, Maryland, showed a complete absence of rate differences among the different socioeconomic areas of the city.[18] Even before this study, Hare in Bristol, England, attempted to determine whether the attractor or the breeder hypothesis best explained schizophrenic rate differentials in the city. He was forced to conclude that, while the issue was not resolved completely, the evidence did seem to favor the attractor hypothesis.[19] The most impressive and monumental study of Leighton et al. showed that as far as the psychoses were concerned, there appeared to be no difference in the rate between disorganized and organized communities.[20]

This analysis has been concerned primarily with the attempt to determine if there are any differences in the size of the schizophrenic rates between the core and the periphery of the city. However, there is the pattern of rates formed by some of the other psychotic groups that Faris and the author did examine in an earlier study. These other mental disorders, such as manic-depressive psychoses, general paresis, alcoholic psychoses, and the old-age group, have not received much attention in recent epidemiological investigations. These studies have concentrated primarily on the schizophrenic disorders, the total psychoses and, in some instances, the psychoneurosis and character disturbances. The contrast between the manic-depressive distribution and the schizophrenic distribution in the earlier study already has been commented on, and it was noted that the manic-depressive cases gave evidence of less residential mobility than did the schizophrenic cases. This is also supported by the recent study in Detroit.[21]

In referring to the distribution patterns of alcoholic psychoses and drug addiction in the earlier study, it was noted that the concentration of cases seemed to be explained largely by the tendency of these cases to select the more anonymous areas in the urban community where they might escape surveillance. Again, in the earlier study the correlation of the general paretic rates with vice areas and syphilitic case rates, while they did not explain the rate patterns, did suggest by implication that proximity to sources of infection might account for the high rates in certain areas of the city. The gradual control of syphilis has reduced cases of general paresis to almost a disappearing point and this may account for the absence of new epidemiological work with this psychosis. Some evidence on this point is shown in Table 5.1.

The early association found between the old-age psychosis and the areas of poverty merely suggested that the families in poverty-stricken areas tended more easily to place their older members in psychiatric hospitals. However, it is being discovered, with the aging of the population, that these psychoses of old age have no relationship to any particular population; rather, they are likely to be related to the number of older people in the population, and numerically are possibly on the increase owing to the increasing age of the population. As the current population of older people, those long-time residents of the city core, die out and are not replaced, there will be a real increase in the geriatric disorders in the peripheral and suburban areas, especially in the oldest areas.

SUMMARY AND PREDICTIONS

This analysis of the pattern of mental illness in large cities has pointed up two positive findings. First, certain forces are at work in the U. S. city that are making obsolete the traditional ecological organization that seemed to characterize cities from their beginnings up to World War II. Thus it is not unexpected that rate patterns for various social problems also will be subject to change. This seems to be true for patterns of mental illness. When the current forces have worked themselves out, a new ecological organization of the city will emerge. In its ideal form it would provide a greater equilibrium in its organization. This means that with respect to the various subcommunities of the large urban centers, population, income, and family size will tend toward a more normal distribution. The rate patterns for all kinds of social deviance, including mental illness, also will shift toward this new equilibrium. It is predicted that, with respect to mental illness, when the new ecological organization of the city is completed, only a few of the subcommunities will have high or low rates; the bulk of the subcommunities will converge toward an average rate. If this trend continues, there will be a grave question concerning the attaching of any significance to the living conditions and cultural organization in subcommunities for explaining the high rates of psychoses, particularly schizophrenia.

In answering the second question, certain evidence has been presented to show how a high schizophrenic rate in a subcommunity of the city has developed. The analysis pointed to mobility as the chief factor to account for the spread of schizophrenia cases in the urban community. The analysis also questioned that any schizophrenic rate in a subcommunity of the city can be regarded as a product of an indigenous population. This means that schizophrenic rate differentials can hardly be explained by the cultural climate in a subcommunity, but are more likely to be accounted for by a social selection process, aided and abetted by the actions of schizophrenics themselves in selecting areas of residence where their chances of survival in the free community would appear to them to be enhanced.

This analysis suggests a greater caution in using differential rate distributions of various forms of pathological behavior to infer a connection between the behavior in question and the surrounding social conditions. It seems most likely that differential rate patterns in cities for various types of social deviance may be significant as a means for studying the organization of the city, rather than as a device for dredging up the etiological factors to account for the deviance in question.

NOTES

1. R. E. L. Faris and H. W. Dunham, Mental Disorders in Urban Areas: An Ecological Study of Schizophrenia and Other Psychoses (Chicago: University of Chicago Press, 1939); and H. W. Green, Persons Admitted to the Cleveland State Hospital, 1928-1938 (Cleveland: Cleveland Health Council, 1939).
2. C. W. Schroeder, "Mental Disorders in Cities," American Journal of Sociology 47 (1942): 40-47.
3. W. F. Ogburn, Social Change with Respect to Culture and Original Nature (New York: Viking, 1950).
4. I. Foster, "Some Facts about the Labor Market in the Sixties," American Child 43 (1961): 5-8; and M. Fuhrman, "School Dropouts and Juvenile Delinquency," Federal Probation 24 (1960): 34-37.
5. H. Gans, Urban Villagers (New York: Free Press, 1962).
6. J. Jacobs, The Death and Life of Great American Cities (New York: Random House, 1961); and E. Wolf and C. Lebeaux, "Studies in Change and Renewal in an Urban Community" (unpublished manuscript, Wayne State University, 1965).
7. Discussion of "Definition of a Case for Purposes of Research in Social Psychiatry," in Interrelations between the Social Environment and Psychiatric Disorders (New York: Milbank Memorial Fund, 1953).
8. L. Srole et al., Mental Health in the Metropolis: The Midtown Manhattan Study (New York: McGraw-Hill, 1962).
9. D. Leighton et al., The Character of Danger (New York: Basic Books, 1959).
10. R. J. Plunkett and J. E. Gordon, Epidemiology and Mental Illness (New York: Basic Books, 1960).
11. J. W. Woodward, "Changing Ideas on Mental Illness and Its Treatment," American Sociological Review 16 (1951): 443-54.

12. G. Gurin, J. Veroff, and S. Feld, Americans View Their Mental Health (New York: Basic Books, 1960).

13. G. M. Crocetti and P. V. Lemkau, "Public Opinion of Psychiatric Home Care in an Urban Area," American Journal of Public Health 53 (1963): 409-14.

14. L. Levy and L. Rowitz, The Ecology of Mental Disorder (New York: Behavioral Publications, 1973).

15. S. Goldsmith, D. Jaszi, H. Kaitz, and M. Liebenberg, "Size Distribution of Income since the Mid-thirties," Review of Economics and Statistics 36 (1954): 1-32.

16. A. Myerson, "Review of Mental Disorders in Urban Areas," American Journal of Psychiatry 96 (1941): 995-97.

17. D. L. Gerard and L. A. Houston, "Family Setting and the Social Ecology of Schizophrenia," Psychiatric Quarterly 27 (1953): 90-101.

18. J. A. Clausen and M. L. Kohn, "Relation of Schizophrenia to the Social Structure of a Small City," in Epidemiology of Mental Disorders, ed. B. Pasamanick (Washington, D. C.: American Association for the Advancement of Science, 1959).

19. E. H. Hare, "Mental Illness and Social Conditions in Bristol," Journal of Mental Science 102 (April 1956): 349-57.

20. Leighton et al., The Character of Danger.

21. H. W. Dunham, Community and Schizophrenia: An Epidemiological Analysis (Detroit: Wayne State University Press, 1965).

PART THREE
THE SOCIAL-CLASS VARIABLE

INTRODUCTION TO PART THREE

The impact of social class on the behavior of persons in the several social classes has been of perennial interest to sociologists. This interest is firmly tied to those democratic cultures where the citizens suffer from heavy guilt feelings concerning the consequences of class inequalities. Numerous past researchers have shown how class variables have had consequences for persons with respect to behavior, education, occupation, health, and personality. Thus it is hardly unexpected that there have been numerous studies that have examined the relationship between social-class structure and specific types of mental disorder. The results of these studies have almost always shown the highest rate for schizophrenia is found in the lowest social class. Kohn has found this to be almost universal.[1] The Dohrenwends, in their review of previous epidemiological studies, uncovered seven studies that reported rates of schizophrenia by social class. Of these seven, five reported the highest schizophrenic rate in the lowest social class, and two reported the lowest rate in one of the other social classes.[2]

Two questions emerge from this finding: Is this correlation valid and reliable? What is the best explanation with supporting evidence to account for this relationship?

In order to establish the reliability and validity of this correlation, the following criteria must be met: the cases used in the research all should be diagnosed as schizophrenia utilizing the same criteria; the cases of schizoprenia uncovered should represent the total number of cases for a given time period in a given community; a measure of social class should be utilized that is independent of the person who develops the disorder; and the social class at birth and the social class at the onset of schizophrenia should be the same for a large majority of cases making up the rate.

It should be clear that there are no research investigations of this relationship that have measured up to these criteria. The third and fourth criteria never have been met. The only measure of social class that is independent of the person who develops schizophrenia is the social class of the father at the birth of the potential schizophrenic. This social-class measure is then compared to the social class of the schizophrenic at the onset of the disorder.

While the studies reported in this section also do not meet these criteria, they do amass selective bits of evidence that cast much doubt on the proposition that schizophrenia is a mental disorder that develops primarily among persons in the lowest social class. Conversely, this would mean that one would hardly expect any schizophrenics to appear in the other social classes; if they did it would be interpreted as some deficiency in the measuring index for social class.

In the research reported here, attention will be focused on several bits of evidence that serve to undermine the proposition that schizophrenia is a psychosis that is found mainly in the lowest social class. In utilizing a test for the significance between rates of the several social classes as reported by Hollingshead and Redlich, it was found that the rates differ significantly only between class V and the other social classes, with no significant differences reported among classes I-II, III, and IV. The same results also are found for the two subcommunities in the Detroit study. In presenting the rates of schizophrenia by social class, one should note that there is no linear relationship. The schizophrenic rates for the combined subcommunities in Detroit show that the rate in the lowest social class is 7.5 times larger than the rate in I-II, 3.4 times larger than III, and ten times larger than the rate in IV. When the schizophrenic cases are distributed in the several social classes in the two subcommunities of Detroit as indexed by fathers' social class the rate is highest in class I and declines to class IV and then increases in class V, but the rate increase is still not equal to the rates in classes I-II. When the fathers are compared with their schizophrenic sons, the fathers show that on the average they are in an occupation much higher than would be warranted by their education, while their schizophrenic sons are in occupations much lower than would be expected on the basis of their education. The rate for blacks in the lowest social class was almost twice the rates for whites. These bits of evidence will be explored and analyzed in the following chapters.

NOTES

1. M. L. Kohn, "Social Class and Schizophrenia: A Critical Review," Journal of Psychiatric Research 6, Supplement 1 (1968): 155-73.

2. B. P. Dohrenwend and B. S. Dohrenwend, Social Status and Psychological Disorder (New York: John Wiley & Sons, 1969), pp. 24-28.

6
SOCIAL CLASS AND SCHIZOPHRENIA

In Chapter 4 it was asked whether two culturally contrasting subcommunities in the city showed any significant differences in relation to the incidence of schizophrenia. It was noted that in the original case count, as the result of intensive screening, the ratio of the incidence of schizophrenia between the two subcommunities was roughly three to one in each year examined, somewhat in excess of the ratio in the nonschizophrenic group but considerably lower than the ratio in the additional category. It was further noted that the residential mobility of the schizophrenic cases in both subcommunities played a definite role in determining the size of the rates, and that when this factor was taken into account there emerged ratios of approximately two to one between the two subcommunities for both schizophrenics and nonschizophrenics. A further examination of the previous residence of the schizophrenic cases revealed that approximately two thirds of the cases found in each subcommunity moved into them from the central areas of the city.

This combination of findings provided a plausible hypothesis that rate differences of schizophrenia between the two subcommunities were in a large part to be explained by the different life-chances of the families at the birth of their potential schizophrenic offspring in Conner-Burbank, as compared to those in Cass. This hypothesis seemed to be compatible with one study that had suggested that the

---

Used with permission from my book Community and Schizophrenia—An Epidemiological Analysis (Detroit: Wayne State University Press, 1965), pp. 172-98.

residential inclination of the families of mental patients to move is of the same general character as that of those families without mental patients.[1] Thus an inference could be drawn: of the families that produce schizophrenics some are and some are not residentially mobile, but they do provide differential life-chances for their offspring and have some similar undetermined quality. Whatever this quality may be, there are families that stay in the slums and families that move away that do not produce schizophrenics.

The evidence presented suggested further that schizophrenics are likely to reflect the characteristics of the population of the community in which they are found. Little evidence was found to support the notion that a difference in the sociocultural climate and organization of a community explains differential incidence rates of schizophrenia. This does not mean that sociocultural factors, acting directly or indirectly, have no role to play in the development of schizophrenia, but only that the role of such factors cannot be determined from the observation of differential incidence rates of schizophrenia in social structures. The general mobility that characterizes U.S. society would appear to be the more telling factor to account for any differential distribution of schizophrenia in a large city. Further, it is noted that the general characteristics of an open society such as the United States would make it possible for some schizophrenics to change their residence if their families do, while other schizophrenics do not change their residences because their families do not.

This summary sets the stage for an inquiry into the role of the social class factor* in relation to incidence rates of schizophrenia, an inquiry that merely shifts previous ecological analyses of mental illness to another framework. A class analysis may provide a sharper delineation of social structure than is the case with a purely ecological or spatial analysis. This may be due to the democratic character of U.S. society that makes residence of little significance in determining the class position of a person. In fact, one of the central assumptions written into this research from the beginning was that both subcommunities would show class differences even though there might be large variations in the percentage of the population falling in the several classes.

---

*In speaking of the social class factor, the author has followed a convention of other reported studies. Strictly speaking, there is no measure of social class but rather a measure of social stratification as determined by applying certain weights to the education and occupation of heads of households in a subcommunity.

The following questions are the central concern of this chapter:

Do incidence rates of schizophrenia vary inversely with social class?

If they do, can these incidence rates of schizophrenia in the various social classes of the two subcommunities be accepted as reliable and valid?

Are there reliable and valid differences in the incidence of schizophrenia with respect to vertical mobility?

What relationships exist between the incidence of schizophrenia by social class and residential mobility?

What is the most plausible interpretation of incidence-rate differences by social class that may be found from the examination of these data?

SOCIAL CLASS AND MENTAL ILLNESS: THE HOLLINGSHEAD-REDLICH STUDY

The emphasis in this work is upon schizophrenia. While data have been presented for other diagnostic groups, this has been done only to achieve a comparison with the schizophrenic group. This position is stated here again because the author intends to examine critically the previous study by Hollingshead and Redlich concerning the relationship of social-class position and mental illness.[2] The two central hypotheses that they advanced at the beginning of their research were that the prevalence of treated mental illness is related significantly to an individual's position in the class structure, and the types of diagnosed psychiatric disorders are connected significantly to the class structure. It does appear that their findings support these two hypotheses, but their use of prevalence rates of treated mental illness does not enable them to deal with the crucial issue involved in the relationship of social class and mental illness. This can only be realized by utilizing incidence rates, as the author has attempted to do in the present work. However, even with respect to their data on treated prevalence of psychoses—which show an inverse relationship—there are certain doubts that arise concerning the validity of their findings. First, they tackle the problem as to whether or not the psychotics were indigenous to the social class in which they came to be recorded. Their evidence on this point shows that practically all of the cases were indigenous to the class in which they were recorded. Hollingshead and Redlich possibly make a more valid interpretation for this finding when they present the hypothesis that the distribution reflects the differential treatment available at the different class levels, with the result that in the lowest classes, where little treatment is available, the cases tend to accumulate.[3] However, this explanation is not available in their findings with respect to the prevalence of neuroses by social class, where they find a direct relationship. This direct relationship would appear to be a function of two situations: neurosis tends to be infrequently diagnosed in the lower class because it is a luxury disturbance and people at the lowest class level cannot afford to recognize it; and the inclusion in classes I, II, and possibly III of those persons who are receiving psychoanalytic treatment from private practicing psychiatrists introduces a certain bias in the class distribution. It is doubtful if many of these cases, who are continuing to function in job and family, can be regarded as clinically neurotic.

A consideration of the prevalence rates of the psychoses calls attention to an item not yet mentioned in the previous critical comments on this study. When Hollingshead and Redlich break up their total prevalence group into three groups of incidence, reentry into treatment, and continuous treatment, it is to be noted that the rates of psychoses in the various social classes are by no means as sharply differentiated in the incidence and reentry groups as they are in the continuance group. In fact, the rates in the incidence and reentry groups are by no means inversely related to the class structure, for the rates in the first three classes for these two groups are not significant when compared. Only by comparing each of the rates in the first three classes with the rate in class V is a significant difference found. This is pointed out because it suggests that the cases appearing in the various class positions of these two groups are not likely to have settled into their final position in the social structure but still have possibilities of downward mobility attached to them, and thus are corroborative (as will be shown) of their own findings of this research with respect to class. These critical ratios are shown in Table 6.1.

The Hollingshead-Redlich findings will be examined now with respect to social class and schizophrenia. In Table 6.1 the same point can be made that was made above with respect to the rates in their incidence and reentry groups.[4] It is recognized that their original figures are only six-month prevalence figures and that when they break their total groups down into different diagnoses, the number in the incidence groups is bound to be quite small. This is true with respect to their schizophrenic distribution; as Goldhamer has noted, the addition of one or two cases in a given class might change the picture somewhat.[5] If one assumes that the same number of schizophrenic cases would appear in the next six months in New Haven, the picture remains much the same. Utilizing a test of the significance of the difference between rates, no significant difference was found between the various classes for incidence rates of schizo-

TABLE 6.1

Matrix of Critical Ratios Resulting from Testing for the Significance of the Differences between Social-Class Rates for Psychoses

Social Class	Incidence Rates			Reentry Rates		
	I & II	III	IV	I & II	III	IV
III	.84	—	—	.56	—	—
IV	1.13	.0001	—	.20	.33	—
V	3.91	3.36	3.61	2.20	4.20	4.2

Source: Data from A. Hollingshead and F. Redlich, Social Class and Mental Illness (New York: John Wiley & Sons, 1958), table 16, p. 235.

phrenia, although the differences were marked for the prevalence rates of schizophrenia, with one exception: there was no significant difference between class III and classes I-II. In the reentry group significant differences were found only between class V and the other three classes. These data can be seen in Table 6.2. This critical consideration of the Hollingshead-Redlich study indicates that while their data tend to substantiate the two hypotheses, there is both a statistical doubt and the same difficulty of interpretation as in the ecological studies. Their incidence rates by social class for schizophrenia have not demonstrated, at least, by a statistical test, that there is any difference in the incidence of this disease at the various class levels and that such differences as found can be easily due to chance.

SOCIAL CLASS AND MENTAL ILLNESS: CASS AND CONNER-BURBANK

The following is an examination of the author's own case data in relation to social class in two subcommunities.* In this examination of the relationship between the incidence of schizophrenia and social class, four sets of data are presented. Examined first is the distribution of psychiatric cases in the three diagnostic groupings

---

*The author has utilized the Hollingshead-Redlich technique for determining the class structure on the basis of special sorts that were furnished us by the U.S. Bureau of Census. The census sort has one less occupational category than the Hollingshead-Redlich scale; hence, the range of social-class index scores tends to be slightly smaller than the range of scores provided by the Hollingshead-Redlich index. In determining the class position of the psychiatric cases in this sample, the author utilized the Hollingshead-Redlich categories and the weights they had assigned. He also gave to each case a social-class index score on the basis of the census categories, again utilizing the same weights for occupation and education as were provided in the Hollingshead-Redlich manual. In the census sort of psychiatric cases by social class it will be noticed that the correspondence between the two systems is not a complete 1-to-1 relationship, but that there is a tendency for the census scores to be somewhat higher than the Hollingshead-Redlich score; hence, some of the cases fall in the class next above. It should be noted that the census index tends to provide slightly higher rates in the top four classes than does the Hollingshead-Redlich index.

TABLE 6.2

Matrix of Critical Ratios Resulting from Testing for the Significance of the Differences between Social-Class Rates for Schizophrenia

Social Class	Incidence Rates			Reentry Rates			Prevalence Rates		
	I & II	III	IV	I & II	III	IV	I & II	III	IV
III	.32	—	—	.86	—	—	2.11	—	—
IV	.72	.40	—	1.19	.02	—	7.04	5.00	—
V	2.71	2.61	2.78	3.60	3.03	3.18	16.70	3.25	10.88

Source: Data from A. Hollingshead and F. Redlich, Social Class and Mental Illness (New York: John Wiley & Sons, 1958), table 17, p. 236.

by social class in the two subcommunities of Detroit. Second, the cases are presented by diagnostic group and social class, combining the distributions for both subcommunities. Third, the social-class distribution in the two subcommunities is presented by grouping them with psychosis and without psychosis, utilizing both the Hollingshead-Redlich scheme and the census scheme. Finally, statistical tests are presented to show those instances where the differences in rate between the social classes are statistically significant.

Incidence Rates by Social Class

The first set of rates for the social classes is shown in Table 6.3,* which points to several findings. First, the rates for each diagnostic group and in both subcommunities—with the exception of the additional cases in the Conner-Burbank subcommunity—do not vary inversely with social class. Second, this absence of inverse variation is also seen in the distribution of total cases in both subcommunities. Finally, in all diagnostic groups—as well as in the total cases for both subcommunities—the rates are highest in class V, again with one exception: the nonschizophrenic group in the

---

*These rates are based upon the total population for 1960, as determined from the United States census. It would have been desirable to secure a more refined estimate of the population in the various class levels, but this was not possible from the census data. However, experience in the study with respect to the computation of various sets of rates in the two subcommunities leads one to believe that a more refined population estimate would not have changed the pattern of the rates much. It should be remembered (see Chapter 4) that when the author computed the rates in the two subcommunities on the basis of the population 15 years of age and over, and on the basis of the total population, the ratio of the rates for each diagnostic group between the two subcommunities was the same. This point becomes much more telling in a special test of significance of the difference between rates. A reduction in the size of the population in each category would reduce the possibility for obtaining significant differences, while an increase in the population means that the distance between the rates would be smaller for obtaining a significant difference. It would seem that in using this test of significance with a larger population, one tends to bias the data in the direction for producing significant differences.

TABLE 6.3

Number and Incidence Rates of Psychiatric Cases by Social Class for Three Diagnostic Groups in Two Subcommunities of Detroit, 1958

Social Class	General Population	Schizophrenic Number	Schizophrenic Rate	Nonschizophrenic Number	Nonschizophrenic Rate	Additional Number	Additional Rate	Total Number	Total Rate
				Cass					
I	1,363	0	—	1	1.47	0	.73	1	2.20
II	1,360	0	—	3		2		5	
III	6,179	4	.65	2	.32	5	.81	11	1.78
IV	21,123	3	.14	8	.38	11	.52	22	1.04
V	16,912	31	1.83	27	1.60	20	1.18	78	4.55
Total	46,937	38	.81	41	.87	38	.79	117	2.47
				Conner-Burbank					
I	2,070	1	.28	1	.57	1	.14	3	.99
II	4,986	1		3		0		4	
III	16,578	6	.36	15	.90	3	.18	24	1.44
IV	37,239	6	.16	18	.48	15	.40	39	1.05
V	10,767	10	.93	7	.65	12	1.11	29	2.69
Total	71,640	24	.34	44	.61	31	.43	99	1.38

Conner-Burbank subcommunity has a lower rate in class V than in class III.

This first analysis of the rates for the social classes in three diagnostic groups and two subcommunities hardly gives any confidence of a class variable in relation to the incidence of functional mental disorder. This is particularly the case with respect to the schizophrenic rates in the several class levels.* Insofar as the central focus of this inquiry is to determine whether social class appears to make any difference in the incidence of schizophrenia, the cases were combined in the two subcommunities and rates were computed for the various classes. These data are seen in Table 6.4. As one would expect, a similar pattern emerges as when the subcommunities were considered separately; here the high rate in class V for all diagnostic groups is very much in evidence.

Incidence Rates for Psychotics and Nonpsychotics

In order to compare the class rates with those of Hollingshead and Redlich, it seemed desirable to present the distribution of cases on the basis of those that were psychotic in contrast to the nonpsychotic. These data are presented in Table 6.5 for both subcommunities, utilizing both the Hollingshead-Redlich scheme and the census scheme. An inspection of this table points to the following findings. Again there is an absence of any inverse relationship between the rates for both psychotic and nonpsychotic cases and the class structure. This holds particularly with the Hollingshead-Redlich scheme. Utilizing this scheme, the highest rate appears in class V for all groups except the nonpsychotic in the Cass community. Utilizing the census scheme tends to provide larger rates for the upper four classes, with the result that the highest rate is never found in class V.

The next test was to determine if there were any significant differences between the rates in the various classes for the three diagnostic groups in each subcommunity. The matrix of critical

---

*The author is disturbed (as Hollingshead and Redlich should have been) that the small number of cases in the upper four classes (and in general for all three diagnostic groups) raises a question as to their reliability. One can do nothing about this except to point out the generally small size of the population in the first three classes in Cass; still, one finds a certain number of cases from these classes. In Conner-Burbank this is more true of the upper two classes.

TABLE 6.4

Number and Incidence Rates of Total Psychiatric Cases by Social Class for Three Diagnostic Groups in Two Subcommunities of Detroit, 1958

Social Class	General Population	Schizophrenic		Nonschizophrenic		Additional		Total	
		Number	Rate	Number	Rate	Number	Rate	Number	Rate
I	3,433	1	.20	2	.82	1	.31	4	1.33
II	6,346	1		6		2		9	
III	22,757	10	.44	17	.75	8	.35	35	1.54
IV	58,362	9	.15	26	.45	26	.45	61	1.05
V	27,679	41	1.48	34	1.23	32	1.16	107	3.87
Total	118,577	62	.52	85	.72	69	.58	216	1.82

TABLE 6.5

Number and Incidence Rates with and without Psychoses for Two Schemes of Social Class in Two Subcommunities of Detroit, 1958*

Social	Psychotic				Nonpsychotic				Total			
	H-R		Census		H-R		Census		H-R		Census	
Class	Number	Rate	Number	Rate	Number	Rate	Number	Rate	Number	Rate	Number	Rate
					Cass							
I	0	—	0	—	1	.73	5	3.67	1	.73	5	3.67
II	0	—	3	2.20	5	3.68	3	2.20	5	2.68	6	4.41
III	4	.65	3	.48	7	1.13	12	1.94	11	1.78	15	2.43
IV	4	.19	12	.57	18	.85	31	1.47	22	1.04	43	2.04
V	34	2.01	24	1.42	44	2.54	24	1.36	78	4.55	48	2.78
Total	42	.89	42	.88	75	1.60	75	1.60	117	2.49	117	2.49
					Conner-Burbank							
I	1	.48	3	1.45	2	.97	2	.97	3	1.45	5	2.41
II	2	.40	1	.20	2	.40	5	1.00	4	.80	6	1.20
III	8	.48	12	.72	16	1.00	20	1.21	24	1.45	32	1.93
IV	16	.43	15	.40	23	.62	29	.78	39	1.05	44	1.18
V	13	1.21	9	.83	16	1.49	3	.28	29	2.69	12	1.11
Total	40	.56	40	.56	59	.82	59	.82	99	1.38	99	1.38

*For population base see Table 6.3.

ratios resulting from these tests is shown in Table 6.6. The results are comparable to those obtained by applying this test to the Hollingshead-Redlich data. Using a critical ratio of three as the determining point of significance, it is observed that for Conner-Burbank only one rate is significant and that is in the total psychiatric group when the rate in class IV is contrasted with the rate in class V. In Cass there are five other significant rate differences, all of them contrasting the rate in class V with the rate in classes III and IV. If one employs a critical ratio of two as the determining point of significance, one can see from an inspection of Table 6.6 that while the number of significant differences is increased, all of them are centered in contrasting the rates in class V with the rates in the other three classes. In other words, out of 45 comparisons between rates, there were only six significant differences and all of them were centered in a comparison of the rate of class V with that of the other four classes.

The small number of cases in classes I to IV raises the issue of rate reliability. Therefore, as shown in Table 6.4, rates are worked out by combining the cases in each diagnostic group for the two subcommunities. Then the test for determining any significant differences between the rates in the various classes was applied, as shown in Table 6.7. The results are clear and support the previous analysis. The only significant differences in the class rates for schizophrenia are found when the class V rate is compared with the rates in the other classes. The same finding also is evidenced in the class rates for the additional group, but not for the nonschizophrenic group with one exception: the significant difference between the rates when class IV and class V are compared.

An analysis of these findings points to several general conclusions. Evidence does not substantiate an inverse relationship between incidence rates of schizophrenia and the class structure. This finding also applies to the other two diagnostic groups as well as to the rates for the total cases in both subcommunities. This finding also applies to the distribution of cases when they are broken down in terms of "with" psychosis and "without" psychosis. The use of the census scheme merely heightens the absence of any inverse relationship among both the psychotic and the nonpsychotic in the class structure. In all diagnostic groups and for both subcommunities, with the possible exception of the nonschizophrenic group in the Conner-Burbank area, the highest incidence rates are to be found in class V. When a test for the significance of the difference between the various class rates is applied, significant differences are found when class V is contrasted with the other classes, but are not in evidence when the other classes are compared with one another.

TABLE 6.6

Matrix of Critical Ratios Resulting from Testing for the Significance of the Difference between Social-Class Rates for Each Diagnostic Group in Two Subcommunities of Detroit, 1958

Social	Schizophrenic			Nonschizophrenic			Additional			Total Cases		
Class	I–II	III	IV	I–II	III	IV	I–II	III	IV	I–II	III	IV
						Cass						
III	—	—	—	1.50	—	—	0.13	—	—	0.40	—	—
IV	—	1.53	—	1.46	0.23	—	0.39	0.73	—	1.25	1.28	—
V	—	2.55	5.00	0.16	3.34	3.64	0.67	0.84	1.99	2.27	3.72	6.23
						Conner-Burbank						
III	0.32	—	—	0.90	—	—	0.23	—	—	0.96	—	—
IV	0.57	1.26	—	0.29	1.62	—	1.53	1.47	—	0.15	1.15	—
V	1.83	1.73	2.57	2.11	0.74	0.63	2.77	2.76	2.09	2.72	2.16	3.11

TABLE 6.7

Matrix of Critical Ratios Resulting from Testing the Significance of the Difference between Social-Class Rates in Each Diagnostic Group Based on Total Cases in the Combined Subcommunities

	Schizophrenic			Nonschizophrenic			Additional			Total Cases		
	I-II	III	IV	I-II	III	IV	I-II	III	IV	I-II	III	IV
III	1.11	—	—	.02	—	—	.18	—	—	.47	—	—
IV	.03	1.96	—	1.22	1.49	—	.71	.66	—	.71	1.68	—
V	4.71	3.86	5.72	1.14	1.70	3.35	3.13	3.85	3.19	4.84	5.12	7.11

VERTICAL MOBILITY AND MENTAL ILLNESS

There has been frequent discussion in the literature with respect to the vertical mobility patterns of the mentally ill. In fact, some of the literature in the 1930s went so far as to suggest that neuroses and perhaps more acute mental disturbances might be related to the striving and competitive tendencies within U.S. culture, resulting in increased frustration, mounting anxiety, hostility, and ambivalence.[6] In the Hollingshead-Redlich study the attempt was made to show that the prevalence rate for treated psychiatric cases could not be explained in terms of either upward or downward mobility.[7] In London, Morris attempted to check on the relationship of schizophrenia to social class and found that while his rates for schizophrenia were inversely related to the class structure, the fathers of his schizophrenic patients were rather evenly distributed throughout the entire class structure.[8] He concluded that the high incidence rates of schizophrenia in the lowest class are possibly a result of the fact that most of his cases never got started in a suitable occupational category before the onset of the disease.

These findings have led to an examination of the vertical mobility patterns for the sample of psychiatric cases broken down by diagnostic group and subcommunity. Vertical mobility was measured by the discrepancy that existed between the occupational category of the father and that of the patient. In the case of married female patients, the occupational category of the husband was contrasted with the occupational category of the patient/wife's father. The mobility of college students was determined by the educational level that the student had reached in contrast to the occupation of the father and the level of education such an occupation demanded. By this technique it was possible to determine from the sample of cases those who were upwardly mobile, those who were nonmobile, and those who were downwardly mobile. These data are shown in Table 6.8 for each diagnostic group in both subcommunities, separately and combined. Using a chi-square test for the three comparisons it is found that in each instance there are no significant differences in mobility patterns of the three diagnostic groups. It is only when one combines all diagnostic groups and compares the distribution of cases in the two subcommunities by vertical mobility patterns (Table 6.9) that one obtains a chi-square at the 5 percent level of significance. The same result emerges when the mobility distributions in the two subcommunities are compared, utilizing only schizophrenic and nonschizophrenic cases. These data are found in Table 6.10. This suggests a tendency for the more upwardly mobile cases to be more prevalent in Conner-Burbank.

TABLE 6.8

Distribution of First Contact Cases by Vertical Mobility Pattern and Diagnostic Group, Detroit, 1958

Mobility Pattern	Schizo-phrenic	Nonschizo-phrenic	Additional	Total
		Cass		
Upward	11	5	8	24
Nonmobile	11	12	9	32
Downward	12	11	11	34
Total	34	28	28	90
	$\chi^2 = 1.948$	df = 4	$p < .70$	
		Conner-Burbank		
Upward	6	22	8	36
Nonmobile	8	9	12	29
Downward	4	10	6	20
Total	18	41	26	85
	$\chi^2 = 4.1761$	df = 4	$p < .30$	
		Both Subcommunities		
Upward	17	27	16	60
Nonmobile	19	21	21	61
Downward	16	21	17	54
Total	52	69	54	175
	$\chi^2 = 1.6051$	df = 4	$p < .80$	

TABLE 6.9

Distribution of Total First Contact Cases by Vertical Mobility Patterns for Two Subcommunities of Detroit, 1958

Mobility Pattern	Cass	Conner-Burbank	Total
Upward	24	36	60
Nonmobile	32	29	61
Downward	34	20	54
Total	90	85	175

$\chi^2 = 6.0159$ df = 2 $p < .04$

TABLE 6.10

Distribution of First Contact Schizophrenic and Nonschizophrenic Cases Combined, by Vertical Mobility Patterns for Two Subcommunities of Detroit, 1958.

Mobility Pattern	Cass	Conner-Burbank	Total
Upward	16	28	44
Nonmobile	23	17	40
Downward	23	14	37
Total	62	59	121

$\chi^2 = 6.200$ df = 2 $p < .04$

While this analysis suggests that the vertical mobility patterns in all three diagnostic groups in both subcommunities are similar, it does not provide any basis for asserting that schizophrenic persons are more likely to be downwardly than upwardly mobile, although this is what might be expected. What is found is that the subcommunities, as might be expected, are dissimilar with respect to the vertical mobility patterns of the psychiatric patients residing in them, irrespective of diagnosis.

This analysis of geographical and status mobility patterns of schizophrenia gains some indirect support through Lystad's investigation of the social mobility of schizophrenic patients.[9] Lystad shows with respect to geographical mobility that nonmentally ill persons who are middle class, white, younger, and have more than a grammar-school education show more mobility than do schizophrenics with these characteristics. Further, she shows that nonmentally ill persons who are lower class, black, older, and have less than a grammar-school education show no more mobility than do schizophrenic patients having these characteristics.

With respect to status mobility, Lystad shows that nonmentally ill persons who are middle class, white, female, and grammar-school educated achieve higher levels than do schizophrenic patients with these characteristics. Contrariwise, the nonmentally ill who are lower class, black, male, and less than grammar-school educated achieve no more than do schizophrenic patients with these characteristics. She observes that middle-class, white, and high-school trained groups place a high value on social mobility and finds that schizophrenics in these groups have more difficulty in achieving than do their nonmentally ill counterparts. In contrast, those schizophrenics and nonmentally ill who are in the so-called deprived groups show the same level of achievement. Lystad admits that her data cannot resolve the issue as to whether failure to achieve in the middle class leads more persons to schizophrenia than does failure to achieve in the lower class, or whether schizophrenia tends to prevent persons from attaining a higher degree of success in the more competitive middle class. While her data may not be able to resolve this dilemma, nevertheless it may be worth pointing out that the total evidence with respect to vertical mobility and the social class of schizophrenics would tend to favor the latter interpretation.

Additional evidence on this point is provided by Robins, Gyman, and O'Neal in their follow-up study of child guidance patients seen originally for severe antisocial behavior.[10] Their evidence strongly suggests that such antisocial behavior interfered with the patients' educational achievement and thus affected their occupational status. Consequently, it follows that if, as in the present study, education and occupation are used to determine social class, it can be claimed, as these investigators do, that continued deviant behavior largely determines class rather than the reverse. These investigators further report that the disproportion of antisocial children in the lower classes can be explained in part by a high rate of antisocial fathers whose own antisocial behavior determined their low occupational status. In the present study the heavy concentration of cases in class V, while a parity for incidence rates is found in the other four classes, at least suggests that the schizophrenic condition may be a factor that affects the possibility of moderate educational and occupational achievement, especially for those cases that have left their parental homes to seek educational and occupational success. Further exploration of this point is no doubt desirable, but it is worth noting that only in a society where class position is measured by criteria independent of education, occupation, and income would one be more certain that a mental condition would not determine class. But in a free, open-class democratic society these categories are likely to continue as a measure of class position, and therefore class position will be largely determined by the health, personality, and energy characteristics of individuals.

An attempt was made to determine if there was any relationship between residential mobility and social class. Residential mobility was measured on the basis of residence less or more than five years in the subcommunity. Again, as in the comparable data on vertical mobility, there seems to be a tendency for longer residence in the subcommunity to be associated with a higher class position. In other words, the higher the social class, the more stable the residence. While the chi-square is significant at the .001 level, it is made up almost entirely by the differences in case distribution in the two subcommunities between classes IV and V. These data are shown in Table 6.11 for both subcommunities combined.

The findings from this analysis attempting to probe the relationship between social class and schizophrenia are:

A critical analysis of the Hollingshead-Redlich findings indicates that while they have shown that treated prevalence rates for schizophrenia and total psychoses vary inversely with the class structure, they have not shown this to be true for their incidence and reentry rates, also based upon cases under treatment.

Incidence rates for schizophrenia, the other two diagnostic groups, and total psychiatric cases for the two subcommunities do not vary inversely with social class. The exception here is the "Additional" group in Conner-Burbank.

The highest incidence rates for all diagnostic groups and both subcommunities are to be found in class V, with one exception.

TABLE 6.11

Distribution of First Contact Cases of All Diagnostic Groups, by Length of Residence and Social Class in Two Subcommunities of Detroit, 1958

Social Class	Under Five Years	Over Five Years	Total
I-II	7	6	13
III	15	16	31
IV	17	40	57
V	59	33	92
Total	98	95	195

$\chi^2 = 16.629$ df = 3 $p < .001$

When the cases are broken down into psychotic and nonpsychotic groups, utilizing the Hollingshead-Redlich scheme, the same two patterns as described in (2) and (3) are found.

When the cases are distributed in these two groups according to the census scheme the highest rate is never found in class V, and the rates do not vary inversely with the class structure.

When a test of significant differences is applied to these rates by diagnostic group in both subcommunities, it is found that the only significant differences that exist are between class V and other classes. In fact, in the 45 comparisons only six differences prove to be significant, using a critical ratio of three.

When the cases in the three diagnostic groups were broken down according to whether they were upwardly mobile, nonmobile, or downwardly mobile, no significant differences were found to exist. Only when the two subcommunities were contrasted, utilizing the total cases, did a significant difference appear at the .05 level. When the two subcommunities were contrasted by combining only the schizophrenic and nonschizophrenic cases, a significant difference also appeared, still at the .05 level.

There was a significant difference when the cases in the two subcommunities were combined and length of residence was contrasted with social class. Here the difference was significant at the .001 level, indicating that residential stability appeared to be associated with a higher class level.

As in Chapter 4, where the relationship of community organization to schizophrenia was examined, the most plausible interpretation of this set of findings is sought. The author is well aware that one of the net results of the Hollingshead-Redlich study was to convey the impression that the social-class variable bears some relationship to mental illness.[11] However, a critical examination of their findings raises doubt concerning any definitive settling of this issue and, consequently, leaves the matter open for further exploration. In the current study such exploration was attempted by carefully constructing incidence rates for schizophrenia and other diagnostic groups by social class in two culturally different subcommunities. As has been shown, the author's data run counter to the Hollingshead-Redlich findings of an inverse relationship between social class and mental illness, but also are quite supportive in the sense that he finds the biggest and most significant difference in incidence rates for schizophrenia to exist between class V and the other four classes. This leads one to infer that schizophrenia will be found in all social classes in about equal proportions, although the bulk of the cases always will be found in the lowest social class, class V. This would imply that class V often is the receptacle for many cases and that the development of the disease actually may prevent the vulnerable ones from being recorded in a higher class position. Thus, as in the case of the relationship of community organization to the incidence of schizophrenia, little evidence is found to support the proposition that the social-class structure bears some functional relationship to the incidence of schizophrenia.

This analysis of the incidence of schizophrenia in relation to the class structure has pointed up two questions: Why are the highest rates for schizophrenia, as well as the other diagnostic groups, always found in class V for both subcommunities while the rates in the other four classes tend toward parity? Why do the schizophrenic cases, as well as the other diagnostic groups, show a parity with respect to their vertical mobility patterns?

To initiate an answer to these questions it should be noted that the rates for schizophrenia in the upper four classes show no significant variation for both subcommunities and for the two subcommunities combined. This finding is critical of any assertion that the incidence of schizophrenia is inversely related to the class structure. The heavy concentration of cases in class V has three possible explanations in line with the requirement to seek explanations geared to a social system level of analysis that account for the distribution of cases in any social structure: first, the heavy proportion of schizophrenic cases is found in class V because for some of them, while their fathers were in a higher class, the schizophrenic sons or daughters failed in their educational and occupational efforts and consequently were recorded as members of the lowest class; second, the heavy proportion of schizophrenic cases is found in class V because for those in the sample that left their parental home, their developing schizophrenic condition prevented the realization of their occupational goal, so that they were recorded as members of class V; and third, the heavy proportion of schizophrenic cases is found in class V because more persons in this class than in the other classes have a genetic structure that prevents them from competing on equal terms with other persons and relegates them to class V through the operation of the social process.

It should be recognized that all of these hypothetical explanations emphasize geographical or vertical mobility patterns that are characteristic of U.S. culture. It may appear to some that the first and second hypotheses contain similar elements; however, such is not the case. The first hypothesis emphasizes that the schizophrenic experiences a decline in class status because of his underlying proneness to schizophrenia. The second points to a salient characteristic of U.S. culture, namely, the tendency, when a certain age is reached, to leave home to seek one's fortune and in general try to better oneself by means of the personality and skills that one possesses. Thus the second hypothesis states that those schizophrenics leaving their parental homes, no matter what the social-class status of the home was, failed to realize their ambitions and hence found themselves with educational and occupational statuses marking them for class V.

POSSIBLE INFLUENCES ON CLASS HYPOTHESES

Age Factor

In the attempt to determine the relative plausibility of these hypotheses, age and previous address were examined with respect to class. In relation to age it was reasoned that the older a person was when he first entered psychiatric treatment, the more likely it would be for him to be recorded in a class other than class V. Combining all cases in both subcommunities and comparing the age distribution of classes I through IV with that of class V, one obtains the results as shown in Table 6.12.

Previous Residence Factor

The almost complete agreement of the age distribution in the two class groups was quite surprising, but lent no support to the

TABLE 6.12

Distribution of Psychiatric Cases by Social Class According to Age

Age	Classes I-IV	Class V
10-29	43	42
30-49	50	50
50+	16	14
Total	109	106
χ^2 = 1.9493	df = 2	1 < .95

TABLE 6.13

Distribution of Psychiatric Cases in Three Diagnostic Groups by Social Class According to Previous Address

Previous Address	Classes I-IV	Class V
Inner city	38	75
Outer city	31	12
Other—U.S.	23	10
Totals	92	97
χ^2 = 25.50	df = 2	p < .001

author's reasoning. In other words, whatever the factors involved to account for the heavy concentration of cases in class V, age does not appear to be one of them. These same data were examined by the two class groups according to their previous addresses before moving into one of the subcommunities. This distribution is shown in Table 6.13. Here one obtains a significant difference, but a difference that adds no support to the second hypothesis. Thus it is seen that a much higher percentage of cases in classes I through IV had previous addresses in the other parts of Michigan, the United States, or foreign countries. Therefore, of those recorded in classes I through IV, a greater number, as compared to class V, left home to seek a better life. It should be apparent, however, that this measure is not a reliable one for getting at those schizophrenics who were on their own.

If one examines stratification such as the author has in the subcommunities from a functional viewpoint, one would face up to the following propositions. Every human society has been found to have some type of stratification structure. This structure has the function of distributing persons in any society into some series of rankings or status positions. The principle governing distribution into rank and class will vary in societies and may be on a basis of birth, achievement, personality, education, influence, or something else. This structure functions in any society to provide some type of hierarchical arrangement with respect to every member of a society. In an open democratic society where individual achievement is rewarded to a high degree, the central process becomes personal competition, both legitimate and illegitimate, and the chief selective agency becomes the educational system. It would be expected that under such a system the genetically defective, the physically handicapped, the chronically sick, the rebels, the criminals, the vice-ridden, and persons with unacceptable personality traits would experience difficulty in being fitted into the hierarchy, except for the lowest rank position. If this analysis is valid, it would be natural to expect that in the United States many persons destined for schizophrenia would be placed in the lowest ranking position unless their respective families provided the fortress to protect them from the cruel judgments of the outside competitive world. Thus they would be protected and sheltered by the humanistic quality of U.S. culture, but not from the consequences of the ranking process once they were cut loose from the protective shield of the family.

METHODOLOGICAL NOTE ON SOCIAL CLASS

As already indicated, the Hollingshead-Redlich two-factor index of social position for measuring social class was used in this research. However, as the author gained greater experience with this measure, he gradually became aware of some of the problems that it posed. These will be examined in detail. This section deals with the procedure used in this research for determining social class that parallels the Hollingshead-Redlich technique; a comparison of the percentage of nonpatients and patients as reported by Hollingshead and Redlich with this research; and certain differences in social class that emerge from the patient population when three different methods of analyses are employed.

Procedure for Determining Social Class

The procedure for delineating social class was achieved by utilizing a special sort of heads of households by occupation, education, and race that was furnished by the United States census, and not by means of a psychiatric survey of a sample population, the method used by Hollingshead and Redlich in New Haven. This tabulation is a distribution of heads of households by education, occupation, and race in the tracts included in the Cass and Conner-Burbank subcommunities. It also includes summary sheets for each of the subcommunities. The educational categories of the census largely correspond to the categories used by Hollingshead and Redlich in determining the index of social position, except for a slightly different classification of the first 11 years of schooling. The occupational categories do not exactly correspond with those used by Hollingshead and Redlich, who have distributed the "professionals" and "owners, managers, and executives" groups of the census in three occupational groups according to the social prestige attached to each occupation. Farm workers were given the same score as unskilled workers, and persons with no education were given the same score as persons with one to seven years of schooling. The Hollingshead-Redlich social-class intervals, as well as their weighing factors (four for education and seven for occupation), were used for the determination of the social class of the heads of households.

On the basis of the data in the summary sheets for each community, the distribution of the heads of households by index of social position was determined for each subcommunity. For Cass, where there is a larger nonwhite population, the distribution also was determined separately for the white and the nonwhite heads of households. The results of this analysis with the score interval used for each are shown in Table 6.14.

In order to determine the distribution of the population in each subcommunity by index of social position, the author multiplied for each tract in each subcommunity the number of heads of households

TABLE 6.14

Number and Percent Distribution of Heads of Households by Index of Social Position Scores

Class	Total		White		Black	
	Frequency	Percent	Frequency	Percent	Frequency	Percent
			Cass			
I (11-17)	127	3.78	115	4.58	12	1.42
II (18-27)	120	3.57	112	4.46	8	0.94
III (28-43)	478	14.22	401	15.96	77	9.08
IV (44-60)	1,506	44.81	1,132	45.05	374	44.10
V (61-77)	1,130	33.62	753	29.96	377	44.46
Totals	3,361	100.00	2,513	100.01	848	100.00
			Conner-Burbank			
I (11-17)	145	2.89				
II (18-27)	354	7.05				
III (28-43)	1,160	23.09				
IV (44-60)	2,601	51.78				
V (61-77)	763	15.19				
Totals	5,023	100.00				

in each position by the average size of household of each tract. Since the average size of the household varies with the tract and race, it seemed that taking those variations into consideration would give a more accurate picture of the distribution of the population by the index of social position.

The distribution of the heads of households (based on the summary sheets for the subcommunities) compared with the distribution of the population in households (based on the tabulations for each tract) by index of social position is slightly different for each subcommunity. This additional step, however, resulted in only minor changes in the percentage distribution of the heads of households by index of social position. The main assumption here, hardly warranted, is that the size of the household in each tract was the same for each social class (index of social position).

Finally, on the basis of the distribution of population in households by index of social position scores, the distribution of the total population, as well as the distribution of the population 15 years and over, was estimated by projecting the percentages of the population in households on the total population figures.

Comparison of Social Classes in the Two Studies

There is a most interesting comparison between the percentage distribution of patients and nonpatients by social class in the Hollingshead-Redlich study and in the Detroit study. It seems interesting, although it should not be completely unexpected, that the percentage of nonpatients, or the New Haven population by social class, which Hollingshead and Redlich present, is for the most part almost identical with this author's own. The largest difference occurs in class V where Hollingshead and Redlich have placed 18 percent of the population as against the 23 percent that was found in the two subcommunities of Detroit. Again, when one examines the percentage distribution of patients as found in both studies, while they are not as similar as is the percentage distribution of population, they are very close. The chief differences are in classes IV and V: where in class IV Hollingshead and Redlich find 40 percent of their patients, the author finds only 28 percent; while in class V they find 38 percent, the author finds 49 percent. In both instances it is slightly double the percentage of population found in that class, an observation to which Hollingshead and Redlich also call attention. This contrast is presented in Table 6.15.

TABLE 6.15

Number and Percent of Patients and Nonpatients by Social Class Compared in New Haven and Two Subcommunities of Detroit

	New Haven			
	Patients		Nonpatients	
	Number	Percent	Number	Percent
I	19	1.0	7,108	3.0
II	133	7.0	19,903	8.4
III	259	13.7	48,336	20.4
IV	758	40.1	117,996	49.8
V	722	38.2	43,597	18.4
Total	1,891	100.0	236,940	100.0
	Two Subcommunities of Detroit			
I	4	1.9	3,433	2.9
II	9	4.2	6,346	5.4
III	35	16.2	22,757	19.2
IV	61	28.2	58,362	49.2
V	107	49.5	27,679	23.3
Total	216	100.0	118,577	100.0

Source: A. Hollingshead and F. Redlich, Social Class and Mental Illness (New York: John Wiley & Sons, 1958), p. 199.

Some Problems of Social-Class Placement

The author's greatest concern and uncertainty has come with respect to the assignment of patients to their respective class positions. He did not attempt, as did Hollingshead and Redlich, to validate his class position by utilizing access to the mass media but rather depended as they did on heterogeneity in the score clusters to determine where one class ended and another began. Because he used the two factors of education and occupation instead of the procedure employed by Hollingshead and Redlich, the index of position scores is somewhat smaller than theirs but still provides a range of 66, or from 11 to 77.

This is all well and good. At the outset one could not determine exactly how Hollingshead and Redlich had assigned a patient to his social class. In certain instances it seems that the patient was assigned to his social class on the basis of education, occupation, and residence of the father or head of household; in other instances it seemed that the patient was assigned to a social class on the basis of his own occupation, education, and residence, especially if he was head of his own family. In the case of married women, the assignment seemed made on the basis of the husband's occupation; in the case of single women detached from their families, it seemed to be on the basis of their occupation, education, and residence. It also was noted that other studies using the Hollingshead-Redlich index of social position have assigned patients on the basis of their own education and occupation. In fact, it gradually became clear that this had been the procedure that had been employed in the current study; consequently, one began to wonder about not only its consistency but also its validity. It was noted that it might well place patients in a lower class position where the determination of class was based upon their education and occupation, in contrast to those patients whose position was based upon the father's or husband's education and occupation. This seemed to offer a special difficulty because one saw clearly that the class position of patients might be strongly affected by the incipient stages of schizophrenia, while in the case of those placed by father's or husband's education and occupation, class position would be independent of their disorder and they therefore might enjoy a more favorable class position. Consequently, in Table 6.16 the procedure used for placing each patient in his class position in the two subcommunities is presented.

At this point it seemed that if class was to be related to schizophrenia, some means independent of the disease process should be found to place the patient in a class position. The only method that would be used in such a case would be that of determining the social class of the patient on the basis of father's occupation and education. In other words, it would be a case of saying that the patient actually belonged to the same social class as his father even though the patient's own education and occupation possibly would place him in a lower class. Because many of the patients in the sample were completely independent of the parental families and had established their own homes, the author failed to secure the father's education in all instances, but did secure the father's occupation for patients in the two subcommunities. Table 6.17 presents the distribution of patients and rates for the five social classes in both subcommunities as determined by the father's occupation. It is interesting to note that the distribution of rates by this measure is quite different from the original distribution. No longer do the rates bulk in class V; in

TABLE 6.16

Basis for Assigning Schizophrenic Cases to Social Class in Two Subcommunities of Detroit, 1958*

Social Class	Cass		Conner-Burbank		Total	
	Patient	Father or Husband	Patient	Father or Husband	Patient	Father or Husband
I	0	0	0	1	0	1
II	C	0	0	1	0	1
III	4	0	3	3	7	3
IV	2	1	3	2	5	3
V	16	15	5	6	21	21
Total	22	16	11	13	33	29

*Index based upon education and occupation of patient, father, or husband.

TABLE 6.17

Number and Incidence Rates of Schizophrenic Cases by Social Class as Measured by Father's Occupation in Two Subcommunities of Detroit, 1958

Social Class	Cass		Conner-Burbank		Total	
	Number	Rate	Number	Rate	Number	Rate
I	1	.73	2	.97	3	.87
II	2	1.47	3	.60	5	.79
III	4	.65	6	.36	10	.44
IV	17	.80	8	.21	25	.43
V	14	.83	5	.46	19	.69
Total	38	.81	24	.34	62	.52

TABLE 6.18

Number and Incidence Rates by Social Class as Measured by Patient's Occupation and Education in the Two Subcommunities of Detroit, 1958

Social Class	Cass		Conner-Burbank		Total	
	Number	Rate	Number	Rate	Number	Rate
I	0	—	0	—	0	—
II	1	.74	1	.20	2	.32
III	3	.49	5	.30	8	.35
IV	3	.14	9	.24	12	.21
V	31	1.83	9	.84	40	1.45
Total	38	.81	24	.34	62	.52

fact, the rates are rather evenly distributed for both subcommunities in the five social classes. When the two subcommunities are combined, classes I and II have considerably higher rates than are to be found in class V.

The above result suggests that the class picture might change if each schizophrenic patient was placed on the basis of his own education and occupation. The results of this tabulation are shown in Table 6.18. Here the social class distribution of schizophrenic patients is very close to the final reported figures, although there is a slight downward tendency of four patients who by this measure lowered their class position, while one patient raised his class position.

This analysis suggests two interrelated conclusions. First, there is a need in studies dealing with the mentally ill to secure some measure of social class that cannot be affected by the person's mental disturbance. Second, the incipient stages of such a disease as schizophrenia have every chance of affecting such a person's educational and occupational level and hence his social class as measured by these factors.[12] These issues are considered in the next chapter.

NOTES

1. H. E. Freeman, O. G. Simmons, and B. J. Bergen, "Residential Mobility Inclinations among Families of Mental Patients," Social Forces 38 (May 1960): 320-24.

2. A. Hollingshead and F. Redlich, Social Class and Mental Illness (New York: John Wiley & Sons, 1958).

3. A. Hollingshead and F. Redlich, "Social Stratification and Schizophrenia," American Sociological Review 19 (June 1954): 302-06.

4. Hollingshead and Redlich, Social Class and Mental Illness, table 17, p. 236.

5. See H. Goldhamer, "Review of Social Class and Mental Illness," American Sociological Review 24 (August 1959): 579-81.

6. See Lloyd Warner, "The Society, the Individual, and His Mental Disorders," American Journal of Psychiatry 94 (September 1937): 275-84; see also Karen Horney, The Neurotic Personality of Our Time (New York: W. W. Norton, 1937).

7. Hollingshead and Redlich, Social Class and Mental Illness, pp. 244-48.

8. J. N. Morris, "Health and Social Class," Lancet (February 7, 1959): 303-05.

9. Mary H. Lystad, "Social Mobility among Selected Groups of Schizophrenic Patients," American Sociological Review 22 (June 1957): 288-92.

10. Lee N. Robins, Harry Gyman, and Patricia O'Neal, "The Interaction of Social Class and Deviant Behavior," American Sociological Review 27 (August 1962):480-91.

11. S. M. Miller and E. G. Mishler, "Social Class, Mental Illness, and American Psychiatry: An Expository Review," Milbank Memorial Fund Quarterly 37 (April 1959): 174-99.

12. This chapter was finished for several months before I had an opportunity to examine the work of Goldberg and Morrison in London. The similarity of their findings and interpretations with my own is most striking. See E. M. Goldberg and S. L. Morrison, "Schizophrenia and Social Class," British Journal of Psychiatry 109 (1963): 785-802.

7

SOCIAL CLASS AND MENTAL ILLNESS: FATHERS AND SONS

During the past decade quite a substantial body of literature has been made available that attempts to explore the relationship between social class and mental illness. In a carefully done study, Hollingshead and Redlich amassed data that tended to support two hypotheses: first, that the prevalence of treated mental illness is related significantly to the individual's position in the class structure; and second, that the types of diagnosed psychiatric disorders are connected significantly to the class structure. Their positive findings have added support for the view that psychoses, particularly schizophrenia, are more prevalent in the lowest social class. Although Hollingshead and Redlich themselves are most cautious in this regard,[1] this finding often has been taken up by others who have made the inference that in general the life-style prevalent in the lower classes has some significance as an etiological and/or precipitating factor in the development of mental illness.[2] The English studies, however, have been somewhat contradictory to these U.S. findings; they have pointed out the discrepancy between the occupational position of the fathers and their mentally ill sons.[3]

As reported in Chapter 6, the author found a similar concentration of schizophrenics in class V by using the same measure for social class as did Hollingshead and Redlich. However, when he worked out the social class position of the fathers and distributed

---

Patricia Phillips and Barbara Srinivasen were both coauthors when this paper was first published. Used with permission from the American Sociological Review 31 (April 1966):223-25.

the cases of schizophrenics in the sample by father's social class, the author found that the rates were at a parity in all five social classes.

The author has not been satisfied with these contradictory findings. Consequently, an attempt was made to devise a method to determine if there is any sound basis for claiming that a significantly greater amount of schizophrenia develops in the lowest social class than in the other social classes. The problem is basically whether it can be shown that persons who develop schizophrenia are found in the same class from birth onward. For U.S. society, however, it is known that there is an undetermined amount of mobility between the classes during and over a generation. This should be true of both the mentally and nonmentally ill. One also has been struck with the fact that the measurement of social class on the basis of education and occupation, as proposed by Hollingshead and Redlich and utilized by others, places the mentally ill person at a distinct disadvantage. Therefore a method is proposed that will attempt to illuminate this disadvantage.

METHOD OF PROCEDURE

In order to determine the extent of this disadvantage, the difference between the education and the occupation of each father was measured in contrast to the difference between the education and the occupation of his patient-son. (For reasons that are obvious in terms of technique, only male patients were included in these samples.) This was done by dividing the educational data into six groups and the occupational data into six groups, numbered one through six as shown on Table 7.1. Then the educational weight was subtracted from the occupational weight for all fathers and for their patient-sons in the samples. If a person received a zero score, it would mean that his occupation was equivalent to his education; if he received a negative score, it would mean that his occupation was lower than it should be according to his education; if he received a positive score, he was in an occupation higher than the education that he had received. This simple subtraction produces a discrepancy index score.

In utilizing this procedure, it was assumed that the formal education of all persons in the samples had been completed. All persons who were students at the time of hospitalization have been excluded from the samples. It was further assumed that while the fathers may have completed their education during a period when educational standards were not as high as today for securing and holding certain jobs, these were sufficient for beginning their work careers at that particular period.

TABLE 7.1

Scales Utilized to Obtain Discrepancy Indexes

Score	Education
1	Did not attend any formal school
2	Attended grade school but not high school
3	Attended high school but not college
4	Attended college
5	Graduated from college
6	Attended graduate school
	Usual Occupation
1	Habitually unemployed or underworld
2	Unskilled or semiskilled laborer
3	Skilled laborer
4	Lower white collar
5	Upper white collar
6	Professional or executive

THE DATA

The data composing the samples have been taken from schedules developed at the Lafayette Clinic and filled out for the first 1,200 patients who were admitted as in-patients to the clinic during the period 1958-62. The Lafayette Clinic is a 145-bed psychiatric research and teaching unit of the Department of Mental Health, State of Michigan, and Wayne State University. Samples were selected from these schedules with respect to the following factors: age, diagnosis, type of psychiatric breakdown (acute or chronic), father's education and occupation, and patient's education and occupation. The patient sample was divided into three experimental groups on the basis of diagnosis: group I, schizophrenics, comprising only patients given a diagnosis of schizophrenia; group II, nonschizophrenics, including primarily cyclothymic, involutional, psychoneurotic, and schizoid personality cases; group III, residual cases, including most of the psychopathies, some addictions, and cases not given any diagnosis.

ANALYSIS OF DATA

The first step was to compute the occupation-education discrepancy index for all patients and controls, fathers and sons. The mean discrepancy index of the three diagnostic groups and controls, for fathers and sons, as well as the mean age of sons in each group, are presented in Table 7.2. Information on age of father was not available.

A two-factor analysis of variance test was performed between fathers and sons (factor A) and across the three diagnostic categories and controls (factor B) to test for significant mean differences in their occupation-education discrepancy indexes. The interaction effect between diagnostic group and father-son category was significant. (All tests of significance in this study were performed at the 0.01 level of confidence.) Subsequent tests for simple effects were performed and these results are presented in Table 7.3.

The mean occupation-education discrepancy index was significantly lower for sons than for fathers only in the schizophrenic and residual groups. There were no significant differences between the fathers of the four groups. Schizophrenic and residual-case sons had significantly lower mean discrepancy indexes than sons in the other two categories.

Although the mean age of the sons in the nonschizophrenic group was about ten years greater than the mean age of the sons in the other three groups, this should not affect the comparison between fathers and sons in this group. In addition, despite an advantage in age and greater length of time in the work force, the nonschizophrenic sons had a mean discrepancy index like that for sons in the control group. This suggests that the ten-year advantage in age of this group may have little relation to the mean discrepancy index, perhaps partly because of the type of scales set up in this study. In this case, the data are not affected to any extent by the age discrepancy of the nonschizophrenic group.

A breakdown of the patient sample into acute and chronic classes was performed in order to gain information as to whether such a patient division would seriously affect the interpretation of the above results. These data are in agreement with the differences noted in the above analysis (see Table 7.4).

INTERPRETATION OF RESULTS

These findings inject a note of caution with respect to those investigations that purport to demonstrate the influence of social

TABLE 7.2

Discrepancy Index Means for Sons and Fathers and Mean Age for Sons, by Diagnostic Group

	Schizophrenic		Nonschizophrenic		Residual		Controls	
	Sons	Fathers	Sons	Fathers	Sons	Fathers	Sons	Fathers
Mean discrepancy index	-.73	+.25	+.22	+.56	-.44	+.35	+.20	+.37
Mean age	29.3	—	41.5	—	32.9	—	31.6	—
Number	110	110	96	96	104	104	60	60

TABLE 7.3

Results of Analysis of Variance between Father-Son Categories and Four Diagnostic Groups

Source		df	F
$A \times B$	Father-son vs. diagnostic groups interaction	3	6.715*
A for B_1	Schizophrenic—fathers vs. sons	1	67.315*
A for B_2	Nonschizophrenic—fathers vs. sons	1	5.696
A for B_3	Residual cases—fathers vs. sons	1	32.463*
A for B_4	Controls—fathers vs. sons	1	.837
B for A_1	Fathers across 4 diagnostic groups	3	1.885
B for A_2	Sons across 4 diagnostic groups	3	23.960*

*Significant at 0.01 level.

TABLE 7.4

Mean Discrepancy Indexes of Acute and Chronic Patients and Age of Sons, by Diagnostic Groups

		Schizophrenic		Nonschizophrenic		Residual	
		Sons	Fathers	Sons	Fathers	Sons	Fathers
Mean discrepancy index	Acute	-.66	.04	.25	.56	-.52	.41
	Chronic	-.76	.35	.17	.56	-.25	.18
Mean age	Acute	29.0	—	41.2	—	31.9	—
	Chronic	29.4	—	41.9	—	35.3	—
Number	Acute	48	48	55	55	72	72
	Chronic	92	92	41	41	32	32

class in the development or precipitation of psychiatric disorders. While their relevance may be confined to social class as measured by occupation and education, one suspects that these findings also would be applicable to other objective measures of social class. The central finding here is the significant difference in the mean discrepancy index between fathers and patient-sons for the schizophrenic group. This finding suggests that while the schizophrenic patient may function long enough to obtain a certain level of education, the real test comes when he enters the job market. Here his traits, attitudes, mannerisms, and verbal reactions become only too obvious and operate against his securing a position in the work force and, if he does secure some position, operate to restrict his advancement on the job. This stands out only too clearly when one notes how successful the fathers have been in their various jobs relative to their education; in contrast, their schizophrenic sons are found, on the average, in jobs of a much lower status than normally would be expected considering their educational attainments.

This same finding applies for the residual cases. The jobs occupied by these sons also are much lower than those of their fathers. However, in the case of the nonschizophrenics and the controls, while the sons have a discrepancy index somewhat lower than the fathers, the difference is never significant. It would seem that the nonschizophrenics are not as handicapped by their disturbance in seeking work as are the schizophrenic patients by their attitudes, and the residual cases on the basis of their frequent court records.

These findings, particularly for schizophrenia, seem to point clearly to the conclusion that it is the nature of the disease that determines the class position of the schizophrenic, and not the class position that influences the nature of the disease. The evidence presented here provides a clear explanation of why the various studies find more schizophrenics in the lowest social class than in the other classes; by this measure of social class, schizophrenics are at a disadvantage. Their premorbid personality characteristics prevent them from securing any position to which their education might entitle them; thus they are more likely to be counted as members of the lowest social class. It has been noted that when schizophrenics are located in the class structure on the basis of their father's social class, their incidence rate is at a parity in each social class from the highest to the lowest. The use of this discrepancy index serves considerably to tighten up this finding, and suggests that future studies should be most careful to seek a measure of social class that is independent of a given abnormal mental condition.

In conclusion, attention is called to an earlier study by Tuckman and Kleiner, which also used the discrepancy index, but with a much more elaborate set of assumptions than is used here.[4] Their study demonstrates most conclusively a grave error in interpretation: they proceed from significant statistical differences to the inference of some dynamic psychological process in the schizophrenic. They used the discrepancy index as a measure for comparing aspiration (education) and achievement (occupation). They showed for whites and blacks, and for Protestants and Catholics, in the skilled, semi-skilled, and unskilled categories, that the percentage of schizophrenics is much greater above the median than below the median for education. They interpreted this discrepancy between aspiration and achievement for schizophrenics as an indication of the extreme frustration experienced by persons who break down with schizophrenia. This is their general conclusion: the more frustration, the more schizophrenia. But this equation obviously can be turned around to read: the more schizophrenia, the more frustration. One persistent problem in such research is which condition is prior. It is no doubt true that any discrepancy between aspiration and achievement is likely to mean a mounting frustration for most people, but it does not follow that greater frustration means more schizophrenia. Schizophrenics, like other groups of people who show such a discrepancy, also experience frustration. Furthermore, Tuckman and Kleiner proceed as if they were unaware of the possible existence of a genetic or constitutional basis for schizophrenia.

The author's interpretation would be that the discrepancy that Tuckman and Kleiner find among their schizophrenic subjects, as with the data presented here, is due to the development of the disease and not the reverse. This position seems to be amply supported by the finding of minimal discrepancy between fathers and sons in the control group as compared with the schizophrenic and residual groups.

NOTES

1. A. Hollingshead and F. Redlich, Social Class and Mental Illness (New York: John Wiley & Sons, 1958).

2. See R. Hardt and S. Feinhandler, "Class and Mental Hospitalization Prognosis," American Sociological Review 24 (December 1959): 815-21; and J. Meyers and B. Roberts, Family and Class Dynamics in Mental Illness (New York: John Wiley & Sons, 1959).

3. E. M. Goldberg and S. L. Morrison, "Schizophrenia and Social Class," British Journal of Psychiatry 109 (November 1963): 785-802. See also J. N. Morris, "Health and Social Class," Lancet (February 7, 1959): 303-05.

4. J. Tuckman and R. Kleiner, "Discrepancy between Aspiration and Achievement as a Predictor of Schizophrenia," Behavioral Science 7 (1962):443-47.

8
SOCIAL CLASS, RACE, AND SCHIZOPHRENIA

Numerous past attempts to explore the relationship between the social class structure and the incidence of schizophrenia have resulted in the emergence of three contradictory positions. First, there are a number of studies that have pointed to a very high incidence rate of schizophrenia in the lowest social class with the rates approximately equal in the other four classes.[1] Second, there are those studies that have pointed to a definite negative linear relationship between the incidence of schizophrenia and the class structure, that is, the tendency of the incidence rate to increase in some proportion while the index for social class decreases in some other proportion.[2] Finally, there is a position that the incidence of schizophrenia does not vary significantly within the several social classes, but is found in about the same proportion in all social classes.[3]

As a consequence, the interpretation of these contradictory findings also varies. Some see in both the first and second positions hypotheses that tie the development of this disease to certain sociocultural factors. Further, it is held that these factors, whatever they may be, are more prevalent in the lowest social class than in the other social classes. Another interpretation of these same findings would explain the distribution of this disease in the class structure as a resultant of a process of social selection. This process distributes persons affected with this disease unequally in the five social classes. Thus if the concentration of cases in class V can be explained by social selection, there then is a tendency to infer that this supports a genetic explanation concerning the developments of this disease.

The third position has emerged as a result of efforts to obtain complete diagnostic coverage of cases within a given population of risk, and from attempts to utilize an index of class (that is, independent of the person who develops the disease). The establishment of the validity of this position would add firm support to a social selection theory with respect to those investigations that show a concentration of cases in class V. At the same time it would reject any hypotheses that would embrace selective sociocultural factors in class V as etiological agents for the disease.

It should be clearly spelled out that a social selection explanation is in no sense an alternative to social causation as some have inferred,[4] but is only an explanation of the differential distribution of the disease within the social class structure of a given social system.[5] This means that the acceptance of social selection as an explanation for the unequal class distribution of the disease within a population of risk does not automatically negate the possibility of developing hypotheses of a social causation type. However, as pointed out above, the explanation would tend to reject social causation hypotheses that encompass sociocultural factors that are indigenous to a given social class or classes.

It should be pointed out that no crucial experiment has evolved that can serve as a completely satisfactory test for the validity of any one of these positions. It would seem rather premature to introduce another variable, such as race, within this constellation of factors. However, the author intends to do just this in order to discover if the introduction of this new variable is at all helpful in giving support to any one of these three positions as well as the contrasting interpretations to which attention has been called. This chapter will examine the rates of schizophrenia for whites and blacks broken down by social class for two sets of data in Detroit. It also will examine certain black-white rate comparisons as found in the literature for any light that such data can throw on the central concern.

There was a time, with respect to the history of these black and white groups in the United States, when there was a marked interest in trying to establish a significant difference in the rate of mental illness between them. Much of these data emerged in the pre-Civil War period and were attempts to establish the fact that the giving of freedom to blacks would enhance their susceptibility to various forms of mental illness.[6] Rather interestingly, it often was overlooked in these studies that the rate of mental illness among whites was in excess to those reported among blacks. This was not because there was no mental illness among blacks, especially under the auspices of slavery, but rather because such mental illness as existed often was ignored due to the limited access that blacks had to community health facilities.[7] When blacks came out from under the chains of slavery and moved North, a frequent device of social control was to place them in mental hospitals, thus inflating the rate among the blacks in the North and providing an argument for certain southerners that this was a consequence of giving them their freedom. Thus in the earlier period the establishment of any valid mental disease incidence rates between blacks and whites proved well-nigh impossible because of a social selection that operated through historical linkages, cultural differences, migration patterns, and intense racial prejudices.[8] In the post-Civil War period these social selection factors continued to operate. These factors also can be utilized to explain the concentration of white persons with mental illness in certain communities and social-class categories.

In this chapter two sets of data are used to examine the interrelationship of race, social class, and schizophrenia. The first set of data comes from an epidemiological study of two community areas within the city of Detroit (see Chapters 4 and 6). One is a so-called ghetto area and the other is a semisuburban middle-class area. The case data for these two communities have been broken down by race and social class for both schizophrenics and nonschizophrenics. However, a race breakdown was possible only in the ghetto area. The second area had no blacks within it and certainly none appeared in the schizophrenic cases for that area.

The second set of data consisted of a group of 1,249 cases that were admitted to Lafayette Clinic between 1958 and 1961, broken down by race and social class for both schizophrenics and nonschizophrenics. It should be pointed out that this sample of cases is by no means a representative sample of schizophrenics within the Detroit metropolitan area, and consequently can provide no basis for arriving at any valid generalizations concerning the relationships of race and class with respect to schizophrenia. All one can say is that the findings are suggestive in pointing in the direction of a particular interpretation in contrast to other possible interpretations.

The analyses of the first set of data are presented in Tables 8.1, 8.2, and 8.3. Because of the paucity of cases, social classes I through IV have been grouped together. In Table 8.1 the rates per 1,000 are presented for the two classes for both whites and blacks for the Cass community, the ghetto area. Here one notes that in the case of both whites and blacks the highest rate occurs in class V. However, for the whites the difference is not statistically significant, but the difference among blacks is at a level of significance suggesting a greater concentration of blacks as might be expected in class V. This same contrast is shown in Table 8.2 for the nonschizophrenic cases. Again the only significant difference is to be found among the blacks between classes I-IV and class V, pointing to a heavy concentration of blacks in class V. It also is of more than passing interest to note that a comparison of the total rates for blacks and

TABLE 8.1

Schizophrenic Incidence Rates per 1,000 by Social Class and Race in Cass, 1958

Social	White			Black		
Class	Population	Number	Rate	Population	Number	Rate
I-IV	20,386	5	.25	9,639	2	.20
V	9,010	9	1.00	7,902	22	2.78
Total	29,396	14	.47	17,541	24	1.37

TABLE 8.2

Nonschizophrenic Incidence Rates per 1,000 by Social Class and Race in Cass, 1958

Social	White		Black	
Class	Number	Rate	Number	Rate
I-IV	14	.68	0	0
V	10	1.11	17	2.15
Total	24	.82	17	1.00

TABLE 8.3

Schizophrenic and Nonschizoprenic Incidence Rates for Whites per 1,000 by Social Class in Conner-Burbank, 1958

Social Class	Population	Schizophrenic		Nonschizophrenic	
		Number	Rate	Number	Rate
I-IV	60,873	14	.23	36	.59
V	10,767	10	1.0	8	.79
Total	71,640	24	.34	44	.61

whites shows that the difference for schizophrenics is statistically significant, while for the nonschizophrenics the difference is not significant.

In Table 8.3 these data are presented for the middle-class suburban area for schizophrenics and nonschizophrenics, for whites only, as there were no blacks in this community. Here, for both schizophrenics and nonschizophrenics, the differences between the two class groups have no statistical significance.

The findings presented in these three tables are suggestive, but hardly conclusive. They point in a very expected direction, namely, that blacks appear to be more heavily concentrated in the lowest social class as compared to whites. This would be expected in view of their less favorable economic position as compared to whites. The fact that blacks appear to have a higher rate of schizophrenia in comparison with whites in this ghetto community certainly cannot be taken as any indication that blacks are more prone to this disease; rather, it is indicative of their much poorer economic situation. While blacks seem to have a higher overall rate than do whites in class V, it should be pointed out that this difference has no statistical significance.

The second set of data that consisted of cases admitted to the Lafayette Clinic between the years 1958 and 1961 have been broken down by race and social class for both schizophrenics and nonschizophrenics. Here an attempt is made to compute a series of rates for these cases, using as a base the population 20 years of age and above broken down by social class for the standard metropolitan statistical area of Detroit. The placing of this population in a social class structure was accomplished by a crude assumption that the class distribution in the two subcommunities in Detroit would be approximately similar for the population in the Detroit metropolitan area. This assumption may not be too far off when it is noted that the black population in the two subcommunities constituted 14.8 percent of the total population, while the black population in the metropolitan area constituted 14.2 percent of the total.

These data cannot form any satisfactory basis for drawing valid conclusions concerning the comparison of schizophrenic incidence rates between blacks and whites. It should be remembered that these admissions to the clinic are composed of self-referrals and professional and agency referrals, and that the clinic at the time of these admissions was mostly serving persons on a higher economic level, and so the admissions are hardly representative of the community population.

The data are presented for both schizophrenics and nonschizophrenics in Tables 8.4 through 8.7, broken down by race and patient's social class and race and father's social class. As pointed out in

Chapter 7, there is a difficulty in basing the class structure on the patient's education and occupation because these factors are hardly independent of the disease in the patient. Thus the assumption that the patient is in the same social class as the father eliminates this methodological difficulty. However, it may not give a very true picture of the patient's current social position.

In Table 8.4 the data, presented in accordance with patient's social class, show that the blacks in this sample come from a generally higher class than in the previous sample that represented total coverage. This is as expected, for the clinic in general was serving patients coming from more affluent economic levels. The same picture is noted in connection with the rates for whites. Further, it is interesting to note that the overall rate for blacks and whites is approximately the same, indicating that blacks and whites in their respective populations were utilizing the clinic approximately to the same degree.

A similar picture emerges at least for the whites when the rates are computed according to father's social class as in Table 8.5. Here one notes that while the overall rates for blacks and whites are equal, the blacks are more heavily concentrated in class V as compared to the whites. Also the blacks, when class is measured by father's social class, are more concentrated in class V than when they are distributed according to their own social class. This finding alone suggests the operation of the social selection process. While the fathers' of blacks are in a much poorer economic situation, their sons in the affluent society have been able to change their class position and are found more frequently on a higher class level. In the nonschizophrenic groups (Tables 8.6 and 8.7), it is interesting to note that the overall white rates distributed by both patient's social class and father's social class are larger as compared to blacks. Again, it is worth noting for both blacks and whites that these non-schizophrenics as compared to schizophrenics are much more widely distributed in the class structure.

At this point it is instructive to examine some of the statistical comparisons in mental illness rates between blacks and whites as reported by other investigators. In a careful prevalence survey of mental disorder conducted in 1952, the investigators report significantly higher prevalence rates for whites in contrast to blacks for psychoses, psychoneuroses, and psychophysiologic disorders.[9] These results come from a subsample of a house-to-house survey of of a probability sample and approximately one quarter of the subsample received a clinical evaluation by a psychiatrist. These black-white comparisons for prevalence rates by diagnostic group are perhaps the best available at the present time. Nevertheless, they are surprising. One might expect a rate for psychoneuroses and

TABLE 8.4

Rate Distribution of Schizophrenics Admitted to Lafayette Clinic by Race and Patient's Social Class

Patient's Social Class	White			Black		
	Number	Population 1960	Rate	Number	Population	Rate
I	7	62,656	.11	0	2,893	0
II	4	123,354	.03	0	3,213	0
III	39	407,264	.09	5	30,520	.16
IV	79	982,916	.08	13	139,750	.09
V	80	381,810	.21	9	144,889	.06
Total	209	1,958,000	.11	27	321,265	.09

TABLE 8.5

Rate Distribution of Schizophrenics Admitted to Lafayette Clinic by Race and Father's Social Class

Father's Social Class	White		Black	
	Number	Rate	Number	Rate
I	24	.38	0	0
II	2	.01	0	0
III	30	.07	2	.07
IV	99	.10	14	.10
V	96	.25	26	.18
Total	251	.13	42	.13

TABLE 8.6

Rate Distribution of Nonschizophrenics Admitted to Lafayette Clinic by Race and Patient's Social Class

Patient's	White		Black	
Social Class	Number	Rate	Number	Rate
I	22	.35	1	.34
II	21	.17	1	.31
III	81	.19	7	.23
IV	184	.18	19	.13
V	176	.46	26	.18
Total	484	.25	54	.13

TABLE 8.7

Rate Distribution of Nonschizophrenics Admitted to Lafayette Clinic by Race and Father's Social Class

Father's Social Class	White		Black	
	Number	Rate	Number	Rate
I	37	.59	1	.34
II	14	.11	0	0
III	88	.21	0	0
IV	253	.25	15	.11
V	251	.66	55	.37
Total	643	.33	71	.22

psychophysiologic disorders more in line with the white rates considering the stresses that are likely to harass blacks as a reflection of their disadvantaged social position.

In a rather interesting contrast, the black-white prevalence rates for total mental disorder as reported by the Monroe (New York) County Register for January 1, 1960, show the black rates for each sex are in excess of the white rates.[10] However, these are cases coming for treatment and reported to the register by private practicing psychiatrists and psychiatric agencies, and thus are in no sense equivalent to the house-to-house Baltimore survey. The findings do suggest, however, that social forces to push persons into psychiatric treatment are stronger for blacks than for whites.

The black-white breakdown of the New Haven data shows results similar to the author's Detroit data, namely, that the blacks are more heavily concentrated in class V.[11] This finding adds support to a social selection hypothesis, for if selective factors did not operate one would expect a distribution more similar to the whites and more in keeping with their population distribution.

Fischer in a recent survey boldly attacks what he considers to be the myth that blacks have higher rates of mental disorder than whites.[12] He concludes that in spite of the adverse circumstances surrounding blacks, they appear to have no higher rate of mental disorder than do whites. He proposes a model whereby mental disorder would be defined as the inability to cope with the difficulties of life. This, he holds, would make epidemiological research less culture bound.

These data taken as a whole would tend to question any proposition that asserts a significant difference in incidence rates of schizophrenia, as well as total mental disorder, between blacks and whites. In general these data would seem to give some support to the social selection hypothesis. This hypothesis holds that the distribution of schizophrenics within the social-class structure has no significance whatever in supporting the argument that one social class has more schizophrenics than does another social class. Further, the findings suggest, in the case of patients admitted to the Lafayette Clinic, that blacks and whites were utilizing the clinic in almost the same proportion as they are found to in the general adult population as shown in Table 8.8. Further, the findings point clearly to a more affluent level of black patients in contrast to their black fathers, who are known from all evidence to have experienced a much poorer economic situation. The very scarce data from the literature also support a social selection explanation for the distribution of cases among both blacks and whites, as well as between them, in the social-class structure.

TABLE 8.8

Number and Percent of Population and Number and Percent of Mental Disorders by Race in the Detroit Metropolitan Area

	Population		Mental Disorders	
	Number	Percent	Number	Percent
Whites	1,958,000	85.8	894	88.7
Blacks	321,265	14.2	113	11.3
Total	2,279,265	100.0	1,007	100.0

While the author does not hold that these data are conclusive, he does hold that they are suggestive, and if anything tend to support a social selection hypothesis with respect to the distribution of schizophrenics within a class structure.

NOTES

1. L. Kohn, "Social Class and Schizophrenia: A Critical Review," Journal of Psychiatric Research 6, Supplement 1 (1968): 155-73; see also P. M. Roman and H. M. Trice, Schizophrenia and the Poor (New York: New York School of Industrial Relations, 1967).

2. A. Hollingshead and F. Redlich, Social Class and Mental Illness (New York: John Wiley & Sons, 1957), p. 236.

3. E. M. Goldberg and S. L. Morrison, "Schizophrenia and Social Class," British Journal of Psychiatry 109 (1963): 785-802; and H. W. Dunham, Community and Schizophrenia: An Epidemiological Analysis (Detroit: Wayne State University Press, 1965), pp. 194-98.

4. B. P. Dohrenwend, "Social Status and Psychological Disorder: An Issue of Substance and Method," American Sociological Review 31 (February 1966): 14-34; and R. J. Turner and M. O. Wagenfeld, "Occupational Mobility and Schizophrenia: An Assessment of the Social Causation and Social Selection Hypotheses," American Sociological Review 32 (April 1967): 104-13.

5. See Chapter 10.

6. B. Pasamanick, "Some Misconceptions Concerning Differences in the Racial Prevalence of Mental Disease," American Journal of Orthopsychiatry 33 (1963): 72-86.

7. Malzberg, in one of the early attempts at a careful assessment of the relation between race and schizophrenia, calls attention to the lack of facilities in the southern states as the chief factor determining the rates for blacks in the South. See B. Malzberg, Social and Biological Aspects of Mental Disease (Utica, N.Y.: State Hospital Press, 1940), chap. 9. At the time Malzberg did show, based on first admissions to New York state hospitals, that blacks did have higher rates as compared to whites. We know now, however, that such reported differences must be examined carefully with respect to social factors and social policies that can significantly affect them before they can be accepted at face value.

8. R. Schermerhorn, "Psychiatric Disorders among Negroes: A Sociological Note," American Journal of Psychiatry 112 (1955-56): 878-82.

9. B. Pasamanick, D. W. Roberts, P. Lemkau, and D. B. Krueger, "A Survey of Mental Disease in an Urban Population: Prevalence by Race and Income," presented at a joint session of the Epidemiology of Mental Disorder, a symposium to commemorate the centennial of the birth of Emil Kraepelin, New York City, December 27-28, 1956.

10. Cumulative Register Study, Monroe County, New York, December 11, 1962 (mimeographed).

11. Hollingshead and Redlich, Social Class and Mental Illness, p. 202.

12. J. Fischer, "Negroes and Whites and Rates of Mental Illness: Reconsideration of a Myth," Psychiatry 32 (1969):428-46.

PART FOUR
SOCIAL SYSTEMS AND MENTAL DISORDERS: A SUMMATION

INTRODUCTION TO PART FOUR

The book has attempted to explore the respective roles of community organization and social class viewed as causative factors in the development of schizophrenia. This possible relationship was approached through an epidemiological analysis when the author examined the incidence of schizophrenia in different types of urban communities and in the several social classes. Wherever possible, attempts were made to sharpen these differential incidence findings for schizophrenia by comparing them with incidence findings for other mental disorders, particularly the manic-depressive psychoses. A careful sifting of evidence for both community organization and social class shows that differential schizophrenic incidence rates that previously were regarded as established fact for both community and social class are largely an illusion. Thus the conviction gradually grows that schizophrenia is to be found in all types of communities and in every social class. This position is an echo of Kraepelin's observation at the end of the nineteenth century that schizophrenia is to be found all over and in every country in the world.

There has been in the past an all too ready response to assume that the finding of differential incidence rates by community and/or class points to the necessity to look for various social factors that might account for the differences. This author frequently has pointed out that there is a logical error in attributing social causation to the finding of differential incidence rates. He has emphasized the necessity to eliminate the possibility that a genetic, biochemical, or environmental factor may provide a more plausible explanation for differential incidence rates. His analysis of the differential incidence rates by community and/or class points to the operation of a process of social selection that enables schizophrenic cases to collect in certain socially disadvantaged communities and in the lowest social class.

There has been a tendency to view social causation and social selection as contrasting polar types.[1] This is as much a logical error as moving from differential incidence rates that are on a social system level to some social-psychological explanation of schizophrenia. Ideas about social causation of mental disorders have been around for a long time and by no means grew out of epidemiological or ecological studies of mental disorder. The theory of social selection seems to best fit the facts relative to the mobility of schizophrenic cases in the community and in the class structure.

This social selection theory does not rule out either factors of social causation or social precipitation, but only states that they cannot be utilized as an explanation of differential rates. Thus with respect to epidemiological studies of mental disorder, the possibility of explanation by way of factors of social causation or precipitation has by no means been exhausted.

The easy and often immediate interpretation, particularly by social scientists, that a social factor accounts for differential rate distribution in communities and social classes has provided a significant support to those investigators who think that a social model would be more appropriate for increasing one's understanding of schizophrenia than the more traditional and widely accepted medical model. This suggestion has come on the heels of countless investigations that have failed to uncover in any conclusive fashion the etiology for schizophrenia, and after much effort has been expended to establish reliable criteria for the diagnosis of schizophrenia. A total substitution of the social model for the medical model at this time not only would tend to obliterate these years of research, but also would widen the diagnostic net in order to include those cases that appear to have some schizophrenic symptoms but in a much milder form. The adoption of a social model for schizophrenia merely would increase confusion about this disorder and make it more difficult to establish a valid etiology for this disease. In fact, something like this has taken place with respect to the nature of mental disorder in general so that a practicing psychiatrist, in his clinical setting, often has great difficulty in distinguishing a psychosis from a psychological adjustment problem or a learned deviant behavior pattern in a person caught up in the vortex of an existing social problem.

The major obstacle to securing a valid incidence count of schizophrenics is related to the possibility that a person who has the disease can remain undetected in the community because he is not recognized by himself or by others as being sick. This possibility argues for a widening of the psychiatric net and the development of some sensitive instrument that can detect those persons who have a disorder but who appear on no patient roles of clinic, hospital, or psychiatrist. This means that another method is available other than a judgment by self or others as to who suffers from a mental disorder. The criterion of judgment by self or others for determining who has schizophrenia can be viewed as a product of the social process, while detection by an impersonal instrument can be viewed as a product of social planning.

These final chapters in Part IV attempt to deal with all of these issues. Chapter 12 attempts a summation of current knowledge with respect to the impact of sociocultural factors in the development of schizophrenia and other mental disorders. From this accumulated epidemiological evidence the author would conclude that if there is a causal linkage between the social system and schizophrenia, it is not accounted for by the discovery of the heavy concentration of cases in certain types of urban communities or in the lowest social class, but rather by other factors unrelated to these findings.

NOTE

1. H. W. Dunham, "Social Causation and Social Selection Theories of Schizophrenia," in Social Psychiatry, ed. J. H. Masserman and J. J. Schwab (New York: Grune and Stratton, 1974), pp. 145-54.

9

SOCIAL STRUCTURES AND MENTAL DISORDERS: COMPETING HYPOTHESES

This chapter will examine critically the kinds of hypotheses that have been advanced to explain the findings of some epidemiological and ecological studies of mental disease. In order to accomplish this task it is necessary to mention three points: the differences between epidemiological and ecological studies; the various theoretical considerations directing these studies; and the value and purpose of both kinds of studies in understanding some of the problems associated with mental health and disease.

As the author has reflected on this problem, it seems that some clarification of the task will result by pointing to the distinguishing features of epidemiological and ecological studies of mental illness.* Epidemiology has been defined as "the sum of what is known regarding epidemics."[1] As such, one most important phase of an epidemiological study is to find out the incidence and prevalence of a disease in a circumscribed community setting or a carefully delimited population group. The general objective in these studies has been primarily an overall count of cases. Furthermore, most of the epidemiological studies, particularly the European ones, have been conducted by

---

Used with permission from Milbank Memorial Fund Quarterly 39 (April 1961):259-97.

*While in the work of epidemiologists and ecologists there is much overlapping of interests and technique, the author has elaborated this distinction, even though it may not be acceptable to some, with the express purpose of sharpening up existing disagreements and expressed viewpoints.

medically trained persons who have regarded their efforts as having some genetic significance. Thus when they compare the results of their surveys, they think that their theoretical position is supported when the statistical differences are at a minimum. For example, the two well-known surveys in this country, the Baltimore[2] and the Williamson County, Tennessee surveys,[3] reported rates for active and inactive cases of 62.0 and 69.4 per 1,000 population respectively. Such results frequently have been interpreted that regardless of the type of area—whether urban north or rural south—the frequency of mental and behavioral disturbances in a delimited population is about the same.

However, epidemiological comparisons in the hands of social scientists may produce a different emphasis. Eaton and Weil, using a standard expectancy method, compared ten surveys relative to the amount of enumerated psychoses.[4] The Hutterites, serving as a norm, had a higher enumerated rate of psychoses than seven of the ten populations upon which they reported. They regard the high Hutterite expectancy ratio as a function of their thoroughness in screening, and think that five of the populations ranking below the Hutterites were not screened thoroughly for their recovered mental cases. After several other arguments, Eaton and Weil conclude that the Hutterites have the lowest frequency of psychoses among the four rural populations, but higher than the frequency found by Tsung-yi Lin in his survey of Formosa.[5] They then point to the limitations of the epidemiological method with its capacity for showing the presence or absence of quantitative differences but without being able to explain them. "Their genetic composition, physical health, psychological tendencies would have to be analyzed in detail with the hope of identifying some patterned interrelationships that could account for the quantitative differences."[6]

Undeterred, the investigators proceed to show that a sociological orientation is useful in accounting for the predominance of the manic-depressive psychoses (73.6 percent of all persons diagnosed as psychotic among the Hutterites). After convincing themselves that their diagnostic judgments were valid, Eaton and Weil develop the role of the "social cohesion factor." From examining various bits of evidence they conclude that the ratio of manic-depressives to schizophrenics varied in different population groups and this fact (they call it an assumption) "would support the general theory that sociological factors play an important role in the way functional mental disorders are manifested in patients."[7] They conclude tentatively: "The extreme cohesiveness of the Hutterites which may contribute to their low frequency of schizophrenia, may be significant for the relatively high proportion of manic-depressive reaction among psychotic members of the sect."[8]

Eaton and Weil are used here to illustrate the fashion in which the orientation of the investigators enters into an interpretation, and also to illustrate the gap between a theory and the evidence to support it (Weil, of course, is a psychiatrist). That they should fasten upon the differential frequency of these two functional diagnoses among the Hutterites to show the relevance of sociological factors is incredibly naive considering the seemingly interminable problems in making the differential diagnoses, and considering also that many different psychiatrists were involved in making the differential diagnoses in the other studies.

It might have proven just as valuable to make something of the fact that Bremer's Arctic Norwegian village had a frequency of psychoses that was twice the Hutterite rate, for in both studies the screening was supposed to be excellent and the data were gathered in extremely isolated communities.[9] If one assumes this difference to be a real one, then one is forced to conclude that the population of the Norwegian village is genetically inferior to the Hutterites, or that the conditions of life provide a more telling impact upon the people of the Norwegian village than different life conditions do in the case of the Hutterites. This, in a final sense, is the big factual question: Can such surveys as counts of prevalence and incidence of total psychopathy or particular disorders show significant quantitative variations between different cultural groups and/or different strata or categories of population within the same society?

Ecology has been defined as "the science of organisms as affected by the factors of their environment," or "the study of the environment and life history of organisms."[10] This means that an investigator who wants to make an ecological study of mental disease will be concerned in locating the mentally diseased person in some position within a culture or social system, and viewing him in relation to the positions occupied by other mentally diseased persons and the nonmentally diseased in that system. An investigator making an ecological study of mental disease, or a single mental disease, is concerned with discovering if the incidence of disease, or a given disease, will vary significantly between different temporal, spatial, or social environments. These environments are frequently delimited as social classes, religious groups, occupations, types of families, types of communities, levels of education, historical time, or special environments such as school, military unit, or prison.

If the ecologist can show conclusively that certain significant rate differentials for mental disease exist between different positions in one of these environments, he faces the task of trying to find some hypothesis derived from a theory that may explain the difference. Thus most of these studies have been largely empirical in character and if any theory is pertinent, it is of the broadest and most general variety.

However, the ecologist focusing on the organism in his environment will be concerned with trying to isolate certain environmental factors that will explain the rate differences and account for the development of the disease in the person. If he operates as an ecologist he will emphasize the processes within the environment and attempt to show the social variable or complex of variables that is associated with the rate differential. If he tries to get at the social factors that are causative or predisposing for persons in that environment, he will be thrown on another level of analysis where his ecological findings will prove indicative only of some factors that he might study as having an etiological significance.

The difficulties and pitfalls that beset the investigator in this area as he strives to make sense out of his findings are well illustrated by Frumkin's study of occupations and mental disorder.[11] He begins by emphasizing that research is needed to investigate the etiology of mental illness. His data comprised all first admissions to Ohio State's prolonged-care mental hospitals for the year 1950 who had an occupation, and who had not been classified as housewife, student, or unknown occupation prior to admission. These data (1,192 males and 347 females) were then broken down by occupation in relation to age, sex, and mental disorder. His basic findings consist of rates per 100,000 for each sex for the major psychoses in 12 general occupational categories ranging from unskilled to professional.

It almost goes without saying that his data, method, and findings raise many questions that should be considered before attempting some theoretical interpretation. The finding that the low-prestige occupations have the highest rates of first admissions for the major mental disorders is, all things considered, hardly startling. However, without even touching on the difficulties here, Frumkin barges joyously ahead and using the "method of Verstehen rather than by strictly empirical methods," proceeds to all kinds of generalizations about man in U.S. society that are not only dubious in general, but also in relation to his findings, which should be boxed in by many qualifications. To illustrate with a few choice quotations,

> A man's occupation, in general, is more important to his mental health than is the occupation of a woman to her mental health.
>
> Thus, we find that the more radical male and female unskilled and service workers have the highest rates of alcoholic and syphilitic psychoses because, next to criminal acts, sexual promiscuity and alcoholism seem to be the best emotional outlets, the best known escape from hostility, the rejection and general frustration which are

> so often encountered among people in the lower socio-economic strata of our society.
>
> To go a step further, one might say that the etiology of lower socio-economic-status-group mental illness (and crime) is generally socio-genic in nature, whereas in the upper strata of society, mental illness is generally more psycho-genic. Thus, the etiology of middle class mental disorders, being somewhere in between, i.e., more or less equally socio-genic and psychogenic, or simply psycho-genic in origin, reflects characteristics of both extreme strata of society.[12]

Frumkin's study is used here not because he reported his findings, but because his study illustrates the trap of excessive sociological zeal as one moves from rate differentials to theoretical interpretation. His quality of interpretation is too strained, and hardly drops as the gentle rain from heaven.

Turning now to the general theories that have directed both types of studies, it already has been indicated that they are of the most broad and general kind. The epidemiological studies, particularly the European, have stemmed from a broad biological basis that attempts to point up differences or similarities that must be inferred about the genetic composition of a given population. Investigators with this orientation are likely to be more intrigued if the rates in a given population group or between different population groups are approximately equal.

The ecological studies, largely American, are by contrast likely to be guided by some broad sociological theory that attempts to show how certain social factors may be psychosis inducing for persons occupying a given position in time or space in a social system. From this broad theoretical basis excitement is high when a distribution of cases in relation to some aspects of social structure shows that the rates vary significantly from the different positions in that structure. The question, then, immediately arises: How certain can one be that one's findings actually depict a true rate difference in the incidence of the disease or diseases under study? This is the rub, for the fact is that with respect to both types of studies controversy has centered around the problem of validity. In general, those investigators with a bio-organic orientation try to show that significant rate differences of incidence in a social structure are not valid and cannot be accepted, while investigators with more of a sociological orientation attempt to show that they do possess a validity. Then there are the stolid empiricists who attempt to examine the evidence with an impartial and objective eye.

The following is a brief comment on the purpose and value of these studies for an understanding of mental health and disease. It seems that these studies, considered jointly, have five central purposes and can be valued to the extent that they prove useful as aids to detection, diagnosis, treatment, and prevention of mental disorders in human society. First, these studies frequently serve the purpose of administration and can be helpful in pointing to the quantity and quality of services and facilities that may be needed in the future. Second, they may serve the purpose of sharpening devices for detecting and screening the mentally ill in any population group. Third, they can provide one with some conception of the size and extent of mental disease in general, or of a specific disease as it may exist in a given population group. Fourth, these studies can add to the current knowledge of social systems by showing those elements of processes within such systems that are associated with high and low rates of mental disturbances. Finally, they sometimes can be suggestive of hypotheses bearing on the etiology of mental disease that must be investigated by other methods and that must serve as a testing ground for the crucial relevance between biological and social-psychological theories.

With these rather lengthy introductory remarks concluded, the author returns to the central task, which is to examine critically the hypotheses utilized to explain findings of selected epidemiological and ecological studies of mental disease. This task has three parts. First is a brief analysis of the central problem with which this type of research is always confronted. Second, some of the characteristics of the data will be pointed out that present much difficulty for this survey-type of research in mental illness, especially in the complex, technologically advanced societies of the West. Finally, there will be an examination of the hypotheses that have been utilized to explain rate similarities or differences in various types of social structures. There also will be an examination of these hypotheses as they have evolved in the numerous studies that purport to find the incidence and prevalence of mental disease in different positions of the social structure or in specific delimited population groups. However, there is no intention here to cover the total literature, which is voluminous, but to confine citations and illustrations to what are some of the most significant studies that have appeared during the last two decades.

The central problem that these studies present is posed by this question: How does one define or delimit the case? This has been examined in other contexts and there is no wish to belabor it here, but the problem continues to be crucial and is brought up when the results of such studies are presented.[13] Currently there are three devices. First, there is the arbitrary definition. Thus one will count all persons who seek help from psychiatrists, clinics, or hospitals for the first time, all persons entering a mental hospital for the first time, or all persons being treated at a given time. However, if one arbitrarily defines the case, how does one know if coverage was complete enough to assert the reliability of the rates as found so that any interpretations of them will have some validity?

Second, one can argue that who is counted as sick in any social milieu is the result of a social judgment made by family members, friends, or neighbors, and is a judgment that the person must accept in some fashion by taking action or having some action taken upon him by others. This means that judgments about who is mentally disturbed or can be regarded as a mental case will vary in different social milieus, communities, and subcultures. This definition stacks the cards and contains within it a built-in explanation for rate variations at the different positions in social structure. This position also implies that the way to reduce mental disturbance in a high-rate group would be merely to conduct some kind of educational campaign to bring about greater acceptance and toleration of human frailties. If this position has any relevance it probably would be to the minor type of disturbances, but this then becomes a clinical problem. How does the diagnostician determine that he deals with a minor personality distortion and not one that is a forerunner of a more severe disturbance?

Third, there always has been the hope that for those types of mental illnesses where etiology is still obscure that biochemical research eventually will find the answer and in so doing will perfect a test so that one can say with complete assurance that a given person has a given mental disease. Some clinicians have felt that these statistical survey-type studies are useless without such an objective test. However, one might say in their defense that while they have contributed little of etiological significance, they have helped to clarify certain issues in the mental health field, have been revealing of social systems, and have pointed up certain hypotheses that might be investigated by other methods.

In addition to the problem of defining the case, there are several other characteristics of the data that make the conducting of this type of research quite difficult, especially with respect to the confidence concerning reliability and validity. Here the author has reference to the following factors: the great mobility of patients that is a reflection of stepped-up mobility in the entire society during the past half century; the discrepancy between the onset of mental disease and the decision to seek treatment; the great spread of age at which patients are first recorded as having mental illness; and the great variety of diagnostic types with numerous remissions in the various categories over the years. In addition, there also are the great differences in policies and administrative practices of states and countries that make it difficult to secure comparable data. Finally, there always are the great variety of theoretical orientations that exist among psychiatrists as they attempt to arrive at a diagnostic judgment.

The central issue in all these studies is whether there are reliable and valid rate differences for mental disease, or for a specific mental disease, between different positions in a social structure or subculture. Consequently, the remainder of this chapter will be concerned with examining the hypotheses that have been advanced to explain rate variations among the different positions within a social system, and also to show the manner in which various studies have tended to classify them or advance them as interpretations of their own findings.* Thus this analysis is not concerned with pointing to the various correlational findings of mental disease rates and different indexes for status, isolation, or population characteristic that have appeared in the literature. The function of these correlations is merely to add support to rate differentials that a particular investigator has found present in a particular social structure. That schizophrenic rates are high in low-income occupations and in occupations of low prestige as Clark has reported,[14] or that the rate of mental disease in certain subregions of Texas shows a correlation with the number of psychiatrists in private practice of .40 as Jaco has reported,[15] will not be of concern here. While such correlations are interesting, they have added nothing with respect to throwing any light on the social etiology of mental disease or a specific mental disease.

The crucial problems concerning rate differentials are three in number. First, with what confidence can one assert the reliability and validity of rate differentials or no rate differentials for mental disease as found in specific social structures? Second, what is the most plausible interpretation of the presence or absence of such

---

*The author has confined his analysis to those studies dealing with position in the social system, and feels constrained to point out that the same problem arises when making cross-cultural comparisons. For example, consider the following questions: Does a given culture have more mental disease than another culture? Does a given culture have a higher incidence of one type of mental disease than does another culture? The problem as to whether all cultures have basically the same kinds of mental disease is relevant to a cultural analysis, but is not pertinent to the present concerns.

rate differentials? Third, does a particular interpretation provide one with some suggestive hypotheses about social causation that one can subject to some crucial test?

There are two classes of hypothetical interpretations concerned with providing adequate explanations for rate differentials of mental disease in social structures: the nontheoretical hypotheses and the theoretical hypotheses. By nontheoretical hypotheses is meant those explanations that stem from no acceptable body of scientific theory but find their raison d'être in some defect of method or some obstacle in the environment. Theoretical hypotheses refer to propositions that derive from or can be derived from some acceptable body of scientific theory. Within the class of theoretical hypotheses are three subclasses: those on biological, social-psychological, and social system levels.

The four nontheoretical hypotheses have been suggested at one time or another for the purpose of showing that rate differentials that have been reported as incidence rates are not true incidence rates. Perhaps the oldest and fairest argument has been the notion of incomplete coverage. From this point of view it is contended that a given investigator has not included in his count all the new cases occurring in an area mainly because he cannot get to them. Thus if he counts only first admission to mental hospitals, his count is off because he does not include admissions to outpatient clinics and private psychiatrists. If he includes these his count is off because he does not take account of those in the community who are sick but who do not get into treatment. This argument has been faced by numerous investigators in their studies in one way or another, including Faris and Dunham,[16] Goldhamer and Marshall,[17] and Hollingshead and Redlich.[18] This is the demand for a true incidence figure, and until it can be secured many are likely to remain skeptical of any significant rate differentials that are reported.

In the nineteenth century the one readily acceptable nontheoretical hypothesis was the law of distance. This law merely asserted that the rate of first admissions to a hospital varied inversely with the distance from the hospital. This is equivalent to a contemporary nontheoretical hypothesis that views variations in the first admission rates by geographical or status positions as merely a reflection of the differential availability of psychiatric facilities, whether hospitals or beds. This was one of Kramer's conclusions when he studied the admission data from 1916-50 at the Warren State Hospital in Pennsylvania.[19] Ødegaard reports that rates of admission vary in the different areas of Norway because the more and better facilities tend to account for the higher rates.[20] However, in another study of the incidence of mental disease during World War II, Ødegaard concludes that loss of facilities cannot explain the 1941-43 decrease in rates.[21]

He notes that decreases were particularly marked in Oslo where facilities were fairly good, and least marked in the northwest where the bed shortage was especially bad. He also notes that if facilities determined the decrease then there should be a decrease in nursing cases and readmissions, but in these series there was an increase. He finally concludes that even though a number of psychoses seemed directly caused by the war, there was a real decrease in psychiatric morbidity and a net gain in mental health. This finding will be of further concern when an attempt is made to assess those theories on the social system level.

Malzberg's evidence on this point for New York State is also negative.[22] He shows that between 1925 and 1935 bed capacity increased 71.4 percent, while first admissions increased only 58.3 percent. He thinks that this fact combined with evidence from other states seriously questions the proposition that bed capacity determines the rate of first admissions. Even so, as Ødegaard has pointed out to the author, an increase of bed capacity at a given point in time is, as a rule, followed by a jump in first admissions the following year.

Finally, there is the statistical criticism. While this stems from an acceptable body of statistical theory, it is called a non-theoretical hypothesis because it disposes of rate differentials by claiming some defect in the collecting of or handling of the data. This hypothesis points to an inadequate sampling, failure to establish significant rate differences, an inadequate number of cases (by increasing the cases by three or four in any cell the entire picture might change), or a mobile population. Any of these items might destroy any rate difference reported.

The first set of theoretical hypotheses, those concerned with a biological level of explanation, will be considered first. In general, these studies have been largely of European origin and have been directed to establishing valid estimates of the true incidence and prevalence of mental disease and specific mental diseases in various populations; collecting statistical evidence for the genetic linkages of mental diseases through specific family groups and/or inbreeding of populations;[23] and obtaining reliable frequency figures for a population in order to compare them with frequency found in hereditary-tainted families.

It is not intended to review all of these European studies, but two of them illustrate the above points. Torsten Sjögren reported on the investigation of the occurrence of psychoses and oligophrenia during the period January 1, 1900 to December 31, 1944, on the island A:bo off the west coast of Sweden.[24] He states:

> The object of the investigation was a thorough statistical and hereditary-biological analysis of psychoses and oligo-

> phrenia as well as genealogical survey of the cases concerned and their facilities as far back as it was possible with the aid of parish registers and archives. . . . Furthermore, statistical investigations regarding heredity and incidence of mental disorders in the parents and siblings of the probands can be made and the extent of inbreeding analyzed.[25]

His data, after diligently searching the records, included 397 persons of which 335 comprised his proband group and 62 were secondary cases (siblings of probands). Of the total of 397 persons, 158 comprising 117 families were assembled into a connective pedigree complex. His findings, broken down by pedigree, parish, birth, and residence, and diagnosis are voluminous; while impressive, Sjögren presents them with no interpretation other than implied genetic explanations. His overall finding showed a prevalence rate of 11.0 per 1,000 population for psychoses and 5.7 per 1,000 for oligophrenia. He finds this in excess of figures for all of Sweden in 1940, which were reported as 4.5 and 2.9 per 1,000, respectively. These latter figures, he thinks, are underenumerated. On the other hand, he finds that his figures are quite close to Stromgren's figures for the island of Bornholm in 1938, reported as 11.4 and 4.2 per 1,000, respectively. This comparison is reminiscent of that reported by Goldhamer and Marshall when they called attention to the fact that Kurt Fremming's expectancy for figures for various causes of mental disorders up to the age of 56 in the same island of Bornholm (1951) are of the same order and magnitude as those expectancy measures that Goldhamer and Marshall calculated for New York State.[26]

In view of the author's distinction between the epidemiological and ecological studies of mental cases, it is of some interest to note the contrast between the distribution of Sjögren's cases in his pedigree complex as compared with those cases outside the pedigree complex in four parishes of A:bo. While Sjögren does not present these figures, a slight computation based on the population of the parishes that he has given us reveals it. The computed rates on Sjögren's figures are shown in Table 9.1.

One notes that the cases in the pedigree complex are more highly concentrated in two of the parishes that are poorest in terms of socioeconomic level, while the cases outside the pedigree complex are distributed rather evenly over the four parishes, although the higher rates are in the other two parishes. This is noted because it seems contrary to what might be expected. Here, the expectation would be that the cases inside the pedigree complex showing hereditary linkages should be distributed more evenly over the four parishes,

TABLE 9.1

Number and Prevalence Rates of Cases of Psychoses and Psychopathy in Four Parishes of A:bo in and outside of Pedigree Complex

Parish	Average Population 1900-44	Number in Pedigree Complex	Rate*	Number Outside Pedigree Complex	Rate*	Total Cases	Rate*
S	4,071	89	21.9	71	17.4	160	39.3
V	1,749	33	18.9	28	16.0	61	34.9
R	2,334	7	3.0	49	21.0	56	24.0
K	1,232	1	0.8	30	24.4	31	25.2

*Rate per 1,000 general population

while the cases that supposedly have no genetic linkage should be more heavily concentrated in the two poorest parishes. This may mean that the sick people on this Swedish island who are sick because of some genetic characteristic find themselves in much poorer circumstances than those who are sick for other reasons. Thus those who are sick for other reasons come largely and somewhat evenly from all the social classes in this particular Swedish island.

Bremer's study of the frequency of psychiatric morbidity in a small fishing village in northern Norway from January 9, 1939, to April 1, 1944, attempts to combine the genetic emphasis that he thinks is characteristic of some U.S. studies.[27] While making his observations, his role was that of the local medical officer for the village during World War II. His findings, like Sjögren's, are quite comparable as he reports an overall percentage of about 12.9 for psychoses and psychopathy combined, and 5.56 for oligophrenia out of a total population of 1,080 persons over the age of ten years. The figure would be reduced slightly if 245 children under ten were included. He further goes on to examine the frequencies of the several types of psychiatric morbidity by occupation, race, migration, and wartime conditions.

His environmental emphasis is seen when he divides the total population into two groups: the secure group defined as self-supporting, 636 persons; and the insecure group described as on relief or spasmodically employed, 689 persons. He finds that the frequency of the psychoses is the same for both groups, the neuroses are more frequent in the secure group, and psychopathy and oligophrenia are more frequent in the insecure group.

In these two studies there is a definite attempt to present evidence showing genetic linkage, although there is a marked caution in interpreting the evidence. The other striking feature is the close agreement of the overall frequency for psychiatric morbidity. In truth, if the fact that no frequency variations for the psychoses and oligophrenia in the different kinds of communities in the Western world could be definitely validated, then there would be every reason to suspect that any variation of these disturbances within the social structures of a given Western society is spurious and could not be explained by social-psychological factors or processes.

Several hypotheses on a social-psychological level have been developed. These hypotheses tend to accept rate differentials by geographical areas and/or social space, and emphasize social factors that are supposed to be causative to a given mental disease or a group of diseases. If the validity of any one of these hypotheses could be established and it could be shown how the factor operates, then one would have a most satisfactory interpretation of any rate differentials by time, geography, or social space. Thus the social-isolation hypothesis, first proposed by Faris[28] and later developed in his work with this author,[29] was most applicable to schizophrenia.

Since the publication of Mental Disorders in Urban Areas, there have been numerous references to the isolation hypothesis in the literature, but only three studies have appeared that provide certain data for appraisal. Lemert attempts to give support to this hypothesis by showing the correlation between first admission rates of mental disease and the percentage of various nationalities by counties in Michigan.[30] His work added nothing and hardly could be taken as any test of the isolation hypothesis.

Jaco,[31] in a somewhat more ingenious fashion, attempts to develop a kind of index of social isolation by interviewing with a prepared schedule a carefully drawn sample of residents in four census tracts in Austin, Texas.[31] Two of these census tracts had high and low schizophrenic first admission rates, and the other two represented high and low manic-depressive first admission rates. He proposes 19 null hypotheses to point up the differences in isolation between high and low schizophrenic census tracts. He rejects 13 of these hypotheses and by this device infers that there is more social isolation in the high-rate schizophrenic tract than in the low-rate schizophrenic tract. In other words, he finds more schizophrenia in an area where persons show less contact and communication with one another. He does not show that persons who break down with schizophrenia are more isolated than those who do not.

This is just the point where Kohn and Clausen begin their study, for they see clearly that if there is anything to the isolation hypothesis, it will have to be established through careful study of persons who develop schizophrenia as against those who do not.[32] They selected a sample of 45 schizophrenic and 13 manic-depressive first admissions to mental hospitals from Hagerstown, Maryland. They then secured a group of controls paired individually with the patients on the basis of age, sex, and occupation. The persons comprising the four samples were then interviewed through a schedule that covered the following topics: residential and occupational history, parental family relationships, friendships and activities of early adolescence, dating patterns, adult social participation, and a brief psychosomatic inventory.

They proceed to make careful qualitative analyses of their interview data and come up with the following findings: about one third of schizophrenic and manic-depressive patients, as compared to none of the controls, show evidence of being socially isolated at ages 13-14; there was no evidence that isolated patients were prevented from interacting with their peers because of lack of playmates, excessive morbidity, severe illness, or parental restrictions; and no difference was found between patients and controls in their perceptions of family relationships.

The investigators recognize that their data are based on retrospective impressions of a group of patients, but find also that their data secured from 26 out of 30 patients check favorably with the material in the hospital records. Their general conclusion is that "the data do not support the hypothesis that social isolation in adolescence is a predisposing factor in either schizophrenia or manic-depressive psychosis." They think that in those cases showing social isolation, there is an indication that a person's interpersonal difficulties are so great that he cannot very well continue to function in this area. Rather, it is a question of how he got that way in the first place so that he takes isolation as a way out. Further research along this line utilizing other research designs is very much needed for the study of isolation in the early years.

Gruenberg in his preliminary report on an ecological study of old-age psychoses in Syracuse, New York, raises the question as to whether the patients who were not living alone were experiencing a process of social isolation. He feels that effort should be directed to discovering if such isolation is symptomatic or causative.[33]

Another hypothesis on the social-psychological level has centered around the issue involved in the migration of peoples. The central questions are: Do persons who migrate from one place to another have a higher rate of mental disease than persons who live out their lives in a given community? If they do, is this higher rate caused by persons who are prone to a given mental disease moving around, or is the higher rate caused by the fact that migratory persons are subjected to more severe stress than persons that have stayed home? These questions have been thought at times to be particularly relevant to schizophrenia.

During the latter part of the nineteenth century much effort was expended by commissions and analysts to show that the higher rate of mental disease among the foreign born was due to the defective character of the biological stock represented by the immigrants. This position was very much undercut by Malzberg when he attempted to analyze first admission data by age, sex, nativity, race, and economic group.[34] His results cast much doubt on the earlier position and at least serve to refute the notion that European countries were dumping their defective stocks on American shores. However, Malzberg's efforts cannot be taken as a disproof of the genetic factor in certain types of mental disease, or as proof that rate differentials between natives and the foreign born are the result of a difference in environmental conditions to which the different nationality groups have been subjected. Even so, it became somewhat fashionable in the 1930s to regard the higher rates of the foreign born and the native born of mixed parentage as due to the difficulties of adjustment to new cultural conditions. Ødegaard challenged this conception in his study of the Norwegians who had migrated to Minnesota.[35] He interprets the higher rate of schizophrenic disorders among Norwegians who migrated to Minnesota as compared to Norwegians who stayed at home as due to the fact that those who are more organically predisposed are more likely to migrate. But, like Malzberg, Ødegaard's evidence for the validity of his interpretation of rate differentials is inconclusive.

Tietze, Lemkau, and Cooper in their study add no new dimension to the problem when they show that higher rates of psychopathy are found among those persons who move frequently, as compared to those who reside for a long period in the same house.[36] They also found that the rates were higher for intracity migrants than for migrants from other communities. Again, one has difficulty in determining whether persons who migrate are more likely to be psychiatrically ill, or more likely to become psychiatrically ill because they migrate. One might develop a cultural integration hypothesis with regard to the above data. Persons who are firmly rooted and integrated in the culture of a community have a minimum probability of developing a functional mental disorder as compared to those who are not so well integrated.

Another hypothesis on this level is one that emphasizes the etiological role of a multiplicity of stress conditions in the social environment. This is a broad general hypothesis, less specific than the two discussed above, and stems in a large degree from the work of Faris and this author.[37] This work was set in a broad theory of social organization-disorganization. It portrayed the city as having certain areas of marked disorganization characterized by cultural conflict, minimum concensus, slum dwellings, high population density, and high land values. The idea was that these areas of social disorganization produced disorganized persons and consequently more crime, delinquency, sickness, mental disease, and suicide were to be expected in these areas.

A. H. Leighton's Stirling County study has been particularly designed to deal with the multiple environmental stress hypothesis. While the final report of this study is not yet available, there have been several accounts in the literature indicative of the trend that the research has taken. Leighton himself has provided a statement of theory with a derived hypothesis that the research supposedly will test.[38] Dohrenwend, a social analyst on the project, has provided a rather complete statement of the theory and objectives of the study. In line with the attempt to get at the etiological significance of certain sociocultural factors, Dohrenwend states the central hypothesis, "that social disorganization impinges on such needs of the individual as those for physical security, sexual satisfaction, the expression and securing of love, the securing of recognition, and the expression of creativity, thereby producing psychological stress and disruption."[39] Again in line with their general objectives, D. C. Leighton reports on the prevalence of psychiatric symptoms in a small town of 3,000 population on the basis of record searches and interviews.[40] She reports that a much wider distribution of psychiatric symptoms exists than is commonly believed, and estimates that approximately 37 percent of the adult population in this town are psychiatric cases whether under treatment or not. This bears a close relationship to the study by Rennie and Srole where they attempt to show the prevalence of certain psychosomatic conditions in relation to social class.[41]

These last three hypotheses derive rather clearly from a type of ecological theory. The hypotheses, broadly considered, can be viewed as inferences from differential rate distributions of mental disease, particularly schizophrenia. The author turns now to a series of hypotheses that derive from what he has designated as the social system level. In this sense society is viewed as a functioning social system through space and time that sifts and sorts certain vulnerable personalities so that they get into either environments where the probability of a mental breakdown is increased or decreased, or certain subcultural pockets that serve either to precipitate or induce a mental breakdown. The general hypotheses here can be designated as social selection. In other words, certain persons because of age, sex, personality traits, intelligence, emotional instability, and psychotic proneness are selected for certain positions in occupational groups, city areas, marital status categories, institutions, and the like in contrast to other positions in these structures as the social system moves through time. This process may be either active or passive as far as the person is concerned, and through it one can account for significant differences in the rates for mental disease.

There are four hypotheses that appear in the literature that represent various ways of stating the more general hypothesis of social selection. These four hypotheses are:

Certain persons because of personality inadequacies or mental disease proneness have a tendency to drift into certain social classes, subcultures, or city areas.

Visibility of, and tolerance for, mental disorder vary with the attitudinal structure of different types of communities.

Certain persons, because of their psychic needs to break their social ties, tend to select and segregate themselves in areas, cultural or spatial, marked by anonymity.

As the size of the city decreases, rate differentials between socioeconomic areas tend to disappear.

The intention at this point is to examine several of the more significant epidemiological studies in this area that have appeared during the last 15 years, and to show the manner in which these studies have called upon these hypotheses for negation or validity of the rate differentials that they have reported. In the earlier Chicago study by Faris and this author, the procedure was primarily empirical even though set in the social organization-disorganization theoretical framework. The study started out with the question as to whether or not the distribution of mental disorder would follow the pattern of rates that seemed to characterize the distribution of other social problems in the city.[42]

The contemporary research worker in this area, being more design conscious, generally sets up a series of statistical hypotheses that he purports to test for validity. This procedure is well illustrated by Jaco's study of the distribution of mental disease in Texas,[43] and the Hollingshead-Redlich study of the prevalence of treated mental disease in the class structure of New Haven.[44]

Jaco begins his study with three hypotheses:

> The probability of acquiring a psychosis is not random or equal among subgroups of the population;
>
> Inhabitants of different areas exhibit different incidences of psychoses; and
>
> Persons with different social attributes or affiliations have different incidences of psychoses.

Jaco finds that his evidence gives support to his three central hypotheses. He is well aware that there may be a significant gap between true and treated case incidence. However, his findings might as easily be interpreted through the general social selection hypothesis as they can be with respect to industrialization, anomie, and enculturation. The interesting fact that his findings in certain instances run counter to the findings of other studies should give one pause. For example, his high rates for both males and females among professionals and semiprofessionals cannot be easily explained away by the marginal status supposedly enjoyed by this group in Texas. Again, his low rates among Spanish-Americans for both males and females are unexpected and contrast rather sharply with the high rates frequently reported for various ethnic groups in northern states. This might be caused by the fact, as Jaco suggests, that the Spanish-Americans are not well integrated into the dominant Anglo-American group and also have a very protective kinship system. It also may be explained by the hypothesis that the visibility and tolerance for mental disorders in this group is at variance with the dominant Anglo-American group. Again, much more research will be needed to show that a closed, intact, integrated group has less mental disorder than one that is less integrated around a common core of values. Eaton's findings for the Hutterites might prove to be an example of a negative case.

The point to be made here is that when Jaco's findings run counter to findings of other studies, like other investigators he tries to account for them by social factors, even though the total evidence is contradictory. His hypotheses are broad statistical statements, which, while no doubt true enough in terms of his evidence, provide one with no basis for accounting for the rate differentials as found in age, sex, marital, occupational, or ethnic groups. He could just as easily have used some hypothesis centering on social selection, which he seems fairly close to doing, when trying to interpret the lower rates among the different age and sex categories of Spanish-Americans.

Examine now the Hollingshead-Redlich hypotheses, also three in number:

> The prevalence of treated mental illness is related significantly to an individual's position in the class structure;
>
> The types of diagnosed psychiatric disorders are connected significantly to the class structure; and
>
> The kind of psychiatric treatment administered by psychiatrists is associated with the patient's position in the class structure.

Much the same sort of criticism can be centered on this study of social class and mental illness. While their organized data give support to their hypotheses, their study is largely of prevalence and the concern here is with incidence rates, for these should give some clues as to whether social factors bear some relationship to the etiology of mental disease. Here the expectancy would be that if social class factors have some relevance for etiology, one would expect that incidence rates for a given disorder would have a significantly inverse relation to the class structure. Further, one would have to establish that the higher rate of persons in the lowest class is made up of persons who originated in that class. This is under the assumption that the conditions of life at a lower class level in society are more likely to be psychosis inducing than other kinds of life conditions enjoyed by the other social classes.

Hollingshead and Redlich do have several tables of incidence rates constructed from those persons who entered treatment for the first time during their six months observation period. When they compute the rates based on these cases for the four social classes, they find, using the chi-square test, that the difference is significant at the 5 percent level. However, the rates do not vary inversely with class as shown by the following:[45]

Class	Rate
I-II	97
III	114
IV	89
V	139

These data are based on all the cases of mental illness that entered treatment for the first time. When this total group is broken up into neurotic and psychotic groups, the incidence rates for the neurotics do not vary with class structure. Class IV has the lowest rate and class III the highest rate, with classes I-II and V having rates of 69 and 66, respectively. However, in the case of the psychotic group the incidence rates vary with the class structure but the differential in the first three classes is probably not significant, while the class V rate is twice that of the other rates. This might indicate that class V contains many more psychotics than might be expected provided that they started in class V. This the authors later try to show in discussing the drift hypothesis. Their Table 17 shows that schizophrenic incidence rates vary with the class structure, although there may be questions of whether or not the differences between the classes are significant or the case basis for the classes is sufficient for claiming a difference.

In this study these data, as presented above, might constitute the evidence for arguing that the influence of life conditions on a given class level plays some role in the development of a particular psychosis. But the case is not proven beyond any doubt. The concentration of the higher incidence of psychoses in class V might just as easily be regarded as due to some form of social selection—a hypothesis that is not stated in their work. The denial that the neuroses are linked to class does not quite stand up as the prevalence rates for neuroses vary directly with the class structure and is certainly a function of the fact that the upper social levels in New Haven society have more money to spend on this type of personality perturbation.[46]

In one of their articles, Hollingshead and Redlich suggest a social selection hypothesis when they state that "current prevalence is a measure of the responses patients in the several classes make to the treatment process." They label this as the "differential treatment hypothesis."[47]

Some data from England serve as a challenge to the New Haven study. In an address before the British Sociological Society, Morris presented the rates for England and Wales shown in Table 9.2.[48]

He then asks the ever-present question: "Is this fact caused by a downward drift of men to Class V or by the social and familial

TABLE 9.2

First Admissions for Schizophrenia (per 100,000 men age 20 and over) in 1949-53 in the Five Social Classes

Class	I	II	III	IV	V
Rate	51	57	93	103	229

environment in Class V that tends to produce an excess of schizophrenia?" He then points to a study that has classified a national sample of schizophrenics, ages 25-34, by occupation and social class, and then classified their fathers by occupation and social class on the basis of an examination of birth certificates. The answer was clear. There was an excess of schizophrenics in class V, but their fathers were distributed rather evenly over the five classes. This seems to indicate that the patients experienced a downward drop because of their illness, which explains their excess in class V. Thus here in this study the schizophrenic illness operates as a selective factor or, from the opposite angle, the social system functions to place these men in class V.

Stein's study of class and schizophrenia is relevant here because her findings also contradict some U.S. results.[49] She proceeds by selecting four East London boroughs (E) outstanding for their high proportion of men in classes IV and V, and five West London boroughs (W) outstanding because of their high proportion of men in classes I and II. She then tabulates the first admissions to mental hospitals from E and W boroughs for 1954-55 by age, sex, and three diagnostic groups: schizophrenic, manic-depressive, and psychoneurotic. The results run contrary to those found for U.S. cities. Her findings showed that the W boroughs had significantly higher rates in practically all age and sex categories as compared to the E boroughs. This held true, in general, for schizophrenia and psychoneuroses; it was less marked in the manic-depressive group. She then proceeds to distribute these data among the social classes in the two sets of boroughs. While the rates still are higher in W, she does find in both areas that they vary inversely and consistently with the class structure and for all three diagnostic groups. While she concluded that there was a real class gradient in the inception of schizophrenia, she thinks these results must be qualified because of the radical differences between the E and W boroughs in the sex ratio, number of persons living alone, types of private households and origins of the population. These differences signify that a single index of social class may not be too meaningful.

In another study from England, Carstairs and Brown attempt to get at the incidence and prevalence of psychiatric disorders in two different types of communities: Rhondda, a coal-mining region, and Vale, an agricultural area.[50] Rhondda had a more densely concentrated population than Vale, which was rural and spread over a wide area. Rhondda was found to have more psychiatric cases than Vale (3.8 to 2.6 per 1,000 population). They also found that in Rhondda psychiatric cases were more heavily concentrated in the nonminer group. This might be regarded as an instance of the vulnerability of a minority group, but the investigators are more inclined to think it is an example of adverse selection. They conclude that the linking of social pressures to psychiatric disorders must wait upon an analysis of the social structure and value system of a community, the circumstances leading to the emergence of declared cases and the carrying of undeclared cases in each community, and the clinical features of the illnesses.

Ødegaard has been one of the most constant proponents of the social selection hypothesis. From his earlier study of emigration where he emphasized the tendency of psychiatrically vulnerable persons to migrate,[51] to his more recent analysis of psychiatric cases in relation to the occupational structure of Norway,[52] he has generally attempted to show that social selection versus environmental stress provides the most enlightening explanation for the rate differentials in various social structures. His study of the incidence of psychoses in the various occupations analyzes 34,457 first admissions to Norwegian mental hospitals, 1926-50. He finds the highest admission rates among those occupations with the lowest social prestige. The highest rate is in the seamen of the merchant marine. This holds for all psychotic groups with the exception of epilepsy, mental deficiency, and manic-depressive psychosis, although in these diagnostic categories the seamen are second from the top rate. Ødegaard explains this by a social selection process as well as a secondary selection that takes place when men around 30 seek other occupations, leaving the unstable and psychopathic types in the seaman's group. His finding that the high rates of manic-depressives are in the more favored occupational groups is in conformity with U.S. results, but the mechanism of social selection is more evident for schizophrenia and for the psychoses with epilepsy and mental deficiency. He also thinks that social stress and protection are not explanatory of the distribution of psychoses in the occupational structure.

It is of some significance to note that the hypothesis of social selection frequently is urged when dealing with such special structured institutions as the army, merchant marine, or prison. Winston in her study of psychoses in the army asks "Does mental disease act as a further selective factor in the already highly selected military group?"[53] While she reports no tendency for mental disease to increase in the army, she does find that the psychological misfits are weeded out eventually so that mental disease tends to decrease as length of service increases. This was the opposite of Ødegaard's findings with respect to the merchant seamen, but probably means only that the seamen make a voluntary choice to leave the service while the army actively weeds out those who cannot fit into the rigors of army life.

Sims, in a study of noncommissioned officers in the British Army, Dominion Army, and prisoners of war, also suggests that the difference in the incidence of the disease in the various groups is due to high selection standards.[54] He further reports that there is, in addition, a secondary selection as many recruits are weeded out in basic training and this lowers the incidence among those who get overseas. Ekblad also supports Ødegaard's social selection hypothesis when he shows that his sample of seamen have higher rates for psychopathy and schizophrenia when compared with non-seamen in naval training.[55]

These studies have been examined to illustrate the application of the social selection hypotheses when applied to certain rate differentials in selected social structures. It seems to be much clearer in application when dealing with occupational, marital status, and specific institutional structures than it is when applied to social classes or geographical areas. In the latter the problem is much more complex, although even here the social selection hypothesis must be considered. In essence it is an hypothesis that explains significant rate variations as due to the manner in which a given social system functions through time, and in its functioning tends to sort and sift persons into class and community positions.

As indicated above, there are a number of more specific hypotheses that stem from this general hypothesis and these will be examined now. Both the drifting and segregation hypotheses are variations of social selection. Drifting implies an involuntary segregation and results from the automatic functioning of a social system through time. Segregation implies a voluntary, conscious selection of a preferred place of residence in a community. The drifting hypothesis came into focus over 20 years ago as an attack on the rate distributions for the various psychoses in Chicago and Providence that Faris and this author presented. At the time Faris and this author argued that the concentration of the younger catatonics and paranoids was quite similar to the concentration of older cases, and this fact argued against the thesis that the pattern could be explained by drift alone. This issue was examined by investigators by locating the addresses of a sample of schizophrenics from Buffalo 20 years prior to their first admission to state mental hospitals during 1949-51.[56] They concluded that the concentration of schizophrenic cases in low-income areas was not the result of downward drift from better areas. They further showed that the high rates are not caused by the drift of men living alone.

Hollingshead and Redlich also faced this issue since much of their results would be dependent upon the fact that mental patients are not excessively mobile by class. They examined for their schizophrenic group four sets of data: the nativity of schizophrenics compared with the nativity of adult population in the community; the birthplace of native-born schizophrenics in relation to class; the past addresses of schizophrenics; and the class position of their families of orientation as compared with their own social class position. From these data they concluded that there was no evidence of a downward class drift of schizophrenics. In fact, the evidence showed that 91 percent of the patients were in the same class as their families of orientation. These data raise certain questions about the class mobility of patients. What is the class mobility of the residents of the community itself? Are schizophrenic patients less mobile by social class than nonschizophrenics in the community? One might well expect that they would be, but how then does one account for those observations that schizophrenics are more likely to be geographically mobile than nonschizophrenics?

Prior to the Buffalo study Gerard and Houston, on the basis of studying an ecological distribution of male schizophrenics in Worcester, Massachusetts, concluded that the high rates of schizophrenia in the low socioeconomic areas are to be largely explained by patients living alone.[57] They found that patients coming from families showed marked residential stability and those patients not in families showed marked residential instability. They suggest the hypothesis that these nonfamily men used residential instability as a means of protecting themselves against involvement in disruptive family relationships. Thus they imply the segregation hypothesis.

Hare uses this hypothesis to explain the concentration of schizophrenic cases in Bristol, England.[58] He starts out by trying to check on the Chicago findings to determine if there is additional evidence for supporting the social isolation hypothesis. He shows, like the Chicago findings, that the schizophrenics were concentrated in the central areas while the manic-depressives were more widely distributed. He points out that the high rate in both good and poor central areas is related to the factor of living alone, thus supporting Gerard and Houston. He also raises the alternative, namely, that the concentration of schizophrenics is to be explained either by segregation or the causal effect of the environment.

Another hypothesis that is a variation on the social selection theme stresses the differential visibility and tolerance of areal populations for mental abnormality that, in turn, accounts for rate differentials in different communities. Owen first raised this question years ago when suggesting that this hypothesis might explain Faris and this author's contrasting distributions of paranoid and catatonic schizophrenics.[59] In a more recent study there was an attempt to test the hypothesis that if a difference in demand for hospitalization causes higher urban rates, the urban excess should be predominantly in the rate for cases whose symptoms are sufficiently tolerable socially that care outside of a hospital would be possible.[60] The investigators then proceeded to examine the rural and urban first admissions in Western Ontario, broken down so as to give rates for severity of symptoms for age groups 45-64 and 65 and over. Their results showed that for the age groups studied, the excess urban admission rate is almost entirely explained by the greater urban tendency to hospitalize cases whose symptoms would be tolerated in a rural community. They conclude that this device may be useful in distinguishing between the real and apparent difference in rates of mental disease.

Finally, there is the hypothesis that as the size of the city decreases, the rates tend to approach a parity for the different socioeconomic areas. This proposition was demonstrated rather sharply by a study of the distribution of first admissions of schizophrenics in Hagerstown, Maryland.[61] The findings are extremely pertinent for they contradict the Chicago findings, and by implication raise questions about the spurious quality of the rate differences found in a large city. The findings show that there is no difference between the schizophrenic rates in Hagerstown and the remainder of the country, and no difference between the rates in five areas of Hagerstown arranged on the basis of a rental value index. They also show that the absence of areal rate differences cannot be explained by shifts in diagnosis or unusual upward or downward mobility. Five possible interpretations of these findings are offered, but the one favored by the investigators is that the differences in socioeconomic areas of a small city, like Hagerstown, are not sharp enough to show the differences that the large cities produce. They conclude with the question: "In the constellation of values, attitudes, behaviors, and relationships that are generally indexed by socioeconomic status, by occupation, education and area of residence, what are the factors that are crucially related to schizophrenia?"

In this review of social structures and mental disorders, the author has attempted to concentrate on the various hypotheses that purport to explain significant rate differentials in selected social structures. The fact that the rate distribution in different social structures varies for the different diagnostic groups makes the attempt to interpret total mental disease rate differentials of doubtful etiological value. From an environmental perspective, interest is greater for the so-called functional disorders, but even here the evidence is highly inconclusive for asserting with any confidence that a high rate in a given position of a social structure is a product of certain stresses, strains, and conflicts in that position.

The author also has attempted to show that certain basic methodological orientations about the nature of individuals in human society enter into the way one views these rate differentials. This is partially reflected in the contrast between the European epidemiological studies and the U.S. ecological studies of mental disease, and between those investigators with a biological orientation and those with a sociological orientation.

Biological, social-psychological, and social system theory have been productive of various hypotheses to account for significant rate differentials in social structure. Biological hypotheses have been largely interested in the comparative count of psychiatric cases in different population groups. Here, rate differentials are to be explained away. In contrast, social-psychological hypotheses are likely to assume that rate differentials have been reliably established and then to validate the hypotheses by other research designs. To date, the results on this level have been inconclusive.

On the social system level, the hypotheses have been generally directed to showing how the rate differentials are functions of the manner in which the social process works in communities and social structures. One has certain sociological hypotheses that give added knowledge about the social system, but are not stated in a form that can show the relevance of sociocultural factors for the production of specific mental abnormalities. The task that the social scientists face here is to be able to show that certain stresses from a given position in a social structure make such an ingression into a given human experience that his mental content and behavior emerge in such bizarre ways that he can be fitted only into the social structure by some form of restraint. Then, too, from the standpoint of prevention there is a need to know the positions in the social structure to which the more bizarre behavior types can become adapted.

It is not without point to note that in addition to trying to correct certain behaviors and make them more acceptable, people also must learn to live with the type of personality structure that, through events and experiences, they have made for themselves. In any event, the task of the social scientist in this area is not likely to be facilitated until the clinician has developed methods for isolating those persons who will not break down with a mental disease no matter how extreme the adverse, traumatic, or discouraging elements in their life will be. On the other side of the ledger, it may be that these epidemiological studies of specific mental diseases can provide some clues for distinguishing between different kinds of abnormal personalities that are caught up in the network of an existing diagnostic category.

NOTES

1. W. A. N. Dorland and E. C. L. Miller, The American Illustrated Medical Dictionary, 20th ed. (Philadelphia and London: W. B. Saunders, 1944).

2. B. M. Cohen and R. E. Fairbank, "Statistical Contributions from Mental Hygiene Study of Eastern Health District: General Account of 1933 Mental Hygiene Survey of Eastern Health District," American Journal of Psychiatry 94 (March 1938): 1153-64; and idem, "Psychosis in Eastern Health District: Incidence and Prevalence of Psychosis in Eastern Health District in 1933," American Journal of Psychiatry 94 (May 1938): 1377-95.

3. W. F. Roth and F. H. Luton, "Mental Health Program in Tennessee; Description of Original Study Program: Statistical Report of Psychiatric Survey in Rural County," American Journal of Psychiatry 99 (March 1943): 662-75.

4. J. Eaton and R. J. Weil, Culture and Mental Disorders: A Comparative Study of the Hutterites and Other Populations (Glencoe, Ill. Free Press, 1955).

5. Lin, T., "Study of Incidence of Mental Disorder in Chinese and Other Cultures," Psychiatry 16 (November 1953): 313-36.

6. Eaton and Weil, Culture and Mental Disorders, p. 78.

7. Ibid., p. 85.

8. Ibid., p. 46.

9. J. Bremer, "Social Psychiatric Investigation of a Small Community in Northern Norway," Acta psychiatrica et neurologica scandinavica, Supplement no. 62 (1951).

10. Dorland and Miller, Medical Dictionary.

11. R. M. Frumkin, "Occupation and Major Mental Disorders," in Mental Health and Mental Disorder: A Sociological Approach, ed. A. Rose (New York: W. W. Norton, 1955).

12. Ibid., pp. 153-55.

13. Milbank Memorial Fund, Interrelations between the Social Environment and Psychiatric Disorders (New York: Milbank Memorial Fund, 1953): 117-57; and S. M. Miller and E. G. Mishler, "Social Class, Mental Illness and American Psychiatry: An Expository Review," Milbank Memorial Fund Quarterly 37 (April 1959): 174-99.

14. R. E. Clark, "The Relationship of Schizophrenia to Occupational Income and Occupational Prestige," American Sociological Review 13 (June 1948): 325-30.

15. E. G. Jaco, "Social Factors in Mental Disorders in Texas," *Social Problems* 4 (April 1957): 322-28. See also idem, "Incidence of Psychoses in Texas, 1951-52," *Texas State Journal of Medicine* 33 (February 1951): 86-91.

16. R. E. L. Faris and H. W. Dunham, *Mental Disorders in Urban Areas: An Ecological Study of Schizophrenia and Other Psychoses* (Chicago: University of Chicago Press, 1939).

17. H. Goldhamer and A. W. Marshall, *Psychosis and Civilization: Two Studies in the Frequency of Mental Disease*. Glencoe, Ill.: Free Press, 1953).

18. A. Hollingshead and F. Redlich, *Social Class and Mental Illness* (New York: John Wiley & Sons, 1958).

19. M. Kramer et al., "Historical Study of the Disposition of First Admissions to a State Mental Hospital: Experience of the Warren State Hospital during the Period 1916-50," Public Health Monograph no. 32, Public Health Service Publication no. 445 (Washington, D.C.: Government Printing Office, 1955).

20. Ø. Ødegaard, "Distribution of Mental Diseases in Norway: Contribution to the Ecology of Mental Disorder," *Acta psychiatrica et neurologica* 20 (1945): 247-84.

21. Ø. Ødegaard, "Incidence of Mental Diseases in Norway during World War II," *Acta psychiatrica et neurologica scandinavica* 29 (1954): 333-53.

22. B. Malzberg, *Social and Biological Aspects of Mental Disease* (Utica, N.Y.: State Hospitals Press, 1940), p. 45.

23. Bremer, "Northern Norway."

24. T. Sjögren, "Genetic-statistical and Psychiatric Investigations of West Swedish Population," *Acta psychiatrica et neurologica*, Supplement no. 52 (1948).

25. Ibid., pp. 12-13.

26. Goldhamer and Marshall, *Psychosis and Civilization*, pp. 14-15.

27. Bremer, "Northern Norway."

28. R. E. L. Faris, "Cultural Isolation and the Schizophrenic Personality," *American Journal of Sociology* 40 (September 1934): 155-64.

29. Faris and Dunham, *Mental Disorders in Urban Areas*.

30. E. M. Lemert, "An Exploratory Study of Mental Disorders in a Rural Problem Area," *Rural Sociology* 13 (March 1948): 48-64.

31. E. G. Jaco, "The Social Isolation Hypothesis and Schizophrenia," *American Sociological Review* 19 (October 1954): 567-77.

32. M. L. Kohn and J. A. Clausen, "Social Isolation and Schizophrenia," *American Sociological Review* 20 (June 1955): 265-73.

33. E. M. Gruenberg, "Community Conditions and Psychoses of the Elderly," *American Journal of Psychiatry* 110 (June 1954): 888-96.

34. Malzberg, Social and Biological Aspects, chap. 6.

35. Ø. Ødegaard, "Emigration and Mental Health," Mental Hygiene 20 (October 1936):546-53.

36. C. Tietze, P. Lemkau, and M. Cooper, "Personality Disorder and Spatial Mobility," American Journal of Sociology 48 (July 1942):29-39.

37. Faris and Dunham, Mental Disorders in Urban Areas.

38. A. H. Leighton, "Psychiatric Disorder and Social Environment: Outline for Frame of Reference," Psychiatry 18 (November 1955):367-83.

39. B. P. Dohrenwend, "The Stirling County Study: A Research Program on Relations between Sociocultural Factors and Mental Illness," American Psychologist 12 (February 1957):78-85.

40. D. C. Leighton, "Distribution of Psychiatric Symptoms in a Small Town," American Journal of Psychiatry 112 (March 1956): 716-23.

41. T. A. C. Rennie and L. Srole, "Social Class Prevalence and Distribution of Psychosomatic Conditions in an Urban Population," Psychosomatic Medicine 18 (November-December 1956):449-56.

42. Faris and Dunham, Mental Disorders in Urban Areas, p. 22.

43. Jaco, "Incidence of Psychoses in Texas."

44. Hollingshead and Redlich, Social Class and Mental Illness.

45. Ibid., table on p. 12.

46. Ibid., p. 235.

47. A. Hollingshead and F. Redlich, "Social Stratification and Schizophrenia," American Sociological Review 19 (June 1954): 302-06.

48. J. N. Morris, "Health and Social Class: Address to the British Sociological Association, January 24, 1959," Lancet 1 (February 7, 1959):303-05.

49. L. Stein, "'Social Class' Gradient in Schizophrenia," British Journal of Preventive and Social Medicine 11 (October 1957): 181-95; and Symposium on Preventive and Social Psychiatry, sponsored jointly by the Walter Reed Army Institute of Research, the Walter Reed Army Medical Center, and the National Research Council, April 15-17, 1957, at the Walter Reed Army Institute of Research (Washington, D.C.: Government Printing Office, 1958), p. 199.

50. G. M. Carstairs and G. W. Brown, "A Census of Psychiatric Cases in Two Contrasting Communities," Journal of Mental Science 104 (January 1956): 72-81.

51. Ødegaard, "Emigration and Mental Health."

52. Ø. Ødegaard, "The Incidence of Psychoses in Various Occupations," International Journal of Social Psychiatry 2 (Autumn 1956):85-104.

53. E. Winston, "Mental Disease and the Army," Mental Hygiene (April 1935): 281-88.

54. M. Sims, "Comparative Study of Disease Incidence in Admissions to Base Psychiatric Hospital in Middle East," Journal of Mental Science 92 (January 1946): 118-27.

55. M. Ekblad, "Psychiatric and Sociologic Study of Series of Swedish Naval Conscripts," Acta psychiatrica et neurologica, Supplement no. 49 (1948): 1-201.

56. R. Lapouse, M. A. Monk, and M. Terris, "Drift Hypothesis and Socioeconomic Differentials in Schizophrenia," American Journal of Public Health and the Nation's Health 46 (August 1956): 978-86.

57. D. L. Gerard and L. G. Houston, "Family Setting and Social Ecology of Schizophrenia," Psychiatric Quarterly 27 (January 1953): 90-101.

58. E. H. Hare, "Mental Illness and Social Conditions in Bristol," Journal of Mental Science 102 (April 1956): 349-57.

59. M. B. Owen, "Alternative Hypotheses for the Explanation of Some of Faris and Dunham's Results," American Journal of Sociology 47 (July 1941): 48-52.

60. C. Buck, J. M. Wanklin, and G. E. Hobbs, "Symptom Analysis of Rural-Urban Differences in First Admission Rates," Journal of Nervous and Mental Disease 122 (July 1955): 80-82.

61. J. A. Clausen and M. L. Kohn, "Relation of Schizophrenia to the Social Structure of a Small City," in Epidemiology of Mental Disorder, ed. B. Pasamanick, Publication no. 60 (Washington, D.C.: American Association for the Advancement of Science, 1959), pp. 69-94.

10

PSYCHIATRIC EPIDEMIOLOGY AND MEDICAL ECOLOGY

The central objective of this chapter is to examine the contributions that epidemiological studies of psychiatric disorders have made to the current knowledge about these disorders. These studies are viewed as contributions to medical ecology as well as to the larger, general area that has been gradually emerging as sociological psychiatry. In order to place the review of these epidemiological studies in proper perspective, it is essential to explore the various conceptions that have been held concerning the nature of human ecology; show the relationship between the broad field of human ecology and medical ecology; point to the distinguishing characteristics between epidemiology and medical ecology; and examine the obstacles that confront any investigator who studies mental illness from an epidemiological perspective.

The term ecology has had an erratic development and also an erratic use, particularly when trying to encompass human life. The term was first used by Ernst Haeckel in 1870 when he attempted to develop some logical framework for the study of animal life.[1] He divided physiology into inner and outer phenomena. The outer physiology was to be recognized as ecology. By this taxonomic device Haeckel intended to study the impact of the animal's inorganic and organic environments upon its physiological processes. The extension of ecology to human life came several decades later.

Used with permission from Archives of General Psychiatry 14 (January 1966): 1-19.

CONCEPTIONS OF HUMAN ECOLOGY

There are three conceptions of human ecology. First, human ecology, from the perspective of medicine, tended to become medical ecology that emphasized the environmental relationships with respect to health and disease of human beings. Health was viewed as the maintenance of a delicate balance between a disease agent, organism, and environment; disease results when this balance is shattered. Medical ecology developed a close affinity with the epidemiological study of various diseases, where an attempt was made to develop etiological hypotheses from any one of a number of theoretical frameworks to explain the concentration of a given disease in a particular environmental setting.

Second, human ecology also has been regarded as coterminous with human geography, which was the discipline concerned with examining the role of climate, topography, and vegetation in relation to the varieties of human behavior and social organization.[2]

Third, human ecology, in the hands of the sociologist, was developed as a discipline that focused upon the study of the settling, growth, and decline of human communities. In sociology, Robert Park is recognized as the founder of human ecology.[3] Borrowing certain concepts from plant and animal ecologists, Park attempted to show their relevance to human society and, as in the case of animal and plant societies, to point to the consequences for human beings resulting from ecological processes. It might be noted that in the latter part of the nineteenth century the application of the Darwinian theory to encompass the growth and decline of societies, by reference to the unrelenting struggle for existence that characterized the state of nature for plants and animals, foreshadowed the development of human ecology.

Park saw that human society differed from the uncontaminated jungle of animal life because each human society had a cultural or a moral order that set boundaries and limitations to the completely free working of the ecological order. Even so, much knowledge could be gained by viewing the individual in what Park termed ecological space, and studying the events and happenings that impinged upon him. Thus ecology, which has been defined as "the science of organisms as affected by the factors of their environment," or "the studies of the environment and life history of organisms," was extended by Park to encompass not only the physical but also the social and cultural environments of human beings.[4] Consequently, human ecology became a study of the individual within a social system, locating his position within that system and examining his position in relation to the positions occupied by others in the system. Therefore human ecology is one possible model for the study of the individual and is concerned with the examination of that balance of environmental elements that would be necessary for survival within the system. It should be clear that ecology, whether plant, animal, or human, is concerned with the phenotype (what the organism becomes) in contrast to the genotype (what the organism is at conception).

The difficulty with the classical statement of human ecological theory is that it posits people as being willy-nilly at the mercy of the inevitable and mechanical operation of ecological processes at the symbiotic level. The theory provided no postulate that would view the individual as an active cultural agent attempting to shape and remold the type of sociocultural environment that has evolved for and by him through time. Thus what is natural in terms of biological ecology ceases to be completely natural, at least in a biological sense, when shifted to the human level. This is aptly noted by the hypothesis of drift[5] as contrasted to the hypothesis of voluntary segregation,[6] both of which have been utilized to explain the differential distribution of schizophrenic rates in an urban setting. In the former hypothesis the person is pictured as rudderless and at the mercy of the impersonal ecological processes. The latter hypothesis depicts the person as actively searching and seeking the kind of environment that will maximize his chances for maintenance and survival. These two hypotheses illustrate quite clearly the original conception of human ecology and the later difficulty it has encountered as a theoretical model for depicting the individual's involvement with his environment in order to explain both his successful and unsuccessful adaptations.

However, this difficulty at the outset was not the concern of the human ecologist. Rather, it was only natural that within this theoretical model the many varieties of human behavior could be examined to determine the extent that they encouraged or discouraged the possibility of the individual's adjustment and survival. Within this framework many kinds of deviant behaviors that are evaluated as disruptive of the social order have been examined (see notes 7 through 14). It was only natural that the various diseases an individual acquires, either through heredity or environment, also should be examined in relation to the ecological order. This was particularly true with respect to the various kinds of mental illnesses because here were instances of mental aberrations and distorted behaviors that, at first glance, seemed to grow out of the kinds of experiences in interpersonal relations that the individual had in selected subcultural environments.

What has been said already should indicate clearly the relationship between human and medical ecology. The human ecologist attempts a study of the individual in relation to his total environment, trying to ferret out those generalizations that explain the ease or difficulty of his adjustments and explain the kinds of communities that develop in relation to the total conditions that surround him. There are difficulties in studying human beings from this perspective because they are both highly mobile and culture-bearing animals. In fact, from the viewpoint of human evolution it is worth noting that in the earliest period the role of geographical factors in influencing and shaping culture was most marked. But as human culture has evolved, especially in relation to the development of technology, it has become so complex and overpowering that it becomes the dominant influence in shaping the human environmental setting.[15] Medical ecology, as a specialized field of human ecology, focuses upon all classes of environmental factors as they cause, influence, and modify the development and spread of diseases in human societies.

EPIDEMIOLOGY AND MEDICAL ECOLOGY

There is a marked distinction between epidemiology and medical ecology. The epidemiological investigator focuses upon his data for any clues that point to causative factors whether encompassed by biological, physiological, psychological, or sociological theory. He also is concerned with the application of any new knowledge gained in order to pave the way for the prevention of a given disease. In contrast, medical ecology provides a narrower focus, projects a model of the social system, and attempts to examine how the human organism, in sickness and in health, maintains himself and survives within a given social system. The medical ecologist also is concerned with cause, but particularly with those causes that stem from the continuing precarious balance among disease agents, persons, and their sociocultural system. Epidemiology is regarded as primarily encompassing a method rather than a field for the study of disease. It represents one method, as Hollingshead has noted in a recent article, on a par with laboratory and clinical methods, for the study of disease.[16] Thus medical ecology is, like anatomy and physiology, a distinct field of medicine that focuses upon all of the possible implications that the total environment has for maintaining a balance that fosters health rather than disease in human beings. In most instances, especially in using statistical procedures, the epidemiologist and medical ecologist will use the same techniques and measuring devices, but their final interpretations may have radically different emphases.[17]

The uncertainty concerning the distinction between epidemiology and medical ecology has produced some amusing results. For example, social scientists initially viewed the study of mental disease within an ecological framework. As they became more acquainted with the work of the medically trained epidemiologist, they have tended to regard their studies as epidemiological in character.[18] In contrast, perhaps partly under the influence of the human ecological model, certain medically trained epidemiologists have tried to focus upon the problem presented by health and disease by seeing diseased states as a result of the disruption of the precarious balance between the person and his sociocultural environment. Human ecology presents a closed model where the environments and the organisms are intertwined and interdependent, very much like the web of life that Darwin described. In contrast, epidemiology, as a method, is not constrained by postulating any theoretical model. Rather, it is a means for studying the disease as it appears in the person and tracing it to any condition or set of conditions no matter where they may lead, be they biological, bacteriological, geographical, psychological, or cultural.

OBSTACLES TO PSYCHIATRIC EPIDEMIOLOGICAL OR PSYCHIATRIC ECOLOGICAL RESEARCH

In terms of the actual operation, it matters little whether an investigator in the mental health field thinks of himself as working in psychiatric epidemiology or psychiatric ecology. The obstacles that he confronts in his research are similar. That is, they are similar if the investigator plans to use a statistical approach and to portray the distribution of a given mental disease in time or space and broken down by age, sex, ethnicity, race, occupation, education, religious affiliation, and the like. In the area of disease recognized as mental, these obstacles are most formidable and they have been of such a character as to raise numerous questions concerning the significance of the results of such studies to date.

These obstacles are five in number. First, the investigator wants to know if the persons that he is including in his survey have the same kind of mental disorder. Second, he wants to isolate certain symptomatic conditions that point to the disease at some point in time and to the social recognition of the disease at another point in time. These essentials in a conventional sense embrace the problems of diagnosis and detection. It is this latter obstacle, referred to as the gap, that is the difference in the point of time that the disease began and when it was officially recognized by others. This obstacle has raised numerous questions as to the reliability and validity of much epidemiological work in mental illness. Unless the investigator can have some assurance on these two points he will have difficulty in dealing with his data in any meaningful way. The third obstacle concerns the matter of coverage. What assurance does the investigator in quest of an incidence rate have that all persons within a community who have the disease have been detected?

A fourth obstacle is represented by the excessive geographical mobility of persons, particularly in the contemporary Western world. This mobility not only makes for difficulty in keeping track of people (particularly in the United States), but it also means an ever-present difficulty in determining the rate of a mental illness in a given population of risk because most populations are not very stable for long, but experience both in- and out-migrations. This makes for difficulty in comparing the rates between populations and has caused some investigators to conduct their epidemiological investigations in isolated locales where they do not have to contend with the mobility factor.

The fifth obstacle has to do with the source of data. An investigator must decide whether he is going to collect his cases from psychiatric facilities where the case has been officially identified, or whether he will include cases that come under the treatment focus of private practicing psychiatrists. The investigator then must decide whether he would go directly to the community to conduct a survey that would get at the number of mentally ill in the community. Also, the multiplication of psychiatric facilities since World War II that receive and treat patients has added grave complications to the epidemiological task. Night hospitals, day hospitals, halfway houses, private outpatient clinics, increase of private practicing psychiatrists, psychiatric wards in general hospitals, rehabilitation centers, and therapeutic clubs all now constitute sources for cases and thus complicate the task of coverage faced by the epidemiologist.

These obstacles are the same for the investigator whether he thinks of himself as making an epidemiological or an ecological study. In addition to work that is similar to that of the epidemiologist, the medical ecologist may approach his task by examining the life history of persons in a community setting in order to examine the ingression of environmental factors into their experience and the impinging of environmental factors in their relationship to one another. The chief obstacle here that confronts the medical ecologist is the extent to which the ecological order will be composed of the same persons in space and time. This is in part the problem of mobility, but it also is in part the possibility that the ecological order might be disrupted by some catastrophic change such as revolution, war, mass migration, or swift climatic changes that would cause the conditions in the ecological order to change markedly, thus affecting the persons. Any one of these factors might produce a situation where people who have fitted in and adapted well to the old ecological order may not fit in with the new one, and persons who have not fitted into the old ecological order would emerge as the adjusted and as leaders of the new one. Thus marked changes of an ecological order might produce the very situations that could reveal in a telling fashion the influence of environmental factors in the production of certain kinds of mental disturbances.

With this account of the nature of human ecology, the interrelationship of human and medical ecology, the distinction between epidemiology and medical ecology, and the obstacles pertaining to the investigation of mental disease whether conducted by an epidemiologist or a medical ecologist, one can focus on the central concern of this chapter, which is to assess the state and significance of the epidemiological studies of psychiatric disorders.

The literature concerned with the investigation of psychiatric disorders from an epidemiological and/or ecological perspective has become quite vast. A major portion of this literature has been developed on the basis of empirical studies that have been conducted since 1920. For example, in a rather comprehensive bibliography of 362 references provided by a report of the Milbank Memorial Fund in 1950, only 28, or 7.7 percent, are before 1920.[19] In addition to the above report, the Milbank Memorial Fund has held two other conferences bearing on investigations in this area.[20] In the 1959 conference the paper by this author contained a bibliography of 88 references, and the paper by Murphy, dealing with studies of social change in relation to mental health, provided a bibliography of 90 references. These reports are cited in order to refer readers to those previous attempts that have been made to organize the literature in this area. This chapter will not be concerned with a review of the literature, but rather will attempt to organize the significant studies along certain lines that will summarize the state of current knowledge in this area and point to some of the inevitable trends of these studies. Thus this survey will present the significant existing material in terms of the empirical findings of epidemiological and ecological studies of psychiatric disorders; hypotheses developed from these findings; experimental epidemiological studies; and evaluation of epidemiological studies of psychiatric disorders.

EMPIRICAL FINDINGS

With respect to the empirical findings, the concern here is with various statistical analyses of mental disorders related to age, sex, marital status, and nativity, as well as certain other studies that have been concerned with the distribution of mental disorders by type in geographical, social, and temporal space. It is these epidemiological findings that have provided whatever factual base there is for the development of different hypotheses to explain the various distributions that are found; an emphasis on certain possible interrelationships between specific types of environment and types of mental disease; and the formulation of certain hypotheses pertaining to etiology.

While it is easy to state what one wishes to include under empirical findings, it is far more difficult to interpret findings and compare one set of findings with another. This is so because investigators have conducted their studies in widely separated areas that provided great variability with respect to mobility, social conditions, psychiatric facilities, and time. Most of the early epidemiological studies in the United States relied primarily upon data based on first admissions to state mental hospitals. For example, the studies by Pollack[21] and Malzberg[22] that have been reported over the last 45 years have relied almost entirely on the data provided by the admissions of the mentally afflicted in New York State hospitals. These studies have been made possible through the early use of IBM equipment to sort the data according to certain individual and demographic characteristics of the cases. While these studies have provided little of theoretical significance, even though Malzberg does attempt some speculative interpretations of certain findings, they did succeed in bringing a certain systematic order to the hospitals' admission data and in providing a stimulus for other investigators to attack the problem of mental disease from various environmental positions. Malzberg attempted to study each type of major psychosis in relation to certain individual and demographic characteristics, and often was able to point out certain differences among psychoses with respect to age, sex, marital status, nativity, race, religion, birth order, economic condition, and literacy. The differences found at least suggested by inference that there was some valid basis to psychiatric nomenclature.

Any attempted examination of the statistical analyses of mental disorder in relation to those individual and demographic factors was complicated by the variety of psychiatric disturbances. Most of these studies have concentrated on the major psychoses to the neglect of the psychoneuroses and the so-called character disturbances. For the most part, these studies are a reworking of the data provided by state and federal annual reports. The major findings are quite well known to workers in this area. In general, it might be said that men exceed women in incidence for schizophrenia, paranoia, senile psychoses, general paresis, and cerebral arteriosclerosis, while women exceed men in incidence of manic-depressive and involutional psychoses and the psychoneuroses. The age pattern varies with the various psychoses, with the schizophrenics in general having the highest incidence among men in the 20-29 age group and among women in the 30-39 age group. The high incidence in the other psychoses, for the most part, is concentrated in the population above 50 years of age. With respect to marital status it usually has been found that rates for all the psychoses are highest in the widowed, divorced, and separated categories, the next highest in the single group, and lowest among the married. This latter finding generally has been interpreted two ways. First, that the marriage state protects one from a psychiatric disturbance, and second, that the incipient character of psychoses is more likely to prevent one from entering the marriage state and, if married, more likely to speed divorce or separation. The latter interpretation appears more plausible in the light of current knowledge about the various psychiatric disorders.

With respect to nativity, it often has been reported, at least in the United States, that the foreign born exceed the native born with respect to the rates of first admissions to mental hospitals. The difficulty with most of these crude statistical studies is that factors such as economic status, social class, education, and religious preference have not been subject to control. One is uncertain of the true picture here for comparisons are crude at best.

However, it is in moving to those epidemiological studies that have focused upon the distribution of various types of mental disorder in time and space that one begins to build up one's epidemiological knowledge. Look at the issue of whether or not mental disease is increasing in the population. This issue is quite complicated and has not been competently resolved because of the difficulty of securing for the various communities comparable data both in terms of diagnosis and of hospital admission policies. In general, two interpretations have been extant relative to this issue. The first is an environmental one emphasizing that the increasing complexity of social organization with respect to numbers, types, density, and social structures is bound to bring about an increase in mental illness. The second position argued that any increase reported by the statistics is more apparent than real and is largely related to the increase in hospital beds, psychiatric facilities, and personnel to treat patients. These conditions have brought about the supposed increase in incidence. In other words, there were mentally ill persons in the population who, in an earlier period, were receiving no treatment. A certain amount of evidence exists that supports this position. For example, the law of distance, developed in the nineteenth century, showed an inverse relationship to exist between first admission rates and the distance from a psychiatric hospital. White, in a 1903 study concerned with the geographical distribution of mental disease in the United States, reported the highest rates of first admissions to hospitals in the longest settled parts of the country with the rates declining as one moved westward from the Atlantic seaboard.[23] In the ensuing 60 years, however, this discrepancy between the east and the west coast has been eliminated with the development and spread of population all across the land, and particularly with equalization of psychiatric care provided by west coast facilities. This author pointed out the disappearance of this difference in a recent survey.[24]

In spite of these considerations, Malzberg in 1941 concluded on the basis of the time span between 1909 and 1935 that there was a real increase of all the major psychoses with the exception of general paresis in New York State. He attempted to tie the controversy to the argument between the eugenicists and the environmentalists; in that period the eugenicists argued that the biological stock was deteriorating, resulting in an increase in mental disease, while the environmentalists argued the reverse.

While this controversy may have had its impact on certain investigations before 1940 (Winston[25] and Elkind[26] presenting data arguing against an increase), it remained for Goldhamer and Marshall to attempt a most careful study that might pin down the issue in a more definitive fashion.[27] They presented for Massachusetts a number of comparisons between age- and sex-specific first admission rates for 1885 and contemporary rates. All comparisons showed a close agreement between the nineteenth century and contemporary rates for both sexes for the age groups under 50. They concluded that their data supported the general hypothesis that "in the central age groups the incidence of the major mental disorders has not increased over the last two or three generations." They interpret the substantiation of this hypothesis by stating that "(a) the stress factors in contemporary life that supposedly might bring about an increase in the psychoses have not, in fact, increased during the last century, or (b) if these factors have increased they are not as relevant to the theory of the psychoses as has been supposed." They did recognize, however, the possibility of short-term fluctuation in the rates and they were quick to point out that their findings have no bearing on the psychoneuroses. This author and Medow, in a more recent survey utilizing the data for the several states as reported by the federal government and using the same procedures as did Goldhamer and Marshall, substantiated their findings by data from the period between 1910 and 1950 as tested by three eastern states, two midwestern states, and two far-western states.[28]

Another aspect of this controversy that makes the solution of the problem difficult is the shifting definition of mental illness. For example, it is interesting to note that in the ten surveys reviewed by Plunkett and Gordon, the surveys after 1950 reported more than four to five times the amount of mental disorder in selected communities than the surveys before 1940.[29] One must remember that the surveys were reporting on total mental disorders and that the huge differences reflect nothing more than a widening of the psychiatric net to include more cases. It is reminiscent of the recent Midtown Manhattan study that reported 80 percent of a sample population in Manhattan as having some kind of psychiatric impairment.[30]

This widening definition of mental disease that has occurred primarily since the end of World War II complicates any attempt to determine if mental disorder is increasing. However, this should not handicap an inquiry into the possible increase of the psychoses provided that complete coverage can be obtained and some uniform standard clinical judgment assured. In fact, Goldhamer and Marshall painstakingly attempted to reassure themselves that the character of the admissions into the Massachusetts hospitals in the nineteenth century were the same as those admitted today.[31]

The author turns now to reporting epidemiological findings from studies concerned with the distribution of mental disease in geographical and social space. Most of these studies, particularly in the United States, have computed their incidence rates for various populations of risk on the basis of first admissions to public and private mental hospitals. These studies have concentrated on total admissions to such hospitals, as well as breaking them down by type of psychosis. They have been frequently criticized on the grounds that their coverage of cases is incomplete, but on the other hand, it could be argued that admission to a mental hospital constitutes an operational definition of mental illness. Even so, from this perspective differentials in admission policies and hospital facility levels in the communities across the land are likely to make comparisons of rates quite unreliable. Nevertheless, these studies have raised many provocative issues and have served as stimuli for further research in this area—research that attempts to take into account the criticisms of the earlier studies.

Prior to the publication of Mental Disorders in Urban Areas in 1939, there were very few epidemiological studies of mental illness based on hospital admissions. True, the Scandinavians and the Germans had conducted epidemiological surveys in isolated risk populations. Loua,[32] Deas,[33] Sutherland,[34] White,[35] MacDermott,[36] Dawson,[37] Malzberg,[38] Green,[39] and Ødegaard[40] reported differential rates by area for total mental disorders in various populations of risk. These studies are of historical interest and pinpoint the isolated investigator who saw the possibilities of epidemiological analysis for throwing light on the etiology of mental illness. MacDermott's question is perhaps significant here when he asks if the wide rate differences in Ireland by area challenge the hypothesis that insanity is inherited.[41]

The Faris and Dunham study was the first to examine area differences in the different types of psychoses. The major findings of this study are well known and it is not necessary to repeat them here. This study served as a stimulus for the additional work carried on in this area after World War II. The central finding of this study, that schizophrenia appeared to be highly concentrated in the impoverished area in the city of Chicago, set the stage for a long period of controversy. Was it really true that a given city population in one area actually produced more schizophrenia than a population in another area? This was the central question. It motivated much argument and some empirical work directed toward ascertaining the truth of such a differential. In his review of the book, Myerson argued that these impoverished areas of the city merely attracted and collected the schizophrenics from other areas.[42] Gerard and Houston, 14 years later, questioned the differential rates by showing that schizophrenics living in families were scattered much more widely throughout the city than were schizophrenics living alone.[43] Three years later another set of investigators attempted to show that the area differential rates of schizophrenia were sound and could not be accounted for by drift alone.[44] The issue for the U.S. city is highly complex, especially in view of the high rate of mobility, differential admission policies, and differentials in available psychiatric facilities. Clausen and Kohn, in their study of the distribution of schizophrenia in Hagerstown, Maryland, came up with a complete absence of differential rates by economic area that questioned further the earlier findings.[45]

In the 1930s U.S. sociologists turned a good share of their attention to the phenomenon of social class in their society. It was almost inevitable that mental illness eventually would be examined in relation to the class factor. This was the monumental contribution of Hollingshead and Redlich when they reported a negative correlation between social class and psychoses, and a positive correlation between social class and psychoneuroses for treated prevalence cases.[46] They also reported the same negative correlation for schizophrenia for both prevalence and incidence. Again, the same issue arises as in the case of the geographical distribution studies. Did their cases originate in the class in which they were found or did they change classes over a period of time? While Hollingshead and Redlich attempt to argue that there was little class shifting, the issue was not resolved beyond the shadow of a doubt.

Morris reported from London in 1959 that a group of male schizophrenics were highly concentrated in class V while their fathers were rather evenly distributed in all the social classes.[47] These results suggested that the measure of social class utilized by Hollingshead and Redlich was faulty because in many instances it hardly could be regarded as independent from the patient that suffered the disease. Therefore it seemed more reasonable to assert that the presence of the disease had a bearing on the class position of the patient rather than the reverse.

While these empirical epidemiological studies by no means exhaust the work that has been done in this area, they do point up the central issues in a variety of possible interpretations. The central question is the uncertainty surrounding the reliability and validity of the data as analyzed, but even so, attempts were made and are still going on to advance the most reasonable interpretation.*

HYPOTHESES AND THEORETICAL INTERPRETATIONS

When it comes to attempts made to make sense out of differential distributions in geographical, social, and temporal space, the picture is quite confusing. It has been made confusing because investigators in this area have presented their data on one level of organization and then have tried to make an interpretation on another level of organization. This is a logical error. That is, the investigators are not content with finding some plausible interpretation of rate differences that also might be supported by other facts, but often barge happily ahead to make inferences concerning the quality of interpersonal relations, the nature of social contacts, the character of family life, or the identification of stress factors that they regard as warranted by rate differentials, whether they be by area, social class, or time.

Currently there are five hypotheses that have been suggested in the literature that have been used to explain rate differentials of schizophrenia in various populations of risk.† Perhaps the oldest

---

*Inasmuch as this review is concerned primarily with epidemiological and ecological studies of mental illness, the author is not including any of the studies that have focused upon the relationship of cultures and cultural differences in relation to mental illness. Many of these studies also are epidemiological in character and might well be considered here, but they often raise the same issues as the studies that already have been cited.

†The intention here is to present these hypotheses as applying only to schizophrenic rate differentials. In fact, this is the way they have been used primarily in the literature. While it is true that there are studies bearing on the rate differentials of other psychoses, they have not received the attention that has been given to rate differentials of schizophrenia.

hypothesis, one that was particularly prominent in sociological literature between the two world wars, stresses the factor of anomie, or social disorganization. Here, social disorganization is regarded as an independent variable and the schizophrenic rate as a dependent variable. It is then necessary to develop measures that will index the instability and disorganization of a community, and to show that when this index is high the schizophrenic rate also will be high in comparison with communities where the index of disorganization is low. If such can be established with confidence, one has an ecological correlation that may help to pinpoint the factors on another level that might be examined. But one hardly has an etiological explanation for the disease.

A second hypothesis, and one of the oldest advanced to account for differential rates of schizophrenia, is that of drift.[48] This hypothesis states that variations in schizophrenic rates by area and social class are to be explained by an unconscious drift of persons with the disease from areas or classes where status conditions are clear to areas where they are unclear; this inflates the rate in certain areas or classes at the expense of other areas and classes to produce highly significant differences.

The chief difficulty with this hypothesis is the image of the schizophrenic that it suggests. The image suggests that the schizophrenic is so incoherent, bizarre, confused, and impulsive that in no situation does he know what he is doing or why he is doing it. This image is most inadequate for it makes no allowance for the fact that the schizophrenic person in his prepsychotic period is often trying like others to make the most of what he has. Further, this hypothesis denies any role for voluntary choice and selection on the part of the schizophrenic, but reserves such voluntarism only for those members of the community who are not going to break down. Because this hypothesis presents a faulty image of the schizophrenic as a person, it does not have much value for explaining rate differentials.

Another hypothesis that has been utilized for explaining schizophrenic rate differentials, and that functions on the same level of organization as the data, is that of differential tolerance.[49] This hypothesis states that a favorable, sympathetic, and accepting attitude toward schizophrenic persons in a given community serves to keep them out of a psychiatric facility and therefore they are not counted. This means that in communities where an unsympathetic attitude exists toward the schizophrenic the rate will be high, and where a sympathetic attitude exists the rate will be low. This hypothesis also has been used to show that families on higher status levels are more accepting and protective of their members than are families on lower status levels. If this is so, it means that the former set of families are less likely to place their mentally ill in psychiatric institutions and consequently they are kept out of the count. However, while this hypothesis has its utility for explaining schizophrenic rate differentials, it can be at best a temporary explanation. It only succeeds in calling attention to a longer gap between the occurrence of initial symptoms and the initial entry into treatment in some communities as compared to others. With an increase in psychiatric facilities in the various communities and a changed attitude of people toward mental illness, one would expect this explanation to lose its relevance. Under such circumstances the gap should get smaller and smaller.[50]

A fourth hypothesis suggested to explain variations in the geographical distribution of schizophrenic incidence rates employs the concept of segregation. This hypothesis, which in a sense is the converse of the drift hypothesis, can be stated as follows: schizophrenics, both potential and actual, voluntarily and actively select certain areas of the community for their residence in order to escape those intense involvements that come with close interpersonal relations. Gerard and Houston, from an examination of their data, inferred that schizophrenics, separated from their families, consciously selected certain anonymous areas as a means of protecting themselves from becoming involved in disruptive family relationships.[51]

Hare, in his first study of the distribution of schizophrenics in Bristol, England, while not so positive as Gerard and Houston, thought that his high rates of schizophrenia were to be explained by the process of segregation or by some as yet undetermined causal environmental factors.[52] In a later study of the distribution of schizophrenic and manic-depressive psychoses, he attempted to determine whether the attraction or the breeder hypothesis accounted for the distribution of schizophrenic rates. He concludes that the evidence gives some support to both hypotheses, but he judges that the evidence is heavily weighted on the side of the attraction rather than the breeder hypothesis.

A fifth hypothesis has been suggested by Clausen and Kohn in their study of the distribution of schizophrenic rates in Hagerstown, Maryland.[53] In this study they noted the almost complete equalization of schizophrenic rates in the five socioeconomic areas that they carved out in Hagerstown. They note that this finding is at variance with that reported for larger cities. This discrepancy causes them to suggest the possibility of a "direct relationship between the size of the city and the degree which rates of schizophrenia correlate with such indices of socio-economic status, area of residence and occupational level." This hypothesis is one that is clearly developed on the level on which the data are presented and, while it probably has little theoretical significance, it may be useful in accounting for such contradictory findings and for making sense out of variations in the patterns of schizophrenic rates in urban centers.

It should be clear that these five hypotheses are directed to the task of explaining the variations in the pattern of schizophrenic incidence rates in various community settings. They are in no sense directed to any etiological possibilities for the development of schizophrenia, but rather focus directly on accounting for the variation in rate patterns. The social disorganization hypothesis is perhaps the only one that might suggest certain inferences about etiology, but the ecological correlations upon which this hypothesis rests could gain significance only if it could be shown that the population in the areas that serve as the units of correlation is relatively stable. This is patently impossible for any U.S. city over the past 50 years. Given stable area populations, this hypothesis asserts that in those areas where poverty, disorganized families, cultural conflict, disproportionate sex ratios, and a large percentage of single adults are found, high rates of schizophrenia also will be found. But as has been indicated, actual conditions in the city would not enable one to embrace this hypothesis with any degree of confidence. This factor accounts for those investigators who have sought relatively isolated and stable populations as locales for epidemiological studies.

The remaining four hypotheses contribute, in one form or another, to the support of the more general hypothesis of social selection that has been less favored by investigators in this country than in Europe. In this country, the general position that the sociocultural environment may contain factors of etiological significance for schizophrenia has caused studies to be used for such a search to the neglect of observations that support the selective character of the social process that sorts and shifts by age, sex, residence, nativity, occupation, education, and institutional affiliations.

In Europe, Ødegaard is a strong advocate of the social selection hypothesis. In his early study of the migration of Norwegians to the United States, he hypothesized that their higher rate of mental illness in Minnesota as compared with Norway was due to the fact that psychiatrically vulnerable persons were more likely to migrate.[54] In a more recent study relating the mental disorders to various occupational groups in Norway, he concludes that social selection in contrast to environmental stress provides the more telling explanation for the higher rate of psychoses among seamen as compared to other occupations.[55] This high rate held for all psychotic categories with the exception of psychosis with epilepsy, psychosis with mental deficiency, and manic-depressive psychosis, where the seamen had the second highest rate. In addition to the initial social selection, Ødegaard notes a secondary selection that takes place around the age of 30 when some seafaring men leave their ships to seek other occupations. By this process the psychiatrically vulnerable types remain among the seamen. He further notes that the evidence of social selection seems most marked for schizophrenia, epilepsy, and mental deficiency.[56] Ekblad tends to support Ødegaard's findings by pointing to the higher rates of schizophrenia in his sample of seamen as compared to his sample of Navy trainees.[57]

This hypothesis also has been utilized by investigators when considering specialized social structures such as the army, the merchant marines, or prison inmates. In her study of the army, Winston asks, "Does mental disease act as a further selective factor in the already highly selective military group?"[58] She concludes that it does. While she reports no evidence that mental disease increases in the army, she does find that psychological misfits tend to be weeded out so that mental disease decreases as the length of service increases. In a study of British noncommissioned officers and prisoners of war, Sims points to social selection as the process for explaining the differential incidence rates for mental disorders in the various groups.[59] He also notes that the elimination of misfits in basic training lowers the incidence rate for those who get into the combat area. Thus one would conclude that social selection is the basic process for accounting for the differential rate patterns of schizophrenia that may be reported for various cities, rural areas, and isolated populations.

These five hypotheses have been viewed as being tenable propositions for the observational level upon which the distribution rates for schizophrenia and other psychoses have been reported. Several hypotheses of a social-psychological nature that have attempted to point to factors of interpersonal relations and conditioning that might have some etiological significance for the development of schizophrenia have been purposely ignored. Hypothetical propositions that have tended to emphasize such concepts as social isolation, role confusion, role strain, interpersonal stress, differential status, mental conflict, frustration, and blocked social mobility have not been considered because they have no value for explaining differential rate patterns, but at best can represent only inferences from such patterns—inferences that are highly subjective because the gap between differential rates and interpersonal experience is too great to be bridged. This is not to say that they have no value for explaining psychiatric reactions, but that they can be utilized only with observations made on the interpersonal level to which they are intended to apply.

EXPERIMENTAL EPIDEMIOLOGICAL STUDIES OF MENTAL DISEASE

Many investigators who conduct epidemiological studies of mental disease have the recurring dream that their initial empirical work will be so rewarding that they will be able to move to experimental epidemiological studies. This is a worthy dream and obviously would take the design of studying the incidence of a given mental disease in a population where an x-factor is present as compared with its incidence in a population where the x-factor is absent. To date the epidemiological knowledge of mental illnesses has not proved reliable, valid, or productive enough to resort to experimental studies. However, there have been a few such attempts. These are reported briefly to indicate the direction that this thinking takes.

Eleven years ago Jaco, taking his cue from the Faris and Dunham study that marked social isolation as a possible etiological factor in schizophrenia, developed an index of social isolation by interviewing, with a prepared schedule, a randomly drawn sample of residents in four census tracts of Austin, Texas.[60] Two tracts had high and low schizophrenic first admission rates and two had high and low manic-depressive first admission rates. Jaco set up 19 null hypotheses to pinpoint the differences in degree of social isolation present in the high and low schizophrenic tracts. By rejecting 13 of these hypotheses, he infers that there is a great deal more social isolation experienced by persons in the high-rate tracts as compared to the low-rate tracts. Even though he finds more schizophrenia in an area where persons have less communication, he cannot show by this device that persons who break down into schizophrenia are more isolated than those who do not.

Clausen and Kohn, in another experimental study, attempt to test the social isolation hypothesis by comparing persons who develop schizophrenia with persons who do not.[61] They selected a sample of 45 schizophrenics and 13 manic-depressive first admissions, paired individually with a group of controls on the basis of age, sex, and occupation. The persons comprising the samples were then interviewed by means of a schedule that covered residential and occupational history, parental-family relationships, friendships and activities of early adolescence, dating patterns, adult social participation, and a brief psychosomatic inventory. In the analysis of their data they report the following: almost one third of the schizophrenic and manic-depressive patients and none of the controls showed evidence of being socially isolated in their early teens; isolated patients were never prevented from interacting with their peers because of excessive morbidity, severe illness, parental restrictions, or lack of playmates;

and patients and controls showed no differences in their perception of family relationships. While the investigators recognize that their data are based upon retrospective impressions, they find that their data on 26 of 30 patients compare favorably with the information in the hospital records. Their final conclusion is that "the data do not support the hypothesis that social isolation in adolescence is a predisposing factor in either schizophrenia or manic-depressive psychosis." They think that the social isolation present in certain cases is a result of interpersonal difficulties whereby the patient tends to select social isolation as his way of adjusting.

There have been several studies that, while they do not quite measure up to the classic experimental design, tend in that direction. These are the comparative studies in two or more culturally contrasting communities. Such was Stein's study of social class and schizophrenia in four East London boroughs comprising a high proportion of classes IV and V, and five West London boroughs comprising a high proportion of classes I and II.[62] She recorded the first admissions to mental hospitals from E and W boroughs, 1954 to 1955, broken down by age, sex, and diagnosis (schizophrenia, manic-depressive psychosis, and psychoneurosis). Her findings run contrary to most U.S. results because she showed that the W boroughs had significantly higher rates in practically all age and sex categories as compared to the E boroughs. This difference was marked for schizophrenia and psychoneurosis, but less marked for the manic-depressive group. She then distributed her case data among the social classes in the two sets of boroughs. She reports that the rates in the W boroughs are still the highest, but in both sets of boroughs the rates vary inversely and consistently for social class in all diagnostic groups. While she finds a real class gradient in the incidence of schizophrenia, she thinks that this result must be tentative because of the radical differences in the population structure of the two sets of boroughs.

In another English study, Carstairs and Brown examine the incidence and prevalence of psychiatric disorders in two culturally contrasting communities: Rhondda, a coal-mining area, and Vale, an agricultural area.[63] Rhondda had more psychiatric cases than Vale (3.8 as compared to 2.6 per 1,000 population). In Rhondda the cases were more highly concentrated in the group of nonminers. While the investigators might have regarded this as an instance of psychiatric vulnerability in a minority community group, they preferred to think of it as an example of adverse selection. They conclude that the linkage of social pressures as causative factors to psychiatric disorders must await the further analysis of the relation between social structure and value systems in the community.

The author's own recent research that attempts to examine the incidence of schizophrenia, other functional disorders, and psychopathies in two culturally contrasting subcommunities in Detroit is another study comparable to the above two.[64] Here the attempt was to determine if one could claim that one urban population actually produced more schizophrenia than another. While the initial contrast maintained the usual 3 : 1 ratio between the deprived area and the more middle-class, better organized one, nevertheless, taking account of the mobility factor reduced the differences to a statistically insignificant point. In the other functional disorders the difference also was not significant. But in the psychopathic disturbances a ratio of approximately 8 : 1 was found between the poorly organized area and the better organized one. While this ratio was reduced to 2.2 : 1 when mobility was taken into account, the difference between the two subcommunities was still significant. Even though the ratio in all instances was reduced, the trend persisted in the original direction; perhaps this difference should be emphasized rather than its tendency to be eliminated. There are many other aspects of this study, but it is commented on briefly only as an example of this experimental direction in epidemiological studies.

Perhaps the most impressive attempt at an experimental epidemiology is that reported by Alexander Leighton and his colleagues in the Sterling County study in Nova Scotia.[65] Leighton reported on the original proposal of this study in 1949 when he outlined his plan of research for studying the sociocultural organization of selected communities in relation to the incidence and prevalence of mental disturbance.[66] He stated then that he was interested in testing the proposition whether a condition of social disorganization appeared to be associated with a high incidence of mental disturbance. In other words, he wanted to find out if mental illness would be high where theory said it should be high, and low where theory said it should be low.

It is difficult to do justice to this monumental study in a few short paragraphs because its vast array of facts and diverse avenues of exploration far outrun its original central focus. Even so, in the final volume where the basic findings are reported they come back to the central question and show the extent to which their recorded facts tend to support the theory. In Sterling County the researchers selected five communities and through various kinds of assessments attempted to establish an index of disorganization for each of them. They came up with two communities that appeared to be markedly disorganized and two communities seemingly well organized as shown by good leadership and high morale. As an overall finding it is interesting to note that they come close in agreement with the finding reported by the Midtown Manhattan study[67] with their finding that, according to the criteria of the American Psychiatric Association's Diagnostic and Statistical Manual for Mental Disorders, approximately two thirds of the entire adult population in Sterling County would be found to have suffered from some type of psychiatric disorder at some time during their lives, and that at the present time, at least half of the adults are currently suffering from a psychiatric disorder.

Conversely, in terms of the kinds of mental disturbances, they report as many nonhospitalized cases of psychoses, brain syndromes, and mental deficiency as are hospitalized. Also, they state very definitely that there is no more indication for the generation of psychoses in the disintegrated communities than is found in the two integrated communities and for the county as a whole.

On the other hand, they found a great deal of psychosomatic, psychoneurotic, and sociopathic disorders in the various communities. It is their prevalence that contributes to the huge bulk of psychiatric symptom patterns among the people of the county. They further report that the prevalence of psychiatric symptoms takes place along sex, age, and area disintegration dimensions. That is, in the two most organized communities there is a much greater prevalence of psychiatric symptoms among women than men. The men are much more adapted to the sociocultural system and have an easier time of it, suggesting the hypothesis that "it is not the culture per se but the extent and rate of acceleration in change of the socio-cultural system that has a differential effect on the sexes." Conversely, in the disintegrated areas the prevalence rates of psychiatric symptoms are much higher but are about the same for both men and women. This results, the authors contend, from the similarity of roles of men and women in these areas. The significance of this differential in prevalence of psychiatric symptoms between the organized and disorganized areas has led them to suggest that if a random sample of symptomatically unimpaired people were introduced into the disintegrated areas in numbers not large enough to effect a change in the sociocultural system, these persons would become in time psychiatrically impaired. They further note that if impaired persons in the disintegrated communities were removed and placed in the integrated communities, they would experience a reduction or a complete disappearance of their impairments.

AN ESTIMATE AND EVALUATION OF EPIDEMIOLOGICAL STUDIES

It is impossible to conclude this evaluative analysis of epidemiological studies of mental disease without calling attention to some of the recurring issues and problems that continue to plague these studies. However, there would seem to be no question about the fact that the continued efforts in this area carried on by many sincere and conscientious workers have contributed to a clarification of the troublesome issues, have sharpened up the methodological tools, and have begun to pinpoint those personality and mental aberrations where fruitful work may be expected in the future.

First and foremost is the problem that centers around the issue of true incidence. Will it ever be possible to develop this measure for all types of mental disease as well as for each particular type? This issue is central to any comparative study because unless one can have assurance that all cases of a given type are secured utilizing some standard of uniform diagnostic procedure for the several areas, it is well-nigh impossible to make sense out of comparative studies. One can recognize clearly, as Kramer does in his proposed model, that a true incidence rate for any given disorder is made up of first admissions for a given year plus cases that developed during that year but were not admitted during the year.[68] But it is difficult to know how to bring this about. It is more likely that one will come closer to a true incidence rate with respect to a given psychosis, say schizophrenia, if one can develop more rigorous ways to objectify the diagnosis. A true incidence rate for total mental disorder is probably impossible at this time, considering the shifting values and preferences as to whom is to be considered mentally ill in the different communities. It is this widening definition of mental illness that has produced so much havoc with epidemiological counts. This widening definition, it seems, has an almost propagandistic function to provide pressure to step up the number and quality of psychiatric facilities available to any community. Proposals have been made to establish a central registry where all persons who come to private or public attention for psychiatric difficulty would be reported on specially prepared forms by private physicians, private psychiatrists, clinics, and hospitals, both public and private. In fact, in Monroe County, New York, one such central registry is functioning.[69]

This issue of true incidence has highlighted the controversy between the population survey and the detection and recording of admissions to any type of psychiatric facility in the community. Those who argue for a population survey in the open community claim that true incidence for mental illness never can be obtained, and therefore the best bet is to rely on the carefully constructed prevalence count by surveying a given population. While such proposed surveys raise the issue of sampling, by far the most crucial problem is the reliability and validity of the instrument that is used to pick up psychiatric cases in the community. If reliance is placed on the use of psychiatrists who would have to conduct diagnostic interviews on the spot, the entire effort becomes very costly and the problem of obtaining uniform and standardized clinical judgments still remains. In other words, the problem of applying uniform criteria for arriving at a diagnosis is much the same whether a sample population is surveyed or whether only first admissions to psychiatric facilities are counted.

A third problem is how to deal with the factor presented by both horizontal and vertical social mobility of people. Thus it becomes almost impossible to pin down a valid rate for a given psychosis in a community where the population changes often. This has the possibility of shifting the focus of attention from a specific geographical area to various social groups, subcultures, classes, and institutional structures within the society. Perhaps one should try to examine the differential incidence in such groups rather than attempt to pin down area rates. Those who still want a community rate because they feel that a community encompasses a certain sociocultural matrix tend to look for isolated stable populations with which to work. The problem becomes most acute for city populations within the United States.

The problem of validity will continue to plague epidemiological workers in the psychiatric field until more objective criteria are developed for determining psychiatric diagnoses so that dependence does not have to be placed upon the clinical judgment of psychiatrists, which apparently vary from region to region and even from one psychiatric facility to another. The Dohrenwends, in a recent thoughtful article, have attempted to examine this issue and have offered a proposal that they think might be helpful in resolving it.[70] The basis for their concern will be most familiar to epidemiologists who have worked in this area, for they note, after examining some 35 epidemiological studies all over the world, that the prevalence rate as reported by these studies varies from 1 percent to 60 percent in the various populations of risk. There would seem to be no doubt that this extreme variation is a result of the different conceptions of mental disorder that have been used in these studies.

This author, in his own work and in examining many of the same studies that the Dohrenwends' examined, found (as they did) marked variations when rates were reported for all psychiatric disorders. When rates for psychoses only were reported, variations between the studies were considerably reduced, and when rates for a specific psychosis (such as schizophrenia) were reported, the variations were reduced still further. These observations point clearly to the notion that psychiatric judgment is most unreliable with the borderline cases presenting various behavioral and emotional aberrations. Such judgments tighten up considerably when faced with the outright psychotic. Judgment here, however, is still by no means in complete agreement. The author's observations show that among persons given a diagnosis of schizophrenia initially, the second diagnosis given by a psychiatrist will be changed in approximately one out of every four cases. Thus it is likely that until some objective test is developed to determine the presence of a specific psychosis, there will continue to be much uncertainty in interpreting the results of epidemiological studies. A true incidence or prevalence rate will continue to hinge on the issue of reliability of diagnosis, even though much headway is being made in uncovering those cases that are not hospitalized and adding them to those that represent hospital admissions.

This problem can be diagramed by expressing the lack of congruence between the clinical judgment and the societal judgment as to whom is to be defined as mentally ill. There are four possibilities here. A person could be defined as mentally ill by his significant others, representing society, and also found to be mentally ill by clinical examination. He could be defined as mentally ill by his significant others and not ill on clinical examination. He could be defined by his significant others as not mentally ill while he would be diagnosed as mentally ill on clinical examination. Finally, he could be defined as not mentally ill by his significant others and not mentally ill on clinical examination. In cell a, where the two judgments agree on the presence of mental illness, should be found all the psychotics; in cell b should be found the behavioral and character disturbances; in cell c should be found the psychoneurotics; and in cell d should be found the normals (see Table 10.1). It is obvious in this scheme that cells b and c are where most of the difficulty lies. For as social

TABLE 10.1

Model of Relationship between Societal and Clinical Judgments

Societal Judgment	Clinical Judgment					
	Mentally Ill			Not Mentally Ill		
Mentally ill	+	+	a	-	+	b
Not mentally ill	+	-	c	-	-	d

Note: a indicates psychotics; b, character disturbances; c, psychoneurotics; and d, normals.

and clinical judgments continue to be determined by values and social preferences, order will be difficult to achieve.

One solid finding appears to be gradually emerging with a more total assessment of those epidemiological studies that have been conducted during the past 30 years. Particularly, Leighton's findings in Nova Scotia and the present author's findings on the epidemiology of schizophrenia in Detroit show that psychoses are not readily identified with any specific social environment but rather that psychosis (with reference particularly to schizophrenia) is likely to crop up in any society or culture. This finding is inferentially supported by observations that attest to the universality of schizophrenia in primitive societies.[71] It also should be noted that if the frequency of schizophrenia does not vary throughout different societies in the world, it should not vary through time.

This finding, if subsequently validated by other studies, suggests that epidemiologists might well turn their attention to the study and analysis of the psychoneuroses and the psychopathic disorders. There is a real challenge here in experimenting with rigorous and loose definitions of these mental states in order to determine if they are differentially tied to contrasting sociocultural environments. The evidence for the social roots of these disorders appears to be much more voluminous than for the outright psychotic, and so might prove a bonanza to the psychiatrically inclined medical ecologist.

Both Leighton and the author have reported that the so-called character and behavioral disturbances are found to be much more prevalent in disorganized communities as compared to the more highly organized and integrated communities. In these disturbances the ratio between organized and disorganized communities in the author's study is approximately 1:8, a considerable increase from the 1:3 ratios that most studies report for schizophrenia. It even may be possible that psychoneuroses and psychopathic disturbances are typical reactions tied to contrasting points along the social class continuum.

Finally, it is necessary to offer a word of explanation with respect to the general theory of social selection that has been utilized to explain the differentials found in rate patterns for schizophrenia and total mental disorders. This theory stems from a structural-functional approach in viewing human society, and projects for any society a social system model with its own built-in dynamics as it moves back and forth between states of equilibrium and disequilibrium. Society, as a total functioning system, becomes in a sense a complete ecological environment for the persons composing it. These persons with their innumerable movements and purposeful actions are constantly striving to locate in social positions that will maximize their chances for adjustment and survival within the system. Some of these persons, approximately one in 1,000, develop schizophrenia. Those persons that are so destined will, like others, move in ways that will enable them to be more adaptive within the environmental requirements. Thus it will be found that in seeking their individual solutions for their problems, they will locate themselves in certain areas of the social system and avoid other areas. Here one has an explanation for differential rate patterns that have been brought about through the total functioning of the system or, one might say, by means of ecological processes. This explanation gives no clue as to how the disorder originated; it only explains the differential distribution of the disorder within the social system.

NOTES

1. E. Haeckel, "Entwicklungsgang und Aufgabe der Zoologie." Jenersche Z. Med. Naturwissenschaft, 1870, pp. 353-70; quoted by B. Marston in "Human Ecology," in Anthropology Today, ed. A. L. Kroeber (Chicago: University of Chicago Press, 1953).

2. H. H. Barrows, "Geography as Human Ecology," Ann. Assoc. Amer. Geographers 13 (1923): 1-14.

3. R. Park, "Human Ecology," Amer. Soc. 42 (1931): 1-15; and idem, "The Urban Community as a Spatial Pattern and Moral Order," in The Urban Community, ed. E. W. Burgess (Chicago: University of Chicago Press, 1926), pp. 5-18.

4. W. A. N. Dorland and E. C. L. Miller, The American Illustrated Dictionary, 20th ed. (Philadelphia: W. B. Saunders, 1944).

5. A. Myerson, "Review of Mental Disorders in Urban Areas," American Journal of Psychiatry 96 (January 1941): 995-97.

6. E. H. Hare, "Family Setting and the Urban Distribution of Schizophrenia," Journal Ment. Sci. 102 (October 1956): 753; and idem, "Mental Illness and Social Conditions in Bristol," Journal of Mental Disease 102 (April 1956): 349-57.

7. C. Shaw and H. McKaye, Delinquency Areas (Chicago: University of Chicago Press, 1929).

8. T. Sellin, "Cultural Conflict and Crime," Soc. Sci. Res. Council Bull., no. 41 (1938).

9. E. Mowrer, Family Disorganization (Chicago: University of Chicago Press, 1927).

10. R. Caven, Suicide (Chicago: University of Chicago Press, 1928).

11. R. E. Park and E. W. Burgess, The City (Chicago: University of Chicago Press, 1925).

12. H. W. Zorbaugh, The Gold Coast and the Slum (Chicago: University of Chicago Press, 1929).

13. E. R. Mowrer, Disorganization—Personal and Social (Philadelphia: J. B. Lippincott, 1942).

14. P. Sainsbury, Suicide in London—An Ecological Study (London: Chapman & Hall, 1955).

15. E. S. Rogers, "Man, Ecology, and Control of Disease," Public Health Rep. 77 (September 1962): 755-62.

16. A. Hollingshead, "The Epidemiology of Schizophrenia," Amer. Soc. Rev. 26 (February 1961): 5-13.

17. J. S. Böök, "Genetic and Neuropsychiatric Investigation of a North Swedish Population, Acta genet. med. 4 (1953): 1-100; and L. Srole et al., Mental Health in the Metropolis: The Midtown Manhattan Study (New York: McGraw-Hill, 1962).

18. R. E. L. Faris and H. W. Dunham, Mental Disorders in Urban Areas—An Ecological Study of Schizophrenia and Other Psychoses (Chicago: University of Chicago Press, 1939); and E. G. Jaco, The Social Epidemiology of Mental Disorders (New York: Russell Sage Foundation, 1960).

19. Milbank Memorial Fund, Epidemiology of Mental Disorder (New York: Milbank Memorial Fund, 1950).

20. Milbank Memorial Fund, Interrelations between Social Environment and Psychiatric Disorders (New York: Milbank Memorial Fund, 1953); and idem, Causes of Mental Disorders: A Review of Epidemiological Knowledge, 1959 (New York: Milbank Memorial Fund, 1961).

21. H. M. Pollock, Mental Disease and Social Welfare (Utica, N.Y.: State Hospitals Press, 1941).

22. B. Malzberg, Social and Biological Aspects of Mental Disease (Utica, N.Y.: State Hospitals Press, 1940).

23. W. A. White, "The Geographical Distribution of Insanity in the United States," J. Nerv. Ment. Dis. 30 (May 1903): 257-79.

24. H. W. Dunham, Sociological Theory and Mental Disorder (Detroit: Wayne State University Press, 1959), chap. 6.

25. E. B. Winston, "Age: A Factor in the Increase of Mental Disease," Ment. Hyg. 16 (October 1932): 650-52.

26. H. B. Elkind, "Are Mental Diseases on the Increase? The Problem of Determination," Psychiatric Quarterly 33 (January 1930): 165-72.

27. H. Goldhamer and A. Marshall, Psychosis and Civilization (Glencoe, Ill.: Free Press, 1959).

28. Dunham, Sociological Theory and Mental Disorder.

29. R. Plunkett and J. E. Gordon, Epidemiology and Mental Illness (New York: Basic Books, 1960).

30. Srole et al., Mental Health in the Metropolis.

31. Goldhamer and Marshall, Psychosis and Civilization.

32. M. T. Loua, "De l'influence des grandes commotions politiques et sociales sur le développement de la folie," Soc. Statistique Paris 15 (1874): 226-30.

33. P. M. Deas, "An Illustration of Local Difference in the Distribution of Insanity, J. Ment. Sci. 21 (April 1875): 61-67.

34. J. F. Sutherland, "The Growth and Geographical Distribution of Lunacy in Scotland," Report of the 71st meeting of the British Association for the Advancement of Science, Glasgow, September 1901 (London: John Murray, 1901), pp. 733-42.

35. White, "Geographical Distribution of Insanity."

36. W. R. MacDermott, "The Topographical Distribution of Insanity," Brit. Med. J. 2 (September 1908): 950.

37. W. R. Dawson, "The Presidential Address on the Relation between the Geographical Distribution of Insanity and That of Certain Social and Other Conditions in Ireland," J. Ment. Sci. 42 (October 1911): 571-97.

38. B. Malzberg, "Trends of Mental Disorders in New York State," Psychiatric Quarterly 10 (October 1936): 667-701.

39. H. W. Green, Persons Admitted to the Cleveland State Hospital, 1928-1937 (Cleveland: Cleveland Health Council, 1939).

40. Ø. Ødegaard, "A Statistical Investigation of the Incidence of Mental Disorder in Norway," Psychiatric Quarterly 25 (1946): 381-99.

41. MacDermott, "Topographical Distribution of Insanity."

42. Myerson, "Review of Mental Disorders."

43. D. L. Gerard and L. G. Houston, "Family Setting and the Social Ecology of Schizophrenia," Psychiatric Quarterly 27 (January 1953): 90-101.

44. R. Lapouse, M. A. Monk, and M. Terris, "Draft Hypothesis and Socio-Economic Differentials in Schizophrenia," Amer. J. Public Health and the Nation's Health 46 (August 1956): 978-86.

45. J. A. Clausen and M. L. Kohn, "The Relation of Schizophrenia to the Social Structure of a Small City," in Epidemiology of Mental Disorder, ed. B. Pasamanick, Publication no. 60 (Washington, D.C.: American Association for the Advancement of Science, 1959).

46. A. Hollingshead and F. Redlich, Social Class and Mental Illness (New York: John Wiley & Sons, 1958).

47. J. N. Morris, "Health and Social Class," Lancet 1 (February 1959): 303-05.

48. Myerson, "Review of Mental Disorders."

49. C. Buck, J. M. Wanklin, and G. E. Hobbs, "Symptom Analysis of Rural-Urban Differences in First Admission Rates," J. Nerv. Ment. Dis. 122 (July 1955): 80-82.

50. M. B. Owen, "Alternative Hypothesis for the Explanation of Some of Faris and Dunham's Results," Amer. J. Soc. 47 (July 1951):48-52.

51. Gerard and Houston, "Family Setting."

52. E. H. Hare, "Mental Illness and Social Conditions in Bristol," Journ. Ment. Sci. 102 (April 1956):349-57.

53. Clausen and Kohn, "The Relation of Schizophrenia."

54. Ø. Ødegaard, "Emigration and Insanity: Study of Mental Disease among Norwegian Born Population in Minnesota," Acta psychiat. neurol., Supplement 4 (1932).

55. Ødegaard, "A Statistical Investigation."

56. Ø. Ødegaard, "The Incidence of Psychoses in Various Occupations," Int. Soc. Psychiat. 2 (Autumn 1956).

57. M. Ekblad, "Psychiatric and Sociologic Study of Series of Swedish Naval Conscripts," Acta psychiat. neurol., Supplement 49 (1948).

58. E. Winston, "Mental Disease and the Army," Ment. Hyg. (April 1935).

59. M. Sims, "Comparative Study of Disease Incidence in Admissions to Base Psychiatric Hospital in Middle East," Ment. Sci. 92 (January 1946): 118-27.

60. E. G. Jaco, "The Social Isolation Hypothesis and Schizophrenia," Amer. Soc. Rev. 19 (October 1954):567-77.

61. J. A. Clausen and M. L. Kohn, "Social Isolation and Schizophrenia," Amer. Soc. Rev. 20 (June 1955):265-73.

62. L. Stein, "Social Class Gradient in Schizophrenia," Brit. J. Prev. Soc. Med. 11 (October 1957):181-95.

63. G. M. Carstairs and G. W. Brown, "A Census of Psychiatric Cases in Two Contrasting Communities," J. Ment. Sci. 104 (January 1956): 72-81.

64. H. W. Dunham, Community and Schizophrenia: An Epidemiological Analysis (Detroit: Wayne State University Press, 1965).

65. A. Leighton et al., My Name is Legion (New York: Basic Books, 1959); idem, People of Cove and Woodlot: Community from the Viewpoint of Social Psychiatry (New York: Basic Books, 1960); and idem, The Character of Danger (New York: Basic Books, 1963).

66. A. Leighton et al., "A Proposal for Research in the Epidemiology of Psychiatric Disorders," in Epidemiology of Mental Disorder (New York: Milbank Memorial Fund, 1950), pp. 128-35.

67. Srole et al., Mental Health in the Metropolis.

68. M. Kramer, "Discussion of H. W. Dunham's Article," in Causes of Mental Disorders: A Review of Epidemiological Knowledge, 1959 (New York: Milbank Memorial Fund, 1961), pp. 271-73.

69. H. C. Miles et al., "A Cumulative Survey of All Psychiatric Experience in Monroe County, New York: Summary of Data for the First Year (1960)," Psychiatric Quarterly 30 (July 1964):458-87.

70. B. P. Dohrenwend and B. S. Dohrenwend, "The Problem of Validity in Field Studies of Psychological Disorder," Journal of Abnormal Psychology 70 (1965): 52-59.

71. P. R. Benedict and I. Jacks, "Mental Illness in Primitive Societies," Psychiatry 17 (November 1954): 379-90; and I. A. Hallowell, Culture and Experience (Philadelphia: University of Pennsylvania Press, 1955).

11
ANOMIE AND MENTAL DISORDER

INTRODUCTION

In this chapter the central purpose is to examine critically the various possibilities that the linkage of anomie with mental disorder has for adding to one's knowledge concerning the etiology of mental disorder, particularly of schizophrenia. In order to examine the possibilities in this proposed linkage, it is necessary to examine critically selected epidemiological studies of mental disorder that supposedly have advanced evidence in support of this relationship. The obstacles to conducting such studies will be noted because these obstacles are a key for showing how tentative and qualified is the evidence that has been amassed. The central contention in this chapter is that many of the epidemiological studies by sociologists have supplied data on one level of organization, and then have made an interpretation of these data on another level of organization. This is regarded here as a logical error, and one that makes it quite difficult to assess the significance of the present state of knowledge in this area. Further, it is suggested that the development of a clinical sociology might prove to be a fruitful means for exploring this ancient linkage. There is no intention of reviewing all the current studies bearing on this linkage, but only an intention to examine certain epidemiological studies that have made this logical error, and other epidemiological studies that have not.

Used with permission from Anomie and Deviant Behavior, ed. Marshall B. Clinard (New York: Free Press of Glencoe, 1964), pp. 128-57.

It has been long recognized that building a bridge between the characteristics of social institutions and the behavior of persons that is regarded as deviant, pathological, or unacceptable by various segments of a community is no easy task. This has been a challenge to seminal minds in every generation, so that this old concern is as compelling today as it always was. It has been a preoccupation of the culture and personality school in anthropology. It also is apparent in many sociological studies of deviant and unacceptable behavior of individual human beings who, for one reason or another, cannot be easily fitted into the approved roles of their social system.

Any attempt to show a linkage between anomie and mental disorder involves a theory of the genesis of deviant behavior and a theory for the functioning of a social system. In turn, this requires a conjunction of empirical findings at the social-psychological level and at the social system level of analysis. This sociological effort is most fruitfully illustrated by Merton's model, which shows that the discrepancy between institutional means and cultural goals present in any society provides a basis for predicting the possible modes of adaptation (namely, conformity, innovation, ritualism, retreatism, and rebellion) as the ways that persons deal with their cultural tensions growing out of this discrepancy.[1] It is in the mode of adaptation that Merton has labeled retreatism that he would expect to find many of the persons who have developed some abnormal mental pathology, such as schizoid types, alcoholics, and psychopaths. While Merton considers all the modes except conformity as deviant in character, he tends to measure deviancy largely in terms of the status quo, for he apparently does not see the possibility that the innovator and the rebellious types can emerge as harbingers of social change. While Merton's model provides a range for various types of deviant adaptation within a given social system, it has not provided one with a sociological theory of deviant behavior, nor has it provided an etiological explanation for the various types of deviant behavior.

The difficulty in bridging the gap between these two sets of theories is not only illustrated by the limitations of the Merton model, but also is seen in Durkheim's classic empirical study of suicide, which has been the stimulus for much empirical work by sociologists concerned with explaining different kinds of deviant and unacceptable behavior. Although Durkheim provided an extremely tight sociological theory with supporting empirical evidence, and although he showed that rates of suicide vary with the integration or lack of integration in a social system, he could not explain why certain persons in that system commit suicide and others do not. While his work has provided new insights, he has been able to portray only certain ecological correlations in showing that suicide rates vary with different types of social structures.[2] Durkheim and many others who have followed him illustrate the difficulty in explaining various types of deviant behavior if one operates exclusively on a social system level of analysis. This suggests that no one has as yet been successful in weaving together a set of theoretical propositions that will show the interrelationship of human experience and the nature of social systems.

CURRENT THEORIES OF MENTAL DISORDER

The difficulties inherent in developing a theory that can connect in a meaningful fashion the individual's biological heritage, his life experience, and the social system's functioning are amply illustrated by the existing viewpoints on the etiology of mental disorder. Currently there are three general, theoretical perspectives from which it is possible to examine the nature of mental disorder. First, one can regard mental disorder, both specifically and generally, as resulting from some biological defect or deficit that has a genetic foundation. This view has been productive of a number of empirical studies in the past, and most texts in biology will have something to say about the evidence for this proposition, though such evidence cannot be regarded as conclusive. These studies will not be of concern here. However, attention should be paid to their existence because of the marked tendency among sociologists to rule out biological considerations when they make interpretations of their findings. Second, mental disorder is regarded as the outcome of certain types of personality that have been forged out of conditioning and learning experiences. Such types display behavior that is inappropriate to situations, and they are triggered into social recognition by the impact upon them of various kinds of interpersonal relations and cultural patterns. This perspective represents a dualism wherein personality becomes an entity separated from its biophysiological base. A third possibility is to view mental disorder largely in behavioristic terms, and see it as a kind of behavior that becomes defined as deviant and unacceptable by the significant others that surround the person. Here, mental disorder as such becomes tied to the values and social preferences operating in a given cultural system. From this perspective it easily could be held that what passes for mental disorder in the society is extremely changeable, for it will tend to vary as values, expectations, and preferences vary.

In each of these perspectives there are a number of hidden assumptions concerning the basic nature of the individual and the relation of that nature to the social order. The first perspective emphasizes a continuous variability in the human biological organism that must be taken into account in assessing the nature of its experiience as it interacts with other human organisms. Thus both the quantity and quality of human behavior must be viewed as being tied closely to the interrelationship of a biological organism and its experience in the world. Consequently, from this perspective the symptoms of a mentally ill person must be seen as a conjunction between certain biological deficits, the accumulated experience of the organism, and the impact of social structures upon this organism at any point in time.

The second perspective takes for granted the biological variability of organisms and centers its attention on the interpersonal relationships in the early years of life and the events and cultural patterns that impinge upon a person during various stages of his development. The emphasis here is on the form and content of the social processes that contribute to the personality structure, as well as on the type of personality that eventually emerges in the adult years. In this view, mental disorder must be seen as a maladaptation resulting from certain inadequate personalities confronting requirements of the cultural order with which they cannot cope.

The third position, one based on cultural relativism, has been prominent in some sociological circles. Like the second position it takes biological variability for granted and then ignores it because of the necessity to see human behavior, both deviant and nondeviant, as a product of learning. From this position, certain behavior forms are identified which, in their integration, point to the emergence of a mental disorder. Thus they are the outcome of a specific type of experience played upon by diverse events and cultural patterns in the social system. This position in its extreme form states that mental disorder is a type of response to the environment that is found only in humans, that mental illness will vary with historical time and circumstance, and that each culture has different types of mental illness that are solely the product of that culture and peculiar to it.

This position became fashionable in the 1920s and 1930s and was given a high degree of respectability by Ruth Benedict's research.[3] There is no question that this work was a significant anthropological study, but there also should be no question that it provided fuel for a cultural relativistic view of mental disorder. In a certain sense this work is a criticism of that psychiatry of the West that attempts to be diagnostic of a given mental condition by merely making a catalog of existing symptoms. In contrast, Benedict maintains that symptoms such as trancelike states, extreme aggression and hostility, homosexuality, and paranoid attitudes are interwoven in the various American Indian cultures that she examined. Indian cultures devised ways to channel these symptoms and make them acceptable, but in the U.S. culture they are regarded as signs of mental disorder. There is the implication that certain primitive cultures provide roles for persons who in most Western societies would be regarded as mentally ill. Benedict further brought out that, if in a culture that emphasizes extreme hostility and competition in subduing one's opponent, there emerged persons who did not conform, then such persons would be regarded with extreme amusement. These persons would be the abnormals in that culture, because they were carriers of traits that in other societies might win a certain approval. In the light of these observations Benedict made suggestions for other societies in handling their abnormals. She suggested the training of the unfit in more objective attitudes and an educational program to bring about a change of attitude toward them.

There can be no question that there are certain forms of behavior, mental attitudes, and even hypnotic states that may be indigenous to a given culture and may be regarded as unacceptable or deviant in another culture. However, the big question is whether these symptoms considered individually have anything to do with bona fide mental illness. Psychiatry in the West to date has been largely descriptive and the symptoms and syndromes it has catalogued can be regarded merely as evidence of some underlying pathology, the causes of which have, for the most part, defied detection. It does not seem likely that any addition to current knowledge will take place until one is sure that in a discussion of attitudes and behavior on a cultural level one is dealing with the same things that are regarded as mental disorders from the more orthodox, psychiatric perspective. The author recalls clearly that years ago, after taking a now well-known sociologist through a chronic schizophrenic ward in a large state mental hospital, that the sociologist stopped and said, "I can't help but observe that these patients we've just seen in the ward hardly seem to be of the same order of phenomena as described by Benedict."

Each one of these theoretical positions insists on its own conception of mental disorder and each one implies a different etiology. Consequently, when research problems dealing with some aspect of mental disorder are carried on within the confines of one discipline, there is a distinct effort for that discipline to develop its own conception of mental illness. Such efforts erect barriers to achieving a unified conception of mental disorder. It can be assumed that when and if the etiology of functional mental disorder finally is established, it will be multidisciplinary in character. The effort in the direction of an interdisciplinary approach to mental disorder is illustrated by attempts of some sociologists to isolate etiological factors for a given disorder from observations made on the level of social system. It should be clear that sociology as a scientific discipline, when it finally develops an acceptable body of theory, must have a series of postulates and propositions that square and mesh with the valid theory from both biology and social psychology. This should be our aim, and we cannot further this goal without a more unified conception of certain behavioral phenomena that cut across the various disciplines. This has been no more clearly demonstrated than by the vagueness and confusion surrounding the nature of mental disorder. To be sure, this confusion is by no means exclusively of the investigators' own making, but they do tend to further it in some of their isolated bits of research. The confusion actually boils down to the fact that there is a lack of clarity about the nature of mental disorder in both psychiatry and social science.

ANOMIE AND MENTAL DISORDER: THE PROBABILITY OF LINKAGE

The focus here is on some problems implied by the attempt to view mental disorder as an outgrowth of an anomic situation. The term anomie often has been used rather loosely by sociologists. Sometimes it refers to a condition in the social system where all usual controls have broken down. At other times anomie implies a lack of equilibrium in a social system. In still other instances it refers to decay and disorganization of an institutional structure in the social system. Anomie also has been used to refer to a condition in which a person seems to be floundering in a normless social environment and life appears meaningless for him. There are a number of implicit value judgments in these notions of anomie. However, the central task should be to discover the essential conditions of anomie in the social system that in turn may produce anomie in the person.

While one can link anomie and mental disorder, the evidence at this point seems to be clear that mental disorder occurs in various occupational groups, institutional complexes, social classes, communities, and cultures, even when there is hardly any evidence of anomie in these same structures, with the exception of probably a small anomic quality that may be indigenous to every social system. Even so, the task here is still to determine if certain kinds of abnormal mental conditions are products of the anomic situation. Should this be the case, the question arises of whether these mental abnormalities constitute bona fide mental illnesses, or whether they merely are another order of phenomena. There is the further question of whether they may be considered as early symptomatic signs of mental disorder. At this point it should be noted that by this question one throws mental disorder on to a continuum that ranges from an absence of mental illness to the most incapacitating type of mental illness.

With these ideas as background, one can examine more specifically some of the findings from epidemiological studies that have in one way or another attempted to connect anomic situations and mental disorder. Mental disorder is a type of deviant behavior that has by no means received as much sociological attention as have other types of deviancy such as delinquency, crime, suicide, family conflict, homelessness, and minority-group prejudice. These types of deviancy as behavior phenomena have yielded themselves more readily for study in relation to social organization because they seem to be so intricately bound up with the organization of any social system as it moves through time. However, when one turns to mental disorder and attempts to consider it from the same perspective and with the same methods that have been used with the other behavioral forms, one runs into many difficulties. So little is known about the real nature of mental disorder. Competing conceptions as to its real nature are a consequence of uncertainty and confusion. Thus the current inadequacies of sociological analyses are seen all too clearly when an attempt is made to provide explanations of differential incidence rates in social structures. Such concepts as anomie, disorganization, cultural conflict, social change, urbanization, and industrialization often have been advanced to further sociological explanations, often without specifying that these same theoretical notions frequently have been used to explain a variety of phenomena on the levels of individual behavior and changing social structure. Here again, one sees only too clearly the difficulty of formulating a theory that will bridge the gap between the analysis of social structures and the development of deviant behavior.

The picture is confused because in some studies, where the data are primarily on a social system level, an attempt is made to provide etiological explanations for mental disorder. In other studies of the same kind the investigators are more modestly content with pointing out the associations that exist between the occurrence of mental disorder and selected characteristics of the social structure. Furthermore, in all of these studies there is still the uncertainty about the reliability and validity of the data. In spite of all efforts, no one has explained satisfactorily the significant differential in the rates of mental disorder both between and within social structures. This uncertainty concerning reliability and validity in epidemiological studies of mental disorders is crucial, but in pursuing their researches, investigators have tended to ignore the matter because they seemingly could do nothing about it and had to depend upon the data that were available. Thus they have drawn certain inferences from available data, knowing full well that the inferences might prove meaningless if the data lacked reliability and validity.

OBSTACLES TO THE EPIDEMIOLOGICAL STUDY OF MENTAL DISORDERS

There are four obstacles to obtaining reliable and valid data for epidemiological studies of mental disorder. First, there is the recognition that any diagnosis of mental disorder is subject to a certain degree of error. This error is due to the fact that many mental diseases of the so-called functional variety cannot be diagnosed by any objective criteria. Consequently, diagnoses reflect criteria that are anything but objective, such as different orientations of individual psychiatrists, the dominant viewpoint stemming from a strong director heading a psychiatric facility, differing cultural bases from which the diagnosis is made, or even the social class of the patient.

Second, there has not been developed a screening net that gives one confidence that all cases of a given mental disorder have been detected in a given population and for a given period of time. In other words, there is no possibility at present of being able to estimate what the error is likely to be. This obstacle that interferes with the detecting of all the cases in a given population at a point in time is particularly pertinent to prevalence studies.

A third obstacle, which also has particular bearing on prevalence studies, is the question of recovery. There not only are no satisfactory criteria to assess the presence of a disorder, but there also are no satisfactory criteria to indicate when a person who once had a given mental disorder has sufficiently recovered to be counted as cured. There is considerable confusion in the attempt to compare prevalence rates for mental disorder between European and U.S. studies. In the European studies there often has been a tendency to include in the prevalence count all those who have ever been mentally ill. In the United States one likes to think in terms of the possibility of recovery, and if a person who once was ill seems to be functioning at a moderate level of efficiency, one would be prone to exclude him from the count. This is a difficult matter that is brought up only in order to be as complete as possible in an assessment of the obstacles that confront any attempt to develop a comparative epidemiology of mental disorder.

The fourth obstacle is the inability to determine when a given mental illness began, as so many illnesses seem to be developmental in character. There are no criteria that would enable one to judge that the degree of pathology in one case is the same as the degree of pathology in another case. Again, as in the case of any objective criteria for diagnoses, one is dependent upon the diverse kinds of psychiatric, clinical judgment, combined often with the well-known medical ethic that any person who says he is in difficulty should be helped. Then too, the present sociocultural climate has been prone to widen the definition of mental disorder, as is most aptly illustrated by the Midtown Manhattan study, which found approximately 80 percent of a sample population to possess some kind of psychological disturbance.[4] This widening of the definition of mental disorder has made the situation even more confusing because it enlarges the gray area between those who are sick and those who are well. This last obstacle is especially cumbersome in the effort to obtain true incidence counts of various kinds of mental illness.

These obstacles in the epidemiological study of mental disorder often were not confronted so squarely in the earlier studies as in the more recent ones in the United States. The recognition of these obstacles has produced a tendency to shy away from incidence studies as being impossible to achieve, and to place a reliance upon prevalence studies for measuring the extent and amount of mental illness present in a given community. This is illustrated by the Hollingshead-Redlich study,[5] which has placed its major emphasis on a prevalence count, and the Midtown Manhattan study, which in a note in its appendix attempts to rationalize its dependence purely upon a prevalence count because the authors think that an incidence count is impossible to achieve.[6] It also is reflected in the Eaton and Weil study that attempted to develop a measure for what was termed lifetime prevalence.[7] This shift of perspective makes the studies less significant because, in the final analysis, the development of any hypothesis about a given psychosis would be greatly enhanced by reliable and valid incidence studies, if such could be made. Many of the recent studies that derive their count of cases from first admissions to psychiatric facilities tried to make the count complete by covering private facilities and private practicing psychiatrists. No study has been able to face the obstacle presented by the lack of objectivity in diagnoses. The present complete reliance upon the clinical impression makes it practically impossible to compare the various studies because so many different psychiatric orientations are at work in deriving the clinical impression.

In the author's own research on the epidemiology of schizophrenia, he has some evidence that race and economic condition bear an influence on the gap between the initial onset of the disease and the decision to seek treatment. In other words, a person who develops schizophrenia and is black or is on a low socioeconomic level is likely to be admitted to a treatment facility sooner than a person who is white or on a higher socioeconomic level. This finding, if valid, would imply that incidence rates in well-ordered middle-class and upper-middle-class communities are likely to be somewhat lower than they would be if this gap did not exist. This also may account for the easier reliance upon the use of prevalence rather than incidence measures, for any such gap should be less significant in carefully conducted surveys to determine the amount of mental disorder present in the community at any given time. The author knows of no prevalence study in the United States that has attempted to deal with the obstacle presented by recovery from mental illness, although some of the earlier studies in the United States have counted both active and inactive cases, as has long been a practice in some of the surveys conducted by the Scandinavians.

The difficulties in securing reliable and valid incidence and prevalence rates are just as serious in working out relationships between such rates and selected characteristics of social structures. Thus reliable and valid data are important because significant correlations between rates and selected characteristics of social structures may be thrown into question since the same correlations show large fluctuations from one study to another. Even though some sociologists have drawn questionable inferences from these correlations, it would seem that it is much too early for the elaboration of grand theoretical schemes that attempt to provide etiological ties of mental disorder with the sociocultural environment. It should be noted that Merton's two modes of adaptation, ritualism and retreatism, might be expected to contain certain neurotics and perhaps even some schizophrenic types, but they also might refer to constellations of personality traits that are incompatible with the personality-trait expectations emphasized by the institutional means and goals of the culture.[8] By this is meant that neuroses and certain psychoses may be of a completely different order from those personality constellations that are depicted by these modes of adjustment, and are only placed in these modes because of the need to encompass all kinds of behavioral outcomes that are to be found in the social system.

For example, if it could be established (and some claim to have done this) that neuroses and certain psychoses are to be found in every culture and under every kind of social condition, then Merton's retreatist mode of adaptation has little relevance with respect to including such kinds of human behavior. Rather, the case might be made that his modes of adaptation are reflections of the various personality structures that emerge in one type of social system, and have little to do with the extreme pathological types of human behavior that may have a universal character. Only to the extent that research might establish that a given type of personality structure provides an underlying foundation for a given mental disorder would the Merton model have any significance for mental disorder. Without such a connection one labors in the dark, and might just as easily emphasize the universality of certain mental disturbances as see them fit a mode of adaptation in a given social system. It is only in the need for being complete in the present state of knowledge concerning the relationship of mental disorder to social conditions, that one finds a rationalization for placing mental disorders in the retreatist category.

A SOCIAL-PSYCHOLOGICAL THEORY OF SCHIZOPHRENIA

The critical perspective with respect to this problem can be sharpened if attention is confined to the schizophrenic disorder, for this is the most frequent psychosis as well as one of the most puzzling in terms of etiology. At this point one should ignore the complexities presented by the detection and diagnostic problems already discussed. Schizophrenia, as currently diagnosed in most psychiatric facilities, actually may represent a number of separate disorders.

During the past quarter of a century most biological and sociological theories concerning schizophrenia have been supported by inferences drawn from several epidemiological studies. In view of the particular relationship with which this chapter is concerned, the author will confine his remarks to certain sociological views. It already has been indicated that such views stem primarily from rate differentials of this mental disorder that are found in various social structures, such as age and sex groups, communities, social classes, cultures, and subcultural groups within a society. It is significant that while numerous studies have reported differential rates in these various kinds of social structures, there is still a gnawing uncertainty concerning their reliability and validity. The question is constantly raised: Do the differential rates as reported represent significant differences in the incidence of this disease within or between various social structures, or are the differential rates merely a reflection of an incomplete coverage of cases; differences in admission policies to facilities; variations in accessibility to facilities; changing fashions in diagnoses and classification; differing orientations of examining psychiatrists; differential tolerance in communities for the mentally ill; mobility of persons in and out of a risk population; or mobility up and down a class structure? These various possibilities for influencing the rates of this disease show that it is far too early to develop any definite propositions concerning the relationship of this mental disorder to a condition of anomie in the society.

Nevertheless, one should be speculative for a moment. Suppose that the various studies conducted in this area have indeed established that there are significant rate differentials for schizophrenia in different types of communities, social classes, cultures, and subcultural groups. If one accepts this assumption, one can project two theoretical explanations as a contribution of sociological thought. In fact, they actually have been advanced to explain rate differentials.

The first theoretical explanation is a social-psychological one. It is geared toward explaining the correlation between selected characteristics of a social structure and the production of a significant, excess number of schizophrenics in that social structure. This explanation would view certain types of sociocultural environments as schizophrenia inducing, and must emphasize that the conflicts, stresses, traumatic events, cultural practices, and isolating processes of the social structure enter into the experience of persons in that structure. These are internalized in such a fashion that the meaning a given person abstracts makes for a kind of personality that places him in opposition, or tangential, to that structure. As a consequence of this opposition or tangential position, there emerge certain incoherent thought processes, peculiarities of behavior, disorientation, withdrawal tendencies, bizarre ideas, and inappropriate affects that, together and observed by a psychiatrist, lead to the identification of the combination of symptoms as a schizophrenic disorder. This view, which has been intentionally weighted in a social-psychological direction, would see schizophrenia primarily as a resultant of a kind of personality-trait organization that would not permit the individual to be fitted into the social structure. While there is little conclusive evidence to support this picture, the fact remains that it could gain some inferential support from the establishment of true incidence rate differentials in or between social structures.

The noteworthy aspect of this explanation is that it tries to show a relationship between observations made at one level of analysis and observations made at another level of analysis. In other words, the gap between incidence rates (even if reliable) and the peculiarities of the behavior of persons in their social setting is tremendous, and is one that even the most plausible inferences can hardly bridge.[9] It may be true that certain sociocultural environments have a schizophrenia-inducing quality, but this hardly can be determined from an examination of rate differentials. This also might apply to other forms of mental and behavioral maladaptations of persons in their cultural milieus but, again, is unlikely to be determined by the examining of rate differences. To arrive at a conception of the validity of this explanation, it would seem necessary to study the process through which various sociocultural elements make their ingression into the person's experience and provide him with meanings that result in schizophrenic-like behavior. This, in a sense, is what the psychiatrist does in the clinical examination of the case. The sociologist is likely to argue that psychiatric training is not sufficiently broad to include knowledge about how sociocultural environments condition and influence human behavior. Therefore, the psychiatrist is unlikely to get at this aspect of human experience when he examines a given case.

This great gap between epidemiological data and sociocultural factors that often are assumed to have some as yet undetermined role in the etiology of certain types of mental disorder, can be illustrated succinctly by certain epidemiological studies carried on by social scientists. The data presented by these studies are on a social system level, but the inferences from them are couched on a level of interpersonal relationships or personality organization. Two sects of theory are involved and the twain do not meet through any chain of evidence.

The first illustration can be taken easily from the research which the author worked out with Robert Faris some 40 years ago.[10] This study is central to the present concern because it stimulated much of the epidemiological work that has been done since in the United States. The data presented in this work were numerous, with significant findings that, if they have done nothing else, have provided many suggestions for additional research. However, it is not unfair to say that when the authors did this they were young, enthusiastic graduate students, highly excited by the implication of Park and Burgess' social theory, and so did not take adequate account of problems that have been a source of difficulty in subsequent studies, especially the difficulties of an adequate definition of the phenomena being studied and a complete coverage of existing cases. However, with respect to the latter, the authors probably were on more certain ground than they suspected because at that time the bulk of psychiatric cases went directly to a mental hospital and were not scattered in doctors' offices, outpatient clinics, general hospitals, diagnostic centers, and nursing homes, as is the situation today—a veritable nightmare to the epidemiologist who must count cases.

The concern here is with the theoretical interpretation at the time and the marked difficulty in substantiating it. The interpretation can be stated in a series of propositions. (1) Communication is essential for normal mental development and lack of communication leads to mental breakdown. (2) In an urban community certain areas appear to be more disorganized than other areas. (3) Disorganization is characterized by excessive mobility, ethnic conflict, breaks in communication, and a lack of consensus. (4) Seclusiveness is a key trait in schizophrenia. (5) Persons who develop seclusive traits do so as a result of isolation or breaks in the communication process. (6) These conditions are found in certain areas identified as being disorganized. Conclusion: Such areas will have the highest rates of schizophrenia.

It is recognized, and this seems to be true of much sociological research, that the interpretation was made after the fact. Consequently, these propositions are actually in reverse order to the reasoning that took place. That is, it was discovered that schizophrenia was differentially distributed in a large urban center, and then an attempt was made to develop an interpretation of a social-psychological nature that would fit the facts. One notes that the gap between a geographical distribution of schizophrenia and the personal experience of isolation hardly could be greater.

As Burgess said at the time, the interpretation was congenial to the sociological mind, but the author must admit that it constructs an image of social life in a large city that probably could not be supported by any set of facts.[11] As is well known, the disorganization concept has come under fire during the past 30 years, with some justification, for there is a question as to whether one is dealing with a real lack of consensus or merely with life-styles of which one may not approve because they differ markedly from one's own. It fails to come to grips with the question of why, in a social milieu with a dense population, any person should be isolated. It also fails to account for the numerous negative cases in areas where supposedly there is little isolation and the communication process proceeds without serious difficulty. One can see here, particularly in this work, the difficulty of jumping from factors associated with high rates to some explanation compatible with social-psychological theory.

Jaco's study faces the difficulty not only of the interpretation of his distributions, but also of inconsistency with previous studies.[12] Take the inconsistencies first, of which two are worth noting. He finds the highest rate of mental disorders among professionals of all occupational categories for both males and females. Instead of trying to understand this divergence from other studies, he proceeds to a social-psychological interpretation by pointing to a so-called marginal status enjoyed by this group in Texas. His further finding of low rates among Spanish-Americans of both sexes provides him with no questions concerning its inconsistency with other findings. On the contrary, he offers another social-psychological explanation by claiming that they form a highly cohesive and integrated group that provides a protection against stress for its members. His utilization of such concepts as industrialization, anomie, and enculturation as containing explanatory interpretations for his rate differences is extremely unconvincing, especially when he finds that the rate is high in one industrialized area and low in another. Ay, there's the rub; it is not industrialization per se that is important, but the kind of industrialization present in a given area. Here again in these interpretations one gets a straining because of the failure to make clear that all that such epidemiological studies can do is to describe as carefully as possible the social conditions that are associated with high and low rates and then to provide clues for other researchable hypotheses.

Perhaps it is in the study by Eaton and Weil that one has an example of the most intense sociological zeal.[13] They attempted to assess the amount of mental disorder among the Hutterites, a sect of 8,542 persons living in the northwestern United States and southwestern Canada. The original idea was that this highly integrated and organized group of people with a common body of tradition and religious beliefs, living an intensely communal life with a strong family base, should have a minimal amount of mental disorder. Much to their surprise, Eaton and Weil found that the Hutterites had an amount of mental disorder that compared favorably with the frequency in nine other surveys from all over the world. But the finding that set the tone for their interpretation was the frequency of manic-depressive psychosis in the Hutterites' communities in contrast to the infrequency of schizophrenia. A social-psychological interpretation must be made at all costs. Here, then, it is not the isolation or breakdown in the communication process, but rather the social cohesive factor that makes the difference. The mere fact that the Hutterites are highly integrated, cohesive, and have a common set of beliefs means that

> many epidemiological findings of the frequency of functional psychoses show a high degree of internal consistency in support of the socio-cultural theory that manic-depression is a disorder most common to persons who have a high degree of social cohesion and who are group centered. On the other hand, this diagnosis is much less common among persons who are social isolates and marginal. The latter category of persons are more likely to show symptoms of schizophrenia.[14]

A contemporary sociological model would impute low rates of crime, suicide, and mental disorder to integrative and cohesive groups with a common body of traditions, and high rates of these phenomena in groups lacking integration and cohesion. However, when Eaton and Weil find evidence that does not support this model, they nevertheless press for a sociological interpretation. One does not know if this model is valid or not; one only knows that it is congenial to a certain sociological theory. This explanation for the manic-depressive rates also was suggested in a slightly different fashion by Faris and the author, and it too can be subjected to the same criticism.[15] Many of these models of sociological theory with respect to deviant behavior are breaking down, and it behooves scientists to assess the facts more carefully and to utilize the most fitting level of theory in making an interpretation.

Again, the point that is being stressed here also is demonstrated by Powell's study of occupation and suicide.[16] Powell makes a series of rather grandiose generalizations from the distribution of suicide rates by age, sex, marital status, and occupational class. Such data always are suggestive and can help to locate a problem, but one should be cautious with interpretations until one has evidence that such rate distributions as Powell found would stand up in other locales. Powell also sees suicide as an outgrowth of anomie, but views anomie as primarily a condition of the person, characterized by the disassociation of the self from a conceptual framework. He regards his version of anomie as a crucial factor in the etiology of suicide and links its development with different status positions in the social system. Thus he advances the notion that a person of one status will have a greater probability of becoming anomic than a person of another status. This may be true, but Powell has hardly established this proposition by his differential suicide rates. Suicide rates by age and sex in a given culture have been used for a long time to show where suicide is more heavily concentrated in a population. They tell one something about a given social system and the functioning of that system, but they cannot explain why persons in a given age and sex group commit suicide more frequently than persons in other age and sex groups. One is merely contending, in using Powell's study, that there is a big gap in essential data between differential rates of suicide in age, sex, and occupational classes, and any adequate theoretical formulation that will explain suicide. Powell does not add anything to the analysis by referring to the person as anomic rather than the society, and he can offer his interpretations only as a series of hypotheses that would have to be investigated on another level. If this were done and positive results obtained, he might be able to account in a satisfactory fashion for the differential rates by occupational class. He, like others, has provided an interpretation that is congenial to sociologists, but he has presented no data to substantiate it. It is highly possible that even in the Western world, at different times, in different places and societies, rates of suicide by occupation would vary from the rates that Powell presents from data secured in Tulsa.

These four epidemiological studies conducted by social scientists were examined briefly and critically in order to show what the author regards as a logical error in the presentation of social-psychological insights from observations confined to the social system level. All these studies have attempted to utilize concepts of interpersonal relations in order to explain variations in rate differentials in various social structures. The contention here is that the kind of epidemiological and statistical evidence amassed by these studies requires researchers to seek for explanations that are geared to a social system level of analysis. Sociological investigators must look to processes and initiating factors that account for significant rate differentials, or even random rate differentials, in different social structures. This can be done only by confining the interpretations to the social system level.

A SOCIAL SELECTION THEORY OF SCHIZOPHRENIC RATE DIFFERENTIALS

In the light of the logical difficulties inherent in these studies and the resulting considerations, the author offers a second theoretical explanation that would place its emphasis on the character and functioning of the social system as it moves through time. This explanation points to the selective character of social structures as they move toward states of equilibrium or disequilibrium at different points in time. This explanation assumes that at any point in the historical time of a social system there are a certain number of persons possessing abnormal genetic makeups, disturbances in metabolisms, physical handicaps, personality organizations inappropriate to the cultural setting, experiences leading toward alienation, or a combination of all these elements, and that among them will be some person who will manifest symptoms that are taken as evidence of schizophrenia. Such persons eventually may be selected out of the social system to play the several identifiable schizophrenic roles at different levels in that system. Consequently, when the various structures in a social system functioning through time develop a breakdown in their controlling and regulatory functions, a condition of anomie may be said to exist. One then would expect that the rates for schizophrenia would be much higher than at another point in time where the controlling and regulatory functions of the structures are more intact.

The significance of the Merton model emerges forcefully by this analysis, for Merton has outlined the types of adjustment likely to occur with respect to a disjunction between culturally prescribed goals and the designated, institutional means for realizing the goals.[17] One might well expect a greater frequency of persons playing out their roles in the deviant modes of adaptation in a given social system at one point in time rather than at another point in time. When the social system manifests a greater equilibrium with respect to the stability and functions of its institutions, one might expect that the conformity adaptation would be more frequent and the deviant modes of adaptation would be less frequent. As a social system undergoes certain changes (for example, those produced by new technology, such as automation) depriving a great number of persons of their means for livelihood and bringing about a disappearance of numerous old roles, one might expect the innovation and rebellious modes of adaptation to be more in evidence.

Dubin's extension of the Merton model provides numerous illustrations of the development of new norms and practices in U.S. society that have brought about many new kinds of behavioral innovations.[18] For example, it might be shown (though Dubin does not use this illustration) that built-in security in the form of pensions, unemployment benefits, old-age security, and paid vacations has produced consequences that might favor the ritualistic mode of adaptation. As security becomes more dominant, aspirations become scaled down, social organization becomes more stratified, and consequently more persons make the ritualistic response in various institutions. One is here reminded of Parkinson's law.[19] However, these new cultural devices tend to multiply the ritualistic responses when people cannot focus upon institutional goals, but become preoccupied with institutional means. Hardly any institutions within contemporary U.S. society have missed the ritualistic responses that these changes have produced. The loss of goals is a forerunner of the loss of means, and when both goals and means become unrecognizable to persons involved in various institutional structures, the retreatist mode of adaptation emerges. This probably is reflected in the number of persons who appear in psychiatric clinics not knowing exactly what is wrong with them, but reporting that life seems meaningless. While Merton tended to place a number of misfits such as the psychotic, the drug addict, and the homeless into this category, it probably has its greatest significance in its application to persons who have been unable to grasp and master the significance of the many changes brought about in contemporary social organizations.[20] Thus, while both Merton and Dubin point to the types that will be selected, they cannot through their models construct the types of experiences that would lead to one mode of adaptation instead of another. The task of research is to show the relationship between changes in the social system and the modes of adaptation that are likely to be more frequent with each given type of change. It would be expected that these responses would vary in the history of a given social system.

The types of persons generally included as examples under all these modes of adaptation have been conditioned over the course of years by a linking of certain constitutional traits with specific kinds of social experience. In a social system at a particular time certain persons whose experiences have already prepared them are being selected by the various social structures for schizophrenic roles. The immediate cause of selection for these roles will always be a flagrant rejection of institutional means and actual behavior necessary in a given social situation, and the failure to find acceptable substitutes. If a person does succeed in finding acceptable substitute behavior, this will sustain him for another short period until the next rejection by his peers occurs and he is finally selected for the patient role. The number of persons selected for this role at any point in time is likely to be related to complex changes in the institutional structure when the system demands new roles and rejects some old ones.

When making criticisms of studies in which social-psychological concepts are used to suggest etiological explanations of schizophrenia, as it derives from differential distributions of this disorder in various social structures, it is necessary to point to some epidemiological studies free of this error. A few investigators have recognized the plausibility of the general theory of social selection and have attempted to develop hypotheses derived from the social system level of analysis that are supportive of the general theory. It is interesting and perhaps significant to note that some of these investigators have not been sociologists.

The hypothesis explaining the differential rates of mental disease in community and social-class structures that has had the greatest currency is the drift hypothesis. It has been largely fostered by psychiatrists.[21] This hypothesis states that personality inadequacies or psychotic proneness of persons causes them to drift into certain social classes, subcultures, or community settings. By this process they inflate the rates in certain social classes, subcultures, and community settings and thus make for significant rate differentials. This hypothesis has had its critics as well as its defenders, and has never been conclusively evaluated. It is recognized that open, free, democratic societies foster both geographical and class mobility, but whether the person who is to develop a mental illness is more downwardly mobile or upwardly mobile than other persons has not been satisfactorily determined. Economic failure affects residence as well, especially in those disturbance-prone persons who are deprived of a family setting. However, the general point is that this hypothesis provides an explanation for schizophrenic rate differentials on the level on which the observations have been made.

A second hypothesis states that visibility of and tolerance for mental disorder varies with the attitudinal structure of different types of communities, social classes, and subcultures. This hypothesis in essence states that a favorable attitude toward the mentally ill in a given social setting is one factor that keeps the person out of a psychiatric facility and hence prevents him from being counted. In contrast, when the attitude in certain social settings is fearful and unaccepting of those persons who are developing a mental disorder, this increases the possibility of having them counted. This explanation has been utilized to account for the differential rates in first admissions in various social structures, and it also has been utilized to account for rate differentials between rural and urban areas.[22]

This hypothesis also has been tied to family structure by the claim that families on higher status levels are more protective and accepting of their members who have developed a mental illness or may develop one in the future than are families on a lower status level. Though this hypothesis has been advanced to account for rate differentials of mental illness, it is most likely to be temporary, especially in modern society. It may tend only to lengthen the gap between the occurrence of the initial symptoms and the first entry into a treatment situation. If this factor were a constant in different social structures it would not be relevant to an interpretation of rate differentials.

A third hypothesis, which is the reverse of the drift hypothesis, states that some social and psychological needs are conducive to the breaking of social ties. Certain people break with their families and actively segregate themselves in social settings that are marked by anonymity. This voluntary segregation would explain why certain areas in a city would have high incidence rates of mental disease in contrast to other areas. This was the explanation suggested by Gerard and Houston in their examination of the differential distribution of male schizophrenics in Worcester, Massachusetts.[23] They show that the high rates of schizophrenia in some impoverished areas can be mostly explained by the large number of patients living alone. Further, schizophrenics living with their families showed definite residential stability in contrast to those not living with their families. They suggest that this residential instability of schizophrenics living alone is a rather conscious device for protecting themselves against involvement with emotionally disruptive family relationships.

In his study of the distribution of schizophrenia patients in Bristol, England, Hare gives support to Gerard and Houston by showing that the high schizophrenic rates in both good and poor central areas of the city are related to the factor of living alone.[24] He further suggests that the high rates in contrast to the low rates of schizophrenia are to be explained either by the process of segregation or by some undetermined causal influence operating in the environment. This hypothesis counteracts the image of the schizophrenic implied by the drift hypothesis and views him as a highly sensitive person who is actively and voluntarily attempting to select a kind of environment that will maximize his adjustment and make survival possible outside of a psychiatric facility. Clearly, there is a close connection between this hypothesis and the general theory of social selection.

A final hypothesis, which also is supportive of the general theory of social selection, states that as the size of the city decreases, rate differentials between socioeconomic areas tend to disappear. This hypothesis emerges from a study of the distribution of schizophrenic first admissions to public and private hospitals in Hagerstown, Maryland.[25] The investigators found that schizophrenic first admission rates tended to approach parity for different socioeconomic areas in the city. This finding contradicted the findings of other studies of the distribution of schizophrenics in large cities. On a social system level of analysis, this hypothesis throws into sharp focus the issue of whether there are any real differences between the incidence rates of schizophrenia in various social structures and population groups. Again, this hypothesis fits with the more general theory of social selection because it focuses on city size as the factor influencing social selection.

These four hypotheses were considered here because they attempt to interpret rate differentials for schizophrenia by hypotheses derived from a level on which their observations are made. They also are derived from the more general theory of social selection that accounts plausibly for rate differences of schizophrenia. Further, the investigators do not make the error of suggesting etiological explanations for schizophrenia; they merely seek to explain differential rates.

CLINICAL SOCIOLOGY AND PERSONALITY VULNERABILITY

This explanation, which emphasizes the selective character of the social system as it moves through time, points to the concept of personal vulnerability in any attempt to determine who is to be selected to play the role of mental patient in the different social structures. Among the elements that enter into this personal vulnerability in any specific instance are genetic structure, the constitutional strength of the organism, disturbances in metabolism, physiological deficits, the role of the family in transmitting a culture, traumatic childhood experiences, and experiences with one's peers in the developmental years. All of these elements enter into emerging behavior forms and developing personality organization, leading to adjustment outcomes that in some instances represent an adequate socialization and in other instances an inadequate socialization in terms of the respective group expectations. Thus the social structures in both their functional and dysfunctional aspects in a social system are constantly confronted by persons ranging from those with a high degree of vulnerability to those with a low degree of vulnerability with respect to filling available deviant roles. Some of these vulnerable types will emerge as schizophrenics, manic-depressives, accident-prone individuals, criminals, suicides, homeless men, prostitutes, pedophiliacs, necrophiliacs, alcoholics, and drug addicts.

However, the genetic and experiential elements are likely to be different in each case. It should be recognized that the terms used to group these vulnerable persons who are selected for official attention in the social system represent categories that are supplied by the culture.

These considerations suggest that if there are ever to develop more adequate explanations of the how and why of deviant behavior, it will be necessary to develop the field of clinical sociology, a field that has been neglected during the past two decades.[26] It is only by an intimate acquaintance with many different kinds of cases—something the psychiatrist and some psychologists enjoy—that one will be able to add to the current knowledge concerning the types of individual and cultural experiences, united to genetic foundations, that fail to prepare persons for acceptable and useful roles in the social system. Then, too, it must be recognized that there always will be certain types in any social system who cannot be adapted to any aspect of a social system and who may, by their very presence, impede the adequate functioning of that system. This is an area to which sociologists have paid scant attention.

However, one must turn to clinical sociology to establish meaningful connections between the almost unlimited variety of human experiences and the various roles that are open to persons in society, and also for the experiences that literally make it impossible for certain persons in a given social system to achieve any of the useful and acceptable roles. As a final observation, it may be worth noting that many of the efforts currently being directed to the rehabilitation of the mentally ill are pointing to the discovery of new social niches and to the development of new roles in which the recovered or partially recovered mental patient can be fitted. This effort may not represent any final answer, but in an indirect way it supplies support for this analysis. As the social process selects out, in a natural fashion, certain vulnerable personalities for the mentally ill roles, the various rehabilitative programs engage in a conscious search for those roles where conflict, stress, and trauma will be reduced to a minimum and the ex-mental patient will have a better chance for maintaining himself in a free society.

Having explored the issue of whether or not valid generalizations can be made concerning possible relationships between anomie and mental disorder, one must conclude that it is far too soon to make any such generalizations. The researches are spotty and show, as of the present, various inconsistencies. The painful question as to the reliability and validity of the data is far from solved. Some epidemiological and statistical studies of mental disorder have produced many farfetched interpretations, representing inferences and conclusions that cannot be made from the underlying data. Inferences and generalizations bearing on inter- and intrapersonal relationships and derived from data that are on a social system level constitute a flagrant error of logic.

On the other hand, the author has contended that the general theory of social selection is the one that appears most plausible in explaining rate differentials or similarities in communities, social classes, and subcultures. He also has recognized those studies where the investigators have been consistent and have offered interpretations geared to the level on which their observations had been made. Further, it has been suggested that if there is anything to the general conception that sociocultural factors may have some etiological role to play, either as causative or precipitative factors, in the development of mental disorder, it will be necessary to develop and exploit the field of clinical sociology. An accumulation of researches from this perspective would enable one to relate in a more significant fashion the social experiences of persons and the characteristics of social institutions composing a social system. It should be clear that such an intriguing concept as anomie is hardly sufficient to reveal how and why the sociocultural elements of social structures can enter into human experience and produce deviant behavior.[27]

NOTES

1. R. K. Merton, in Social Theory and Social Structure (New York: Free Press of Glencoe, 1949), 125-50; see also R. Dubin, "Deviant Behavior and Social Structure: Continuities in Social Theory," American Sociological Review 24 (April 1959): 147-64; R. K. Merton, "Social Conformity, Deviation and Opportunity-Structures: A Comment on the Contributions of Dubin and Cloward," American Sociological Review 24 (April 1954): 177-89.

2. E. Durkheim, Suicide—A Study in Sociology, trans. J. A. Spaulding and G. Simpson (New York: Free Press of Glencoe, 1951).

3. R. Benedict, Patterns of Culture (New York: Houghton Mifflin, 1934); see also A. Irving Hallowell, "Psychic Stress and Culture Patterns," American Journal of Psychiatry 92 (1936): 1291-1310. For a different perspective see R. Linton, Culture and Mental Disorders (Springfield, Ill.: Charles C. Thomas, 1956).

4. L. Srole et al., Mental Health in the Metropolis: The Midtown Manhattan Study (New York: McGraw-Hill, 1962).

5. A. Hollingshead and F. Redlich, Social Class and Mental Illness: A Community Study (New York: John Wiley & Sons, 1958), p. 442.

6. Srole et al., Mental Health in the Metropolis, Appendix C.

7. J. Eaton and R. J. Weil, Culture and Mental Disorders—A Comparative Study of the Hutterites and Other Populations (New York: Free Press of Glencoe, 1955).

8. Merton, "Social Structure and Anomie."

9. Certain sociologists have been keenly aware of this issue. See A. Leighton and J. H. Hughes, "Cultures as Causative of Mental Disorder," in Causes of Mental Disorder—A Review of Epidemiological Knowledge, 1959 (New York: Milbank Memorial Fund Quarterly, 1961), 340-65, esp. 359; see also D. R. Cressy, "Epidemiology and Individual Conduct—A Case from Criminology," Pacific Sociological Review 3 (Fall 1960):47-48; and W. D. Robinson, "Ecological Correlations and the Behavior of Individuals," American Sociological Review 15 (June 1950):351-57.

10. R. E. L. Faris and H. W. Dunham, Mental Disorders in Urban Areas (Chicago: University of Chicago Press, 1939).

11. Ibid., see "Introduction."

12. E. G. Jaco, "Social Factors in Mental Disorders in Texas," Social Problems 4 (April 1957):322-28. In The Social Epidemiology of Mental Disorders (New York: Russel Sage Foundation, 1960), Jaco shows greater caution in his interpretative remarks.

13. Eaton and Weil, Culture and Mental Disorders.

14. Ibid., pp. 85-86.

15. Faris and Dunham, Mental Disorders, 172-73.

16. E. H. Powell, "Occupation, Status and Suicide," American Sociological Review 23 (April 1958):131-39.

17. Merton, "Social Structure and Anomie."

18. Dubin, "Deviant Behavior."

19. C. Northcote Parkinson, Parkinson's Law (Boston: Houghton Mifflin, 1957).

20. Merton, "Social Structure and Anomie."

21. A. Myerson, "Review of Mental Disorders in Urban Areas," American Journal of Psychiatry 96 (January 1940):995-97.

22. C. Buck, J. M. Wauklin, and G. E. Hobbs, "Symptom Analysis of Rural-Urban Differences in First Admission Rates," Journal of Nervous and Mental Disease 122 (July 1955):80-82; see also M. B. Owen, "Alternative Hypotheses for the Explanation of Some of Faris and Dunham's Results," American Journal of Sociology 47 (July 1941):48-52. Owen was the first to call attention to "visibility of symptoms" as a factor that might influence rate differentials.

23. D. L. Gerard and L. G. Houston, "Family Setting and Social Ecology of Schizophrenia," Psychiatric Quarterly 27 (January 1953):90-101.

24. E. H. Hare, "Mental Illness and Social Conditions in Bristol," Journal of Mental Science 102 (April 1956):349-51.

25. J. A. Clausen and M. L. Kohn, "Relation of Schizophrenia to the Social Structure of a Small City," in Epidemiology of Mental Disorder ed. B. Pasamanick, Publication no. 60 (Washington, D.C.: American Association for the Advancement of Science, 1959), pp. 69-94.

26. L. Wirth, "Clinical Sociology," American Journal of Sociology 38 (July 1931):49-66.

27. Melvin Kohn notes the same issue in a recent study. See his "Social Class and Parent-Child Relationships: An Interpretation," American Journal of Sociology 68 (January 1963):471-80.

12
SOCIETY, CULTURE, AND MENTAL DISORDER

The central objective of this chapter is to effect a critical examination of those theories and hypotheses that purport to explain the process by which selected sociocultural factors make their ingression into the personality and emerge as mental symptoms and/or mental disorders. The focus here will be on the specific ways society or culture or both cause mental disorders. This problem is not new. It has assumed many forms over the centuries: devil possession, lunar cycle, masturbation, birth trauma, brain injury, environmental stress, upward mobility, cultural roles, culture conflict, migration, atypical child training, social change, social isolation, and social class. This incomplete catalog of environmental factors provides support for the proposition that the elements composing the genotype have been regarded as necessary but not sufficient for explaining the phenotype.

In posing this question with its focus on cultural and societal variables, the author does not intend to commit himself to any methodological dualism. He views human beings as biopsychic-social entities. An organized and integrated unity of these elements of the individual's nature can be achieved through the socialization process. This process, however, often is not all of one piece and is affected and influenced by inputs of a genetic, psychological, societal, and

---

Read before the Michigan Psychiatric Society Meeting honoring Dr. Jacques S. Gottlieb, Ann Arbor, April 18, 1975. Used with permission from Archives of General Psychiatry 33 (February 1976): 147-56.

cultural character. Consequently, in any human society behavior can emerge that is fragmented, disordered, guilt ridden, unintegrated, inflexible, or deviant by prevailing cultural standards. To explain any one of these behavior patterns requires various research strategies that focus on both single and multiple factors affecting this socialization process.

The difficulty in the past of isolating specific environmental factors and their pattern of operation stems from two unresolved methodological concerns. First, there is the uncertainty as to whether functional mental illness can be differentiated into several qualitatively distinct syndromes or whether it forms a unity of a more generic character. The second concern stresses the failure to establish from the several competing social-psychological theories the most valid theory that can demonstrate empirically the mechanism or mechanisms by which environmental factors penetrate the biological organism to contribute to the molding of the phenotype.

The character of the current zeitgeist makes an examination of the potential role of societal and cultural factors in mental disorder both timely and relevant. It is timely in the sense that the cultural climate in the United States has continued to place a strong emphasis on the role of social factors in the causation and therapy of mental illness. (For example, the 1966 annual meeting of the prestigious American Psychopathological Association was entirely given over to papers in social psychiatry.[1]) This is reflected in the development of specific theoretical schemes that are predictive of explanatory hypotheses for certain mental illnesses. Here one refers to the continued ferment that both psychoanalytic and learning theories have contributed to the conceptualization of certain factors in interpersonal relationships that supposedly explain some of the mental disorders found in man.

Its timeliness also is shown in the frequent emphasis on the possibility of preventing various forms of mental illness under the assumption that empirical investigations have isolated the underlying causative factors. Caplan has proposed that prevention be divided into primary, secondary, and tertiary phases.[2] Thus, while the psychiatrist often cannot engage in primary prevention (the eradication of the cause of a psychiatric condition), he can at least attempt secondary prevention (the control of the course of the mental illness). Then, through rehabilitative techniques, he can build up new habits in the patient that may counteract and even prevent further disability, which is called tertiary prevention. The preventive stance has developed in part out of epidemiological studies of mental illness, but these studies have not been able as yet to advance hypotheses about social causation that have proved valid. Even so, numerous attempts have been made to develop various programs of prevention.[3]

Finally, the timely character of this analysis is found in the community psychiatry movement.[4] This movement is a product of various unvalidated positions concerning environmental factors in mental illness. However, as with notions about prevention, there is a tendency to push steadily ahead with various programs of community psychiatry in the faith that future results will justify them. In the ideal form of community psychiatry, the psychiatrist is divorced from his one-to-one contact with the patient and enters into a new contract with a community or an institution.[5] In this new role he counsels with respect to those policies, practices, and interpersonal relationships that would encourage a high level of morale that might prove conducive to a high level of mental health for the persons involved. Along with an evolving community psychiatry, there has been a parallel development of community mental health centers, which are to provide a continuity of therapy for all patients.[6] Community-based therapeutic facilities enable the patient to stay with his family as long as possible. This family involvement is viewed as essential for maintaining his mental health.

Such an examination is relevant because of the numerous theories in both psychiatry and social science that emphasize the role of sociocultural factors and their psychological counterparts in the etiology, diagnosis, treatment, and prevention of mental disorders. Conceptualizations of this type are elaborated by numerous investigators, but one looks in vain for the hard evidence to establish the causative role of sociocultural factors in mental illness. However, even if proof now eludes one, there are sound reasons for believing that these factors, taken in connection with biological inputs about human behavior, eventually will have definite relevance for selected psychiatric disturbances.[7]

Finally, this examination is relevant because of the various new therapies that operate within a framework of social causation. These therapies are recurrent and ubiquitous. For example, they would include varieties of psychotherapy, varieties of group therapy, milieu therapy, encounter groups, and community psychiatry. The current fashion of encounter-group therapy is the latest device for separating persons from their dysfunctional, psychological hang-ups. Here, psychological hang-ups are equated with neurotic tendencies and deviant behavior patterns, but seldom represent bona fide types of mental illness.

The problem to be examined here is found in every psychiatric textbook. Each mental illness is viewed in part as the interaction of genetic and environmental factors. The division of scientific labor requires the biologist to investigate the role of genetic factors through experiments with animals and statistical manipulation of psychiatric diagnoses found in human families.[8] For his part, the social scientist is expected to design studies to show how selected environmental factors enter into the causation or precipitation of mental illness. The epidemiological experiment of Leighton and coworkers provides an excellent example.[9]

Irrespective of what eventually may prove to be the relative influence of genetic and environmental factors, the reality of the present situation is that in both therapy and education, some type of environmental explanation is favored. Thus the preference in the social sciences is to view mental illness quantitatively as a variation along a continuum from very normal to very abnormal. From this perspective much of the therapeutic attention is directed to a reduction and elimination of symptoms. This view fits with the optimistic quality of U.S. culture and enables therapists to equate remissions with cures more easily. For example, the European epidemiologist in his investigations counts both active and inactive cases, while his American counterpart usually counts only active cases. In the U.S. setting, inactive cases are more likely to be equated with therapeutic successes.

While a qualitative view about mental illness also is present in the literature, it does not enjoy the popular support a quantitative one does. A qualitative view has its roots in genetic theory. Here, the mentally ill person is biologically different from the not mentally ill. From each perspective the unit of observation also is different. From a quantitative perspective, the unit of observation is a specific trait or behavior. From a qualitative perspective, the unit of observation is some biological or physiological substance. However, both views are still essential for research in mental illness.

In the assessment of researches to date that have attempted to isolate those social factors that are causative, an examination shall be made of their philosophical foundation, level of operating analysis, and data base. The approaches used in these researches encompass events in the real world that selectively register in persons as human experiences; epidemiological correlations that relate specific social situations to high or low incidences of mental disorder or specific types of mental disorder; and the bearing of cultural patterns on the type and frequency of specific mental disorders.

THE SOCIAL-PSYCHOLOGICAL APPROACH

The position that mental disorder is a resultant of the interaction of genetic and environmental factors has been continually emphasized. In certain specific abnormal mental states, the influence of environmental factors can be clearly recognized. For example, in alcoholism the role and acceptance of the use of alcohol that the culture provides is patently clear. What is not so clear, however, is its differential effect on persons—why some persons become addicted and others do not. Environmental factors also seem relevant in acquiring a syphilitic infection that could lead to general paresis. The environmental influence in this case is that the person who becomes infected moves in a cultural milieu where the risk of infection is high. An even more direct environmental impact is reflected in the traumatic psychosis where the disorder can be traced directly to a severe brain injury. The psychoneuroses, under the impact of psychoanalysis, have been viewed as products of unresolved conflicts engendered in the early family years and then repressed into the deep recesses of the unconscious. Likewise, the various forms of psychotherapy often have been assessed as environmental products even though the specific social factors involved are still obscure. In sharp contrast to these disorders, Huntington's chorea, with a demonstrable genetic base, has an explanation practically independent of environmental influences.

Turning now to the functional psychoses—the schizophrenias and the depressions—the problem becomes much more complex. In these psychoses environmental factors embedded in interpersonal relations and/or cultural variables have been emphasized as having some etiological significance. But their influence and how they operate never have been made clear. Even so, countless man-hours of research have attempted to isolate relevant social factors with respect to etiology and function. In an effort to clarify the nature and role of sociocultural factors in these psychoses, selected types of social research that have had an impact on psychiatry will be examined. The general objective is to determine exactly what has been demonstrated about social causation in these psychoses, particularly schizophrenia.

Studies of these psychoses utilizing one of several varieties of the social-psychological approach range all the way from rigorously designed experiments to a dependence on the methods of direct observation and interviewing.[10] Any attempt to evaluate the significant results from these studies is complicated by the voluminous literature, ambiguity in the concepts used, differing conceptual orientations of the investigators, and the intellectual and social contacts of the researchers in their early professional years. There has been much cross-fertilization by the disciplines involved: theories derived from psychoanalysis, biological psychiatry, general psychology, sociology, and cultural anthropology occasionally become enmeshed in a single mind to emerge as one variety of a social-psychological approach.

In this attempt to isolate the solid finding of this social-psychological research, attention must be called to the fact that persons trained as psychiatric physicians and persons trained as social scientists share equal billing in those empirical investigations that attempt to explain the behavioral psychopathology that emerges from the interpersonal relations of family life. However, the entanglement of psychiatrists and social scientists in a social-psychological approach probably would not have emerged as it did if it had not been for the vital impact that Freudian thought made not only on the social sciences, but also on all areas of intellectual endeavor.

Freud's basic ideas were grounded in biology via the instinctual life of the organism.[11] The basic notion that the development of the psychic life emerged as a consequence of the struggle between the id impulses and the patterns of Victorian culture was at the time so daring that it could hardly fail to attract the attention of other investigators interested in personality growth. The postulation of the unconscious and the emergence of the ego, with its extension, the superego, as a consequence of the repression of id strivings, provided a structure of theory for explaining behavior and personality that could not be ignored. The idea that neurotic symptoms emerged as a consequence of the repression in infantile sexuality and early sexual traumatic episodes emphasized the significance of interpersonal relations for molding behavior. Again, Freud's attempt to view paranoid responses as an escape from painful unconscious homosexual drives reinforced the necessity to explore the psychic experience as nurtured within the family.

The concern here is not whether this theory has been conclusively validated, but rather that its imaginative structure seemed to clarify much about the experiences within the family that previously had been hidden. Freud and his students were avid in amassing and utilizing clinical data that purported to support the theory. However, it was generally overlooked that such data were always used to illustrate the correctness of the theory rather than to test the theory. Even so, this theory penetrated deeply into existing social-psychological thought. It proved so attractive that when the theory spread widely in the United States during the 1930s, several alert and distinguished social scientists decided that a personal psychoanalysis would add tremendously to their insights and skills for analyzing human behavior.

In the United States during the period when Freud was developing his ideas, Adolph Meyer, conditioned by the pioneering and pragmatic characteristics of U.S. culture, was developing his own psychiatric theory, which he labeled psychobiology.[12] Meyer viewed the individual in his development as learning certain faulty habit patterns that made for very unsatisfactory adjustments in his social relationships. The accumulation of faulty habit patterns led the person to verbal and behavioral distortions that were not understood by others. These distortions gradually developed into a schizophrenic reaction type. Thus the task of the clinician was to unravel the sense in the nonsense in order to understand the behavior expressed. Meyer's theory, like Freud's, gradually meshed with some existing social-psychological theories.

An attempt to fuse Freudianism and social-psychological theories can be seen clearly in an early article by Bingham Dai.[13] Dai was influenced by the ideas of sociologists Robert Park and W. I. Thomas, and also had had the experience of a personal psychoanalysis. In his article he attempts to reconcile and interrelate the symbolic interactional theory of Mead and Cooley with the psychoanalytic theory of Freud. What emerges is an imaginative, humanistic account emphasizing the necessity to view the disturbed patient as a person rather than a clinical entity.

In the 1930s many distinguished psychoanalysts were escaping from Hitler's Germany and coming to the United States. As they began their therapeutic and scholarly efforts in their new country, the theory of these newly arrived immigrants underwent certain revisions as a result of their American experience. These revisions are reflected in the works of Karen Horney and Harry Stack Sullivan.[14] Horney argued that the Freudian emphasis on the unfolding of the sexual impulse was too narrow, and that if the neuroses were to be explained the investigator must take into account the competition and values of U.S. society. In retrospect, Horney's work appears to be tied to the depression zeitgeist of the 1930s. At the time, her ideas enjoyed a popularity among some social scientists and psychiatrists but not among the orthodox Freudians. This popularity did not last and her ideas, while still around today, are hardly recognized except by a few hard-core disciples.

The work of Sullivan has fared somewhat better and lives on in the Washington School of Psychiatry, which he helped to establish. Sullivan, like Horney, enlarged the narrow focus implicit in orthodox psychoanalytic theory. He viewed psychiatry as a study of all the interpersonal processes that are involved in and go on between people. He further attempted to show that personality can never be an entity isolated from the complex of interpersonal relations surrounding one from birth to death. While his theory closely paralleled the social-psychological theory of Cooley and Mead, Sullivan further emphasized that the primary aspect of the evolving interpersonal relations is the basic anxiety present in all humans. While the roots of Sullivan's Freudian revisionism cannot be completely explained here, it is not without point to note that in his early professional life Sullivan had contact with several leading social scientists, notably Thomas, Park, Edward Sapir, and Harold Lasswell.[15] On this background of Freud and two of his revisionists, the author will consider the research studies of two social scientists and two psychiatrists that represent an amalgamation of psychoanalytic theory and social-psychological theory as developed by social scientists.

Numerous empirical investigations of families have been conducted with the purpose of isolating the social-psychological factors responsible for schizophrenia. Examples of such investigations are found in the works of Lidz, Wynne, Bateson, and Lu.[16] Utilizing methods of observation such as interviewing—diagnostic and therapeutic—life-history material, family therapy, prepared schedules, and selected psychological tests, they have attempted to isolate the family situation or event that might account for selected schizophrenic symptoms, particularly a thinking disorder. Even though Lidz and Wynne are medical men, in their approach to schizophrenia they have elected to repudiate the medical model and focus their attention on those events within the family out of which the self and personality are born. Lidz states his repudiation of the medical model clearly:

> I wish . . . to present a different way of regarding man and schizophrenia. I say "man and schizophrenia" pointedly, to suggest that schizophrenia, instead of being a process that has inserted itself into a person and possesses him, depriving him of reason, is rather one of the potential fates to which man is subject in his efforts to find a way of life as an independent person amid the many potential hazards that beset his path from infancy to maturity.

Bateson and Lu, as social scientists, come to this concern more directly and so approach the problem of schizophrenia largely by default, that is, because of the failure to date of finding a valid explanation of schizophrenia via the medical model.

The concern here is not to review the contributions of these investigators, but rather to point to their convergence with respect to theory, method, and data. But above all, it is to point to a type of research that has attempted to isolate certain variables in the interpersonal relations of families that are related to primary schizophrenic symptoms. As such, they constitute investigations that probe the role of societal factors with respect to schizophrenia and possibly other types of mental disturbances as well.

Each of these investigators has been concerned with trying to isolate the event, process, or situation within the family that would account for the emergence of schizophrenia. They also share the same arena for their observations: the interpersonal and intrapersonal relationships within the family. In turn, each investigator on the basis of his observations and interview data attempts a conceptualization of the social-psychological variables that account for the central schizophrenic symptoms. Each investigator in his theory emphasizes learning behavior—both conscious and unconscious—in one form or another. Each conceptualization, as might be expected, has a different emphasis due to a combination of differences in theoretical orientation, terminology, and volume of interview data.

While such differences separate these investigators, their reported findings concerning the sociogenic factors antecedent to schizophrenia bring them very close together. Bateson, utilizing direct observations of physical gestures and expressions, emphasizes the contradictory injunctions leading to the double bind. Lu and Wynne attempt to combine both subjective and objective data for their final conceptualizations of contradictory expectations for behavior and pseudomutuality of emotional exchanges. Finally, Lidz probes the unconscious levels of the members of his research families to get at the psychic factors responsible for the distorted identity development of the schizophrenic member.*

Another example of an environmental emphasis to unravel the cause of mental illness is provided by labeling theory.[17] It is traceable directly to Mead's ideas concerning the emergence of the self. Mead shows that an individual in interaction with another acts in accordance with the intention implied at the beginning of the other's act, and in getting set to respond, he responds not only to the other, but also responds to himself. He can do this, according to Mead, by "taking the role of the other," that is, by putting himself in the other person's place. He thus becomes both subject and object to himself. In this self-other interaction the individual develops a conception of himself that is in part a reflection of the conception the other has of him.

Labeling theory is based on this idea: the process of diagnosing or affixing a label to a person causes other persons to act toward him according to the label. On the basis of such actions, he develops a conception of himself that conforms to the label given to him. The implication of this theory is that the mental and emotional symptoms that one sees in a person are a result of affixing the diagnostic label.

---

*There are other investigators such as Alanen and Laing who, utilizing a social-psychological approach, have concentrated on this area of interpersonal relations in the attempt to locate those sociogenic factors that might prove to be both sufficient and necessary to the development of schizophrenia. However, the work of the investigators considered above is sufficient for providing the quality and flavor of research efforts in this area.

The person becomes as he is defined. Labeling theory has some value as a reinforcing psychological device, but the author submits that it has no value in explaining the observed initial symptoms of a mental disorder.[18]

These differing theoretical positions subtly have formed a foundation for a sociocultural explanation of bona fide mental disease. They have provided support for those persons who view mental disorder as a matter of degree, that is, as ranging from a hypothetical normal state through the mild neuroses to the severe psychoses.

THE EPIDEMIOLOGICAL APPROACH

The author turns now from these studies that attempt to locate mental disorder (particularly schizophrenia) in the human experience to the epidemiological studies that attempt to locate specific types of mental disorders at various positions in the social structure. These studies differ from the social-psychological studies in four respects. First, they have not been initiated by any specific theory. They are studies in search of a theory for an existing mental illness. They are guided by an implicit faith that an analysis of the distribution of mental disorders in time and space should provide clues to etiology. Second, their data are composed of objective events: first admissions to mental hospitals, cases seen by clinics, verbal responses to survey items, and diagnostic judgments, each broken down by demographic and cultural categories such as age, sex, race, nativity, education, income, residence, and mobility. Third, the technique used is primarily statistical on descriptive, analytic and experimental levels. Finally, these studies are carried on within the framework of the medical model. They have been guided by the utility and success of this model in dealing with the infectious diseases. They accept psychiatric diagnoses as real entities even though they sometimes prove to be variable.

As in the examination of the social-psychological studies, the intention is not to review the literature, but to isolate from the several key investigations those significant findings and interpretations that throw some light on the relevance of societal and cultural factors to the cause of mental disorder and its specific types. The investigators considered here also include psychiatrists and social scientists. They have devoted a large part of their professional lives to epidemiological studies of mental illness and all of them span the contemporary period.

Ødegaard's well-known study compared the rates of mental illness (especially schizophrenia) among Norwegians who migrated to Minnesota with the comparable rates of those who stayed at home.[19]

His findings of the higher rates among migrants caused him to conclude that those who were most prone to schizophrenia tended to migrate. It is interesting to note Braatoy's challenge to Ødegaard's interpretation.[20] Braatoy argued, on the basis of significant rate variations in various populations, that the discrepancy in rates between migrants and nonmigrants might be explained in terms of the differences in environmental stresses.

In the 30 years that followed his initial work, Ødegaard continued his epidemiological studies in which he accounted for a significant difference between two rates as due to some policy decision, such as an increase in hospital beds or the operation of the process of social selection.[21] Thus Ødegaard found an explanation for the variations in the distribution patterns of mental illness in the interplay of social forces.[22] He viewed the tremendous changes in family life along with the aging of a population as partly responsible for the increase of the senile psychoses. He found that occupational preference, diminishing status occupations, and social mobility operate as selective factors to account for variations in the rate of schizophrenia in diverse populations.

This author's work, like Ødegaard's, spans the past 30 years. His investigation in collaboration with Faris has been regarded as an epidemiological classic.[23] The work raised this important question: Did the culturally and economically impoverished areas of the city produce more schizophrenia than those areas that were not impoverished? While the study provided no satisfactory answer to this query, it did stimulate various spin-off studies that attempted an answer. These research studies provided different answers to the question—some affirmative and some negative.

In the Faris and Dunham study, the suggested hypothesis was that social isolation was the factor that could account for the high rates of schizophrenia at the center of the city. This hypothesis was a rather farfetched inference and stemmed more readily from existing socialization theory than it did from the several distribution patterns. But in the authors' excitement over the initial findings, they skipped lightly over this faulty logic and tried various techniques for manipulating the available data in order to give support to this hypothesis. While this inference did not flow easily from the data, isolation was a social condition found among individuals that could be subjected to empirical examination. This is exactly what Clausen and Kohn did some 20 years later when they reported no evidence of isolation or conditions making for isolation in the early adolescent years in two thirds of a small sample of schizophrenics.[24]

The findings of the Faris-Dunham study were reviewed, debated, and criticized over the next 30 years. The social scientists tended to view the findings as providing support for a social-causation explanation of schizophrenia, while the biologically oriented psychiatrists viewed them as an artifact resulting from the drift of schizophrenics and potential schizophrenics to those impoverished areas at the city's center.

Twenty years later the author constructed a research design that was intended as a definitive test as to whether a community at the center of the city produced more schizophrenics than another culturally dissimilar community on the periphery of the city.[25] The evidence suggested rather definitely that with a careful attempt to secure complete coverage of all cases coming to official attention during a given year, the schizophrenic rate difference between the two communities decreased. When mobility was taken into account, the differences between the rates in the two communities were reduced to a statistically nonsignificant point. It also began to be definitely clear, as Ødegaard had pointed out, that the differential patterns were to be explained by a selection process that was operating in the larger community. Thus, if this inference was valid, an investigator had to proceed very cautiously before he made any generalizations from rate data about the behavior of individual persons or the kinds of patterns that would emerge in various combinations of interpersonal relations. The central conclusion of this research was stated as follows:

> That the selective process was one that operated through a social necessity for maintaining a balance between the needs of persons and the central characteristics of social organization and that the initiating factor was the life chances of the family at the birth of a potential schizophrenic. This process and initiating factor should be central for explaining the incidence of schizophrenia in any geographical unit of society in the United States.[25]

Another study that has made a substantive contribution to the epidemiology of schizophrenia is the one by Goldhamer and Marshall. On the basis of age- and sex-specific rates, they were able to demonstrate that there has been no increase in the psychoses of the central age groups over the period of the past 100 years.[26] On their initial assumption that the mode of social existence should be related to an increase in psychoses of the central age groups, they were forced to conclude that

> (a) whatever may be the peculiarities of contemporary life these factors as a total conjoint force have not in fact increased during the last century, or (b) that as these factors which are alleged to have a pathic affect,

> have increased, they are not as relevant for the theory of the psychoses as has been supposed.

In a subsequent study, Medow and the author were able to substantiate the above findings for three eastern states, two midwestern states, and two western states on the basis of age- and sex-specific rates for first admissions to mental hospitals for 1910, 1923, and 1950.[27]

The author has reviewed the Goldhamer-Marshall study with his own supporting evidence because the establishment of the absence of an increase in the incidence of schizophrenia over the past century did at least cast much doubt on the hypothesis that the changing characteristics of contemporary civilization accounted for the increase in this disease. One may argue as to whether the point has been proved conclusively, but the evidence so far certainly negates the hypothesis.

As in the case of the Goldhamer-Marshall study, the epidemiological study of Hollingshead and Redlich proved to be another landmark.[28] As in the earlier studies of the community distribution of schizophrenia, these investigators established the fact that the highest incidence of schizophrenia was found in the lowest social class. The trend, however, was not a linear one, for the bulk of the cases was found in the lowest class position. These investigators were most cautious concerning an interpretation of this finding, but other investigators were not so constrained and have attempted to maintain that social class position has an etiological significance with respect to schizophrenia.[29] In another study (see Chapter 7), the author has shown that the evidence supports the proposition that schizophrenia accounts for one's class position rather than the class position accounting for schizophrenia.[30]

Gruenberg, over the past quarter of a century, has directed his research efforts to the study of the epidemiology of mental illness. In addition, he has been a significant influence in directing the research interests and energies of numerous social scientists and psychiatrists to the epidemiological field. In one of his early articles, where he was concerned with the relationship between community conditions and the psychoses of the older age groups, he pointed out the necessity of exploring the actual living conditions of the elderly when his findings showed a heavy concentration of such cases close to the center of the city.[31]

His later work at the Hudson River State Hospital involved a detection and description of the social-breakdown syndrome.[32] This syndrome emerges as a person's irrational and disturbed behavior resulting from the expectations and demands that others place on the person who is being defined as mentally ill. This syndrome, Gruenberg and his coworkers found, appears particularly in schizophrenia, mental retardation, and some organic psychoses. In most cases the disturbed behavior (the social-breakdown syndrome) will clear up within two months. When these expectations and demands on the patient are removed, he will continue with more orderly and undisturbed behavior in the hospital until released.

THE CULTURAL APPROACH

As in the case of the other two approaches already examined, the cultural approach to mental disorder is utilized in the research efforts of both social scientists and psychiatrists. The exploration of the cultural anthropologists with respect to mental disorder has taken numerous directions. Their achievement in delineating the nature of culture in both its evolutionary and functional aspects intrigued and challenged certain psychiatrists, particularly those with psychoanalytical training.

The cultural factor has been viewed as an independent variable in the causation of mental disorders from several theoretical positions. First, culture has been seen as a causal agent in the direct production of mental disorders. This position is most pointedly apparent from a perspective of cultural relativism. Second, culture change has been singled out as an agent responsible for both an increased rate of mental disorders and a specific etiological factor in the clinical examination. Finally, culture has been viewed as a causative agent in the formation of a personality structure that eventually develops psychotic reactions. From this perspective, child-training practices, unhygienic behavior patterns, severe penalties, and an all-pervasive cultural theme have been examined for their possible role in the formation of that personality type vulnerable to a mental disorder.

The position of the cultural relativist with respect to the culture-mental disorder equation will be examined first. It was most natural that cultural anthropologists, with their focus on culture as a real entity complete in itself, would eventually come to view the appearance of mental aberrations and deviant behavior as indigenous to a particular culture. Thus, if a given culture was a unity in itself, any mental aberration or deviant behavior observed would be regarded as indigenous to that culture. For if all norms were to be only viewed and understood within a given culture, so was all behavior—even that behavior regarded as not acceptable in the culture. It is worth noting that if a complete relativistic position is assumed, then specific emotional and mental maladaptations would be indigenous to a particular culture, making them unique as compared to those maladaptations appearing in another culture. From this proposition two corollary propositions follow. First, persons in a given culture perceive and identify such maladaptations in their culture, but could not do the same for another culture. Second, it follows that the general structure and ethos of one culture would be more conducive to producing maladaptations as compared to the structure and ethos of another culture.

Two disorders that appear to be localized have been documented by several observers. One is the windigo, a disorder characterized by a cannibalistic desire on the part of the person suffering from it.[33] It has been reported as appearing among the Cree and Chippewa Indians of Canada. The appearance of this condition is preceded, however, by an extreme depression and a definite anxiety and fear concerning possible starvation.

Another localized disorder is koro, which has been reported in Indonesia and West Borneo.[34] This disorder apparently is recognized by an acute anxiety state in which the suffering person feels that his penis will withdraw and disappear into his abdomen, resulting in his death. To prevent this, he holds his penis tightly in his fist and is assisted by his wife and other relatives because he dare not let go of it, even for a second.

The local character of this disorder is strengthened by the fact that a female type of koro also has been reported. Here, the patient feels that her breasts are shrinking, her labia are being sucked inward, and her female sex characteristics are shriveling.

However, while these two disorders are localized and indigenous to the cultures in which they appear, it may well be that future clinical reports of them will show that the content of the fears and anxieties are determined by the culture, but that the underlying pathological condition is equivalent to certain functional disorders described in the West. In this connection it is interesting to note that Linton, after his work with Kardiner and as a result of his later work at Yale, points out "that all the fundamental types of psychoses which are recognized by Europeans occur in other societies." Thus, as Linton states, this is one way of indicating that all psychoses have an organic base, but that the content of the symptoms is, for the most part, determined by cultural factors.[35]

There have been numerous observations in relatively isolated cultures that specific mental and emotional aberrations both in form and content are tied neatly to the culture of a specific society. When Benedict years ago showed that certain deviant behaviors and paranoid outlooks were prevalent in certain American Indian tribes, she merely made a case for the relativity of certain behavior deviations; she did not establish a case for the relativity of the functional psychoses that, as Linton and other investigators report, are to be found in every culture.[36]

In the same vein, when Hallowell raised the question, "Are there or are there not any significant differences in personality adjustment to be observed if, by using an optimum concept of integrated behavior as a measure, we examine the consequences of one set of the culturally indicated value systems as compared with another?," he obviously was inquiring about the interrelationships of culture and personality adjustment by posing a standard of personality integration.[37] But he could not be speaking about the psychoses, even though he may have had them in mind. There is no question that the culture and personality school that flourished in the 1930s had something to tell about the impact of culture on personality, but, as the literature of the period demonstrates, the school had no success in delineating the specific cultural factors that were necessary or sufficient to the causation of the major psychoses.

However, while it is easy to argue from a position of cultural relativity, the position is untenable on two counts. First, at an earlier historical period when travel and communication between cultures were minimal, it might be said that each culture had a distinct and unique form. But in the present time where such travel and communication are central characteristics of the world, cultural barriers are falling fast. As a result, anthropologists are fast losing their traditional data. Second, a cultural relativistic position denies the theory of psychic unity for all mankind. Certainly, numerous observations of humans worldwide attest to a basic similarity among men and women as opposed to their differences.

Perhaps the most significant effort to explore the interrelationship between culture and personality, both in its structural and adaptive forms, is found in the collaborative work of Kardiner, a psychoanalytic psychiatrist, and Linton, an anthropologist. The timing of this joint effort (the end of the 1930s) is significant for it took shape from the background of the research of Benedict, Bunzel, DuBois, and Linton. These investigators attempted to demonstrate that a particular culture could explain the appearance of certain personality types that could be regarded as deviant by persons from outside the culture. Additional support of this effort came from the theoretical writings of Horney, Fromm, and Alexander, who were working out revisions of classical Freudian psychoanalysis. In their revisions they showed that the different cultural influences in which the person is enmeshed from birth to death must be taken into account in explaining the disturbed emotional behavior observed in individuals.

From this background Kardiner invited Linton to the New York Psycho-Analytic Institute for a series of seminars to explore their respective observations, conceptual differences, and research methods in order to focus more effectively on the interrelationship of culture and personality. This collaboration emphasized the utility of the psychoanalytic exploration of human experience in order to discover the manner in which such cultural elements as values, ideals, religion, and child training were instrumental in forming the personality.

In his first volume, Kardiner achieved a conceptualization of a basic personality structure viewed as a modal personality around which all personalities within a culture could be grouped.[38] The problem was to determine for any culture, on the basis of a psychoanalytic exploration of individual human experience, the primary traits of the modal personality. Any variations from this modal personality can be accounted for by constitutional differences and by a parental training markedly different from that generally found in the culture. He attempted to draw a sharp distinction between the differential influence of primary institutions—sexual taboos, toilet training, infant feeding, in-group formation, and mating patterns—and secondary institutions—religion, folktales, rituals, and customs. In a second volume, Kardiner attempted to utilize these conceptualizations in analyzing the personalities as found in the culture of the Comanche (supplied by Linton), the Alorese (supplied by Cora DuBois), and Plainville, a small Kansas town, (supplied by James West).[39]

From a perspective of 30 years since these works appeared it is, of course, easy to be critical. The effort at its inception certainly had high promise, but one that has not been realized in terms of pointing to the role of culture in the development of mental illness. This focus was never sharply centered; Kardiner and Linton had a more general purpose of developing the essential conceptual tools for showing the penetration and integration of cultural forms in developing the personality structure. Thus Kardiner's contribution has been in his conceptualization of the internal ego structure and the basic personality. This collaboration provided much supporting material for the culture-personality school as shaped by the primary institutions that in turn shaped the structure of the secondary institutions.

This basic personality structure as a modal type in a culture, as developed by Kardiner and associates, has resulted in numerous studies utilizing this concept for its relevance to mental disorder. For example, Prasop, in his studies in Thailand, attempts to show that Thai culture produces a schizoid type of personality.[40] He then supports his position by pointing out that 70 percent of admissions to mental hospitals are schizophrenic, as against 30 percent in the United States. In another context, Jewell, in presenting a case of a psychotic Navaho Indian, points out that he cannot be understood unless one takes into consideration the cultural environment in forming his abnormal personality.[41] Jewell indirectly claims that psychiatrists show an ethnocentrism if they try to evaluate such a case in terms of their conception of a normal personality.

In the catalog of cultural factors that have been studied for their etiological role in mental disorder, the nature and impact of social change have been examined by numerous investigators. Thus the following questions often have been posed: Do persons who migrate from one culture to another have a higher rate of mental disorder as compared to nonmigrants? Do these migrants have a higher rate of mental disorder as compared to the natives of the culture where the migrants settle? If both questions are answered in the affirmative, the question still remains: Are migrants more prone to mental disorder than nonmigrants?

This issue was examined under the rubric of epidemiology when Ødegaard's earlier study was considered, and these questions were posed but not conclusively answered. The role of cultural change as an etiological factor in mental disorder is the collective aspect of this issue. Here the investigator raises the question as to whether persons in a society under the impact of sudden cultural changes are more likely to develop a mental disorder than persons in a society where cultural changes are more gradual.

This problem, intriguing as it is, has been around for over a century, as H. B. M. Murphy has demonstrated in his thoughtful review of the literature.[42] Murphy clearly points out that to establish a case for social change, it is necessary to show in all instances studied that persons subject to social change have higher rates of mental disorder than persons not experiencing such changes. If, on the other hand, there are instances of social change where persons experience no adverse effect, then social change must be rejected as a hypothesis and attention directed to other factors. This would be so in spite of the fact that there are clinical studies that point to social change as the crucial factor in the diagnosed psychopathology.

After reviewing the numerous epidemiological findings in situations of social change—immigrations, internal migrations, war and peace, acculturalization to Western civilization—Murphy concludes that the available evidence is definitely against "the theory of social change as a general mental health hazard," and favors the theory of other more involved associated factors. Murphy does report one situation, acculturalization of non-Western people to Western civilization, where the evidence is fairly unanimous that those peoples experiencing rapid social change to Western ways have higher rates of mental disorder than those people where the pace of change is very slow. Murphy thinks that this finding is not supportive of the social-change factor, but rather supports the state toward which the change is directed, because the people who embody this Western state pattern have a still higher rate of mental disorder. Even though Murphy's review is about 20 years old, the author knows of no new evidence that would contradict his general conclusions.

Two additional observations can be made about the selective effects of social change. First, there seems to be no doubt that rapid social change brings about changes of behavior among all persons subjected to it. Such changes of behavior will show differential influence by such factors as age, sex, income, and group affiliations. In the rapid-change situation, some persons will be advantaged and others will be disadvantaged. But in either case, it should be clear that the effect is a behavior change and not a mental disorder. Second, it also is fairly well established that rapid social change will provoke anxiety for many people. Such anxiety patterns are likely to be carried in the social-psychological climate of a society for some time and could give rise to selected neurotic traits as well as changes of behavior. This possibility is shown in a survey on Taiwan, 15 years after Lin's epidemiological study, where another investigator found a 100 percent increase in psychoneuroses, but no increase in psychoses.[43]

Leighton and Hughes in 1959 had as much a final word as anybody with respect to the problem when they attempted a summation of the various ways that culture might be thought to produce mental disorder.[44] The interesting aspect of their formulation is that while culture takes on a specific meaning, mental disorder is conceived in a broad, generic fashion. Thus, if culture has any role to play in the production of mental disorder, it may produce mental disorder in a general sense. Leighton and Hughes enumerate the ways that this might happen by the following propositions, each prefaced by the phrase, "Culture may be thought to"

Determine the pattern of certain specific mental disorders;

Produce basic personality types, some of which are especially vulnerable to mental disorder;

Produce psychiatric disorders through certain child-rearing practices;

Affect psychiatric disorders through types of sanction;

Perpetuate psychiatric malfunctioning by rewarding it in certain prestigeful roles;

Produce psychiatric disorders through certain stressful roles;

Produce psychiatric disturbances through processes of change;

Affect psychiatric disorder through the indoctrination of its members with particular kinds of sentiments;

Produce psychiatric disorder per se;

Affect the distribution of psychiatric disorders through patterns of breeding;

Affect the distribution of psychiatric disorder through patterns that result in poor physical hygiene.

These propositions of Leighton and Hughes have been presented to show how tenuous and uncertain specific knowledge is in this area. Further, it is suggested that this problem arises because some try to do the extreme and are not content with limiting themselves to those forms of behavioral maladjustments that can be more easily explained by the influence of culture and interpersonal processes.

Perhaps the most significant contribution from the studies that have examined the role of culture in mental illness has been a negative one. That is, the failure to recognize cultural differences sometimes has resulted in diagnosing as mentally ill a person who is living in a culture radically different from his own. His behavior, which stems from his own culture, is so different that he is viewed by others as being mentally ill when he is merely behaving in ways that are appropriate to his culture. Kroeber called this situation to the attention of psychiatrists over 40 years ago.[45]

In this account the author has tried to be both comprehensive and critical with respect to the research that has attempted to clarify the interrelationships of society, culture, and mental disorder. As has been seen, the evidence from the social-psychological and cultural approaches is inconclusive. The findings from the epidemiological studies appear to be more substantive and concrete, but even here the solid findings fail to isolate any factors that show the influence of the culture or the social structure in causing the psychoses. It is largely with the milder mental disturbances, the psychoneuroses and some character disorders, that one can make a case for the influence of culture. Certain maladaptive habits, attitudes, and behavior patterns that make for a precarious social existence have been learned from culture. But even here the evidence falls short of proof and consists primarily of psychotherapeutic interviews where some prevailing theory already predetermines the interpretation of the verbal productions. With respect to the more severe disorders—the functional psychoses—it has been indicated that the results appear to be more negative than positive.

CONCLUSION

In conclusion, the author has summarized the definitive findings that have emerged from these studies that have focused on the role of the social environment, broadly conceived, in the causation of mental disorders.

Schizophrenia and manic-depressive psychoses are differentially distributed in any community.

Like the concentration of schizophrenia in certain local areas in the community, schizophrenia is heavily concentrated in the lowest social class.

Patterns of rate distribution of any mental disease provide no foundation for inferences concerning the interpersonal relations of persons who develop the disease.

Selective social forces account for the distribution patterns of schizophrenia in the community.

Social class is not an etiological factor in the development of schizophrenia.

The psychoses of the central age groups have not been increasing over the past century.

No social-psychological factor has been conclusively demonstrated to play a role in the development of schizophrenia.

A syndrome describing the social breakdown of a person's behavior has been isolated from neuropathological features of the more severe psychoses.

The social-breakdown syndrome appears when demands on the person are greater than his capacity to cope with the demands, and disappears when demands are decreased.

Social change does not produce a situation that causes mental disorder.

The culture of a society forms a basic personality that becomes a modal point for examining the range of personalities found in the culture.

Cultural relativism is of no value in explaining the psychoses.

Schizophrenia is found in every culture of the world.

The culture of a group can determine the content, but not the form, of a psychosis.

A lack of awareness and recognition of cultural differences can account for a diagnosis of mental disorder by a psychiatrist.

These are the generalizations that have been validated and supported by the empirical studies. From time to time various social factors have been hypothesized as causative of certain mental disorders, but in all such cases the evidence has been vague, contradictory, and inconclusive. The emphasis here has been on the various unresolved methodological problems that have made it almost impossible to pin down in conclusive fashion those societal and cultural factors that cause or precipitate specific mental disorders.

While this discussion of methodological issues has been conducted primarily within the framework of the medical model, the author is well aware that some psychiatrists attempt to free themselves from the implications of this model, while other psychiatrists are merely confused and try to force all types of problems that a person confronts into the confines of this model. This confusion can be noted clearly in the failure of clinicians to distinguish among the medical, psychological, and social problems that confront all persons.[46]

It is well recognized that any one of these problems may interrupt, inhibit, confuse, or prevent the acceptable functioning of a person in his various social roles. However, this merely pinpoints the necessity of arriving at the correct diagnosis in order to determine the essential therapy. This observation does not intend to sidestep the central concern of this chapter, which has been to examine the evidence on the etiological role of societal and cultural factors in the production of mental disorders. Eventually the problem may be clarified if it can be demonstrated that the psychoneuroses and some character disorders are social products through and through. The tendency in some psychiatric circles to include juvenile delinquency, race prejudice, prostitution, homosexuality (which recently has been eliminated as a disease by the American Psychiatric Association), and skid-row habitués in the psychiatric net illustrates clearly this inability to distinguish between social and medical problems. This does not mean that persons with these problems are never psychotic; it only means that not all of them are psychotic. The process through which societal and cultural factors play an etiological role in the development of the psychoses still remains to be clarified. The author hopes this book will prove to be a contribution to this goal.

NOTES

1. J. Zubin and F. A. Freyhan, eds., Social Psychiatry (New York: Grune & Stratton, 1968), pp. xii, 382.

2. G. Caplan, Principles of Preventive Psychiatry (New York: Basic Books, 1964).

3. L. C. Kolb, V. Bernard, and B. P. Dohrenwend, eds., Urban Challenge to Psychiatry (Boston: Little, Brown, 1969); and E. M. Gruenberg, "Can the Reorganization of Psychiatric Services Prevent Some Cases of Social Breakdown?" in Psychiatry in Transition 1966-67, ed. A. B. Stokes (Toronto: University of Toronto Press, 1967), pp. 76-99.

4. H. W. Dunham, "Community Psychiatry: The Newest Therapeutic Bandwagon," Arch. Gen. Psychiatry 12 (1965):303-13.

5. Group for the Advancement of Psychiatry, Education for Community Psychiatry, circular letter no. 344.

6. H. W. Dunham, "Community Mental Health Centers: Therapeutic and Sociological Problems of Transition," paper presented at the Sixth International Congress of Psychotherapy, London, August 27, 1964.

7. D. Rosenthal, Genetic Theory and Abnormal Behavior (New York: McGraw-Hill, 1970).

8. S. S. Kety et al., "The Types and Prevalence of Mental Illness in the Biological and Adoptive Families of Adopted Schizophrenics," in The Transmission of Schizophrenia, ed. D. Rosenthal and S. S. Kety (Oxford: Pergamon Press, 1968), pp. 345-62.

9. D. C. Leighton et al., The Character of Danger (New York: Basic Books, 1963).

10. E. G. Mishler and N. E. Waxler, "Family Interaction and Schizophrenia," Arch. Gen. Psychiatry 15 (1966): 64-74; and H. W. Dunham, Sociological Theory and Mental Disorder (Detroit: Wayne State University Press, 1959), chaps. 10, 11.

11. S. Freud, The Complete Introductory Lectures on Psychoanalysis, ed. and trans. J. Strichey (New York: W. W. Norton, 1966).

12. E. E. Winter, ed., The Collected Papers of Adolph Meyer (Baltimore: Johns Hopkins University Press, 1951).

13. B. Dai, "The Patient As a Person," in Social and Psychological Studies in Neuro-Psychiatry in China, ed. R. S. Lyman (Peking, 1939), pp. 1-30.

14. K. Horney, The Neurotic Personality of Our Time (New York: W. W. Norton, 1937); idem, New Ways in Psychoanalysis (New York: W. W. Norton, 1939); and H. S. Sullivan, "Conceptions of Modern Psychiatry," Psychiatry 3 (1940): 1-117.

15. H. S. Sullivan, The Fusion of Psychiatry and Social Science, ed. H. S. Perry (New York: W. W. Norton, 1964).

16. T. Lidz, "Schizophrenia and the Family," Psychiatry 21 (1958): 21-27; idem and R. Lidz, "The Family Environment of Schizophrenic Patients," American Journal of Psychiatry 106 (1949): 332-45; L. Wynne et al., "Pseudo-mutuality in the Family Relations of Schizophrenics," Psychiatry 21 (1958): 205-20; idem and M. T. Singer, "Thought Disorder and the Family Relations of Schizophrenics: I. A Research Strategy: II. A Classification of Forms of Thinking," Arch. Gen. Psychiatry 9 (1963): 191-206; G. Bateson, "Minimal Requirements for a Theory of Schizophrenia," Arch. Gen. Psychiatry 2 (1960): 477-91; idem et al., "Toward a Theory of Schizophrenia," Behav. Sci. 1 (1956): 251-64; Y-C. Lu, "Mother-Child Relations in Schizophrenia," Psychiatry 24 (1961): 133-42; and idem, "Contra-

dictory Parental Expectations in Schizophrenia," Arch. Gen. Psychiatry 6 (1962): 219-34.

17. T. J. Scheff, Being Mentally Ill: A Sociological Theory (Chicago: Aldine, 1966).

18. W. R. Gove, "Societal Reactions as an Explanation for Mental Illness: An Evaluation," Am. Sociol. Rev. 76 (1970): 873-84.

19. Ø. Ødegaard, "Emigration and Mental Health," Ment. Hyg. 20 (1936): 546-53.

20. T. Braatoy, "Is It Probably that the Sociological Situation is a Factor in Schizophrenia?," Acta psychiatr. neurol. 12 (1937): 109-38.

21. Ø. Ødegaard, "The Distribution of Mental Disease in Norway," Acta psychiatr. neurol. 20 (1945): 247-84.

22. Ø. Ødegaard, "Epidemiology—Its Aims and Results," in First Pan African Psychiatric Conference, Abeokuta, Nigeria, November 1961, ed. T. A. Lambo (Ibandan, Western Nigeria: Government Printer, 1961).

23. R. E. Faris, L. Dunham, and H. W. Dunham, Mental Disorders in Urban Areas (Chicago: University of Chicago Press, 1939).

24. J. A. Clausen and M. L. Kohn, "Social Isolation and Schizophrenia," Am. Sociol. Rev. 20 (1955): 263-73.

25. H. W. Dunham, Community and Schizophrenia (Detroit: Wayne State University Press, 1965), p. 230.

26. H. Goldhamer and A. W. Marshall, Psychosis and Civilization: Two Studies in the Frequency of Mental Disease (Glencoe, Ill.: Free Press, 1953).

27. H. W. Dunham and H. Medow, "Trends in Mental Disease in the United States 1910-1950," in Sociological Theory and Mental Disorder (Detroit: Wayne State University Press, 1959), pp. 95-114.

28. A. Hollingshead and F. Redlich, Social Class and Mental Illness (New York: John Wiley & Sons, 1958).

29. M. L. Kohn, "Social Class and Schizophrenia: A Critical Review," J. Psychiatr. Res. 6, Supplement 1 (1968): 155-73.

30. H. W. Dunham, P. Phillips, and B. Srinvasin, "A Research Note on Diagnosed Mental Illness and Social Class," Am. Sociol. Rev. 31 (1966): 223-27.

31. E. M. Gruenberg, "Community Conditions and Psychoses of the Elderly," Am. J. Psychiatry 110 (1954): 888-96.

32. E. M. Gruenberg et al., "Social Breakdown Syndrome: Environmental and Host Factors Associated with Chronicity," Am. J. Public Health 62 (1972): 91-94.

33. J. M. Cooper, "The Cree Windigo Psychoses," Primitive Man 6 (1933): 20-24; and A. L. Hallowell, "Fear and Anxiety as Cultural and Individual Variables in a Primitive Society," J. Soc. Psychol. 9 (1938): 25-27.

34. P. P. Van Wulfften, "Psychiatry and Neurology in the Tropics," in A Clinical Textbook of Tropical Medicine, ed. C. D. De Langen and A. Liechtenstein (Amsterdam: G. Kolff, 1936).

35. R. Linton, Culture and Mental Disorders (Springfield, Ill.: Charles C. Thomas, 1956), p. 70.

36. R. Benedict, Patterns of Culture (New York: Houghton Mifflin, 1934).

37. I. Hallowell, "Values, Acculturation and Mental Health," Am. J. Orthopsychiatry 20 (1950): 739-49.

38. A. Kardiner, The Individual and His Society (New York: Columbia University Press, 1939).

39. A. Kardiner et al., The Psychological Frontiers of Society (New York: Columbia University Press, 1945); C. DuBois, The People of Alor (Minneapolis: University of Minnesota Press, 1944); and J. West, Plainville U.S.A. (New York: Columbia University Press, 1945).

40. R. Prasop, Studies of Mental Illness in Thailand (Bangkok: Rongphim Phakdi Pradit, 1957).

41. D. P. Jewell, "A Case of a Psychotic Navaho Indian Male," in Sociological Studies of Health and Illness, ed. D. Apple (New York: McGraw-Hill, 1960), pp. 107-17.

42. H. B. M. Murphy, "Social Change and Mental Health," in Causes of Mental Disorder: A Review of Epidemiological Knowledge, 1959 (New York: Milbank Memorial Fund, 1961), pp. 280-329.

43. T-Y. Lin, "Mental Disorders in Taiwan, 15 Years Later: A Preliminary Report," in Mental Health Research in Asia and the Pacific, ed. W. Caudill and T-Y. Lin (Honolulu: University Press of Hawaii, 1969).

44. A. H. Leighton and J. H. Hughes, "Culture as Causative of Mental Disorder," in Causes of Mental Disorder: A Review of Epidemiological Knowledge, 1959, pp. 341-65.

45. A. L. Kroeber, "Cultural Anthropology," in The Problems of Mental Disorder, ed. M. Bentley and E. V. Cowdry (New York: McGraw-Hill, 1934), pp. 346-53.

46. H. R. Huessy, "Some Historical Antecedents of Present American Mental Health Dilemmas," paper presented at the Ninth International Congress of Anthropological and Ethnological Sciences, Chicago, September 1973.

INDEX

ABOUT THE AUTHOR

DR. H. WARREN DUNHAM currently holds an appointment as professor of psychiatry (Medical Sociology) in the Department of Psychiatry at the State University of New York at Stony Brook. Dr. Dunham is also a professor emeritus of sociology, Wayne State University. During his final five years at Wayne State he held an appointment as professor of sociological psychiatry in the Department of Psychiatry in the medical school. In 1956-57 he lectured under a Fulbright Grant at the University of Amsterdam and in 1966-67 he taught under a second Fulbright Award at Ain Shams University in Cairo.

In 1955-56 he was chosen as a holder of the Leo M. Franklin Memorial Chair in Human Relations at Wayne State. In 1972 he was selected by the Mental Health Section of the American Public Health Association as the first recipient of the Rema Lapouse Memorial Award.

Dr. Dunham is well known for his lectures on the epidemiology of mental disorders, sociological psychiatry, and the control and treatment of the mentally ill. His most recent books include, Community and Schizophrenia: An Epidemiological Analysis and Social Realities and Community Psychiatry.